JONATHAN EDWARDS, PASTOR

JONATHAN EDWARDS, PASTOR: Religion and Society in Eighteenth-Century Northampton

PATRICIA J. TRACY

AMERICAN CENTURY SERIES

🅤 Hill and Wang, New York

A DIVISION OF FARRAR, STRAUS AND GIROUX

Published simultaneously in Canada by McGraw-Hill Ryerson Ltd., Toronto
ISBN (clothbound edition) 0-8090-6195-3
ISBN (paperback edition) 0-8090-0149-7
Printed in the United States of America
Designed by Nancy Dale Muldoon
First edition, 1980

Library of Congress Cataloging in Publication Data
Tracy, Patricia J.
  Jonathan Edwards, pastor.
  (American century series)
  Includes bibliographical references and index.
  1. Edwards, Jonathan, 1703–1758.
2. Congregational churches—Clergy—Biography.
3. Clergy—Massachusetts—Northampton—Biography.
4. Northampton, Mass.—Biography. 5. Sociology, Christian—Massachusetts—
Northampton. I. Title.
BX7260.E3T72   285.8'092'4 [B]   80-12356
ISBN 0-8090-6195-3
ISBN 0-8090-0149-7 (pbk.)

To my mother and father

Acknowledgments

THE directors and staffs of the following institutions have generously given me assistance in my research and permission to quote from manuscripts in their keeping: the Franklin Trask Library, Andover Newton Theological School, Newton Centre, Massachusetts (Jonathan Edwards and Edwards Family papers); Beinecke Rare Book and Manuscript Library, Yale University (the major collection of Jonathan Edwards MSS); the Connecticut Historical Society; the Connecticut State Library; the Massachusetts Historical Society; the New York Public Library (the Joseph Hawley Papers); the First Church of Christ and the Storrs Library, Longmeadow, Massachusetts (the diary of the Reverend Stephen Williams); Forbes Library, Northampton (the Northampton town papers, the Sylvester Judd and James Russell Trumbull MSS). I am greatly indebted to Mr. Stanley Greenberg and Mrs. Elinor Shea of Forbes for their help and kindness over many years, and to Mr. Blaise Bisaillon, Director of the Library, for permission to use the original drawing by Maitland de Gogorza which is reproduced on the cover of this book. Thanks and acknowledgment are also due to the following publishers for permission to quote from their books: Houghton Mifflin Company, *Jonathan Edwards: The Narrative of a Puritan Mind;* Texas A&M University Press, *The Writing of Jonathan Edwards: Theme, Motif, and Style;* the Macmillan Publishing Company, *Jonathan Edwards 1703–1758;* and Yale University Press, *The Works of Jonathan Edwards.*

A slightly expanded version of Chapter 5 has appeared under the title "The Pastorate of Jonathan Edwards" in the *Massachusetts Review,* XX (Autumn 1979).

My debts to my fellow historians are great in number and depth. I have profited immeasurably from conversations with Richard L. Bushman, David D. Hall, Christopher M. Jedrey, Wilson H. Kimnach, David Levin, Thomas A. Schafer, Kathryn Kish Sklar, Kevin Sweeney, and Robert J. Wilson III. In early drafts of this book I had the benefit of criticism from David Hall and David Levin, and a later draft was improved when Michael D. Bell and Robert F. Dalzell, Jr., pounced on it with both inspiration and common sense. Stephen Nissenbaum and R. Jackson Wilson have provided so many good ideas and so much encouragement over the years that I can't imagine this book ever being realized without them. None of these generous people is at all responsible, of course, for the strange uses to which I have put their wonderful insights or for the obstinacy with which I have persisted in my errors.

My former students and research assistants, Paul V. Rogers and Jeanne Boyle, were of great help at critical stages of this project, and many students from my Colonial America course at Williams College contributed to whatever clarity this book may possess by asking devilish questions. Mrs. Georgia Swift has typed my manuscript with grace under pressure. Arthur Wang and his staff have been exceptionally understanding and helpful.

Robert James Tracy drew the map and diagrams for this book and never once complained about "Jonathan" when I groused about geology field trips. In many ways and over many years, he has earned that most honorific of titles, which Abigail Adams bestowed on her husband, "Dearest Friend."

Contents

"MINISTERS should be Sons of Thunder: Men had need have Storms in their hearts, before they will betake themselves to Christ for Refuge."
—Solomon Stoddard, *The Defects of Preachers Reproved* (1723)

"AND IF it was plain to all the world of Christians that I was under the infallible guidance of Christ, and I was sent forth to teach the world the will of Christ, then I should have power in all the world. I should have power to teach them what they ought to do, and they would be obliged to hear me . . ."
—Jonathan Edwards, "Miscellanies," entry No. 40 (ca. 1723)

JONATHAN EDWARDS, PASTOR

Introduction

SHORTLY after Jonathan Edwards arrived in Northampton, Massachusetts, in 1726* to assist his maternal grandfather in the duties of the ministry, Solomon Stoddard wrote the name of his new colleague in the list of Northampton church members as, simply, Jonathan Edwards. When Stoddard died two years later and his grandson became the church's sole minister, Edwards added the title Pastor next to his own name. Stoddard's shaky handwriting reflected his eighty-three years, and his inscription of the name without a specific category of membership symbolized what he had achieved in his six decades as a minister in Northampton. Edwards was only twenty-five when he received his new title, his hand was vigorous and assertive, and the word he wrote represented all that he hoped to be—and all that would prove so difficult for the heir of Solomon Stoddard to achieve.

During his years in Northampton, Edwards became famous for effective Calvinist preaching that led most of his congregation to have "conversion experiences." From Northampton, in part through Edwards's example to other ministers, the revivals of religion spread throughout the Connecticut Valley in New England; and as a result of similar efforts by other evangelists from Maine to Virginia, the local revivals spread to join in a Great Awakening of

---

*Because the year officially began on March 25, until about 1750 in America, dates were often written as February 16, 1715/16; I have changed all such to the year as we give it, 1716 in the example. Except where the flavor of the language is important, spelling and punctuation have been modernized in quotations.

piety in the American colonies in the late 1730s and early 1740s.

We already know a considerable amount about the Great Awakening as an ideological movement among the clergy and as a political movement among organized churches and denominations. Jonathan Edwards, the most famous revivalist of the eighteenth century, has been extensively studied as a philosopher-theologian; but, strangely, his career as a *pastor*—preacher, counselor, disciplinarian—has received only minimal attention.[1] His theology has a timeless appeal that makes it fascinating today as philosophy, but his importance to his own era—both to the laymen who responded to his preaching and to the ministers who tried to copy his success—lay in his ability to reach the hearts of his congregation. His chief professional concern was the saving of souls, and most of his intellectual activity revolved around an attempt to restate the Calvinist dogma he had inherited so that its meaning would be clear and emotionally affecting when preached in the meetinghouse. One purpose of this book, therefore, is to offer a supplement to the standard portrait of Edwards, to interpret the neglected pastoral implications of his ideas and activities.

A second purpose is to use Northampton as a case study of an "awakened" community. As yet, we know surprisingly little about the Great Awakening as a social movement among lay men and women—the constituency for Calvinist sermons, the makers of individual decisions to endorse one minister or magistrate over another.[2] Because the timing and results of the revivals tended to derive from variable local conditions, it is necessary to turn to the community setting. In this context, the Awakening can be seen as a manifestation of and a release from the tensions that accompanied social change, and Northampton provides a microcosm in which to observe the evolving relationship of minister to people and the changing role of the church in reflecting or influencing the social structure. Edwards's success as an evangelist was a product of his ability to perceive, articulate, and satisfy the emotional needs of his flock, especially the young people. Many ministers who had revivals in their churches in the 1730s and 1740s commented on the important role played by the youth, especially unmarried males from sixteen to twenty-six years of age, whom we would call adolescents. Their rise as an object of concern to the ministers and the community at large signals particular kinds of social changes, especially economic developments which made for difficult transitions between the social categories of child and adult in eighteenth-century New England.[3]

The parallels between the Awakening in Northampton and the revivals in other places can only be suggested briefly within the limits of this book, but readers familiar with the growing literature on the social history of early America will, I hope, find those suggestions compatible with the emerging information on other towns and other colonies. And while Jonathan Edwards's life and ideas were in many ways unique, the professional challenges that he faced were much like those encountered by other Protestant clergymen in eighteenth-century America. Although it is a commonplace to note that the highly literate clergy were not average Americans, it is nevertheless true that their role as spokesmen for popular values was not seriously challenged until the Revolutionary era brought the politician to center stage. It is therefore no trivial issue that we address when we pursue the interaction of a minister with his constituency.

In this type of study, the current consensus about Edwards's place in the intellectual life of early New England is both an advantage and a disadvantage. Long regarded as America's first systematic philosopher, Edwards is credited by many historians with devising doctrines in the mid-eighteenth century that represent the intellectual apogee of the Calvinism that came to the New World with the Puritans in the 1620s and remained a major force in American thought until the nineteenth century. Edwards's great achievement was to use the new scientific concepts of Isaac Newton and John Locke to reformulate classic Reformed dogma: Newtonian principles gave a physical reality to the immanence of an omnipotent God, and Lockean psychology helped to explain how man experienced God directly but passively. Edwards's statements, as published in his lifetime and as they survive in manuscript, gave a renewed intellectual integrity and emotional power to the Calvinist doctrines of man's inherent depravity, God's absolute sovereignty and predestination of all souls, and the free and unearnable gift of His irresistible Saving Grace to the elect.

The intellectual force of Edwards's ideas has always been seen as a sufficient explanation for the broad popular response to his doctrines. Life on the American frontier, it is usually assumed, fired the embers of traditional piety. Faced with a practical lesson in the awesomeness of nature and man's smallness in silhouette against limitless vistas of virgin woodland, the eighteenth-century New Englander (son of the Puritan and father of the Yankee) heard his spiritual needs expressed in the stark vision of Jonathan Edwards.

Edwardsean theology was, we realize in retrospect, the Western world's last emphatic statement of man's utter depravity. For decades Edwards debated with the liberal theologians of New England, who were gradually coming to see man as essentially good and capable of moving under his own power along the road to heaven. Those debates could never be won, because neither side would admit defeat; but in the long run of historiography, although his opponents were the spokesmen for the Enlightenment that forever changed the course of Western thought, Edwards has been declared the victor. His opponents are often regarded as lesser minds, simply unable to understand the subtleties of Edwards's thought or too sentimental to live with a Calvinist view of the universe. The modern temperament finds liberal Christianity to be naïve and applauds Edwards's emphasis on man's potential for evil. The Calvinist view of man and the universe has even been described as a prescient parallel to modern scientific analysis, with Edwards's omnipotent God standing as a metaphor for the fundamental forces of physics and psychology that we still barely understand.[4]

The urge to enhance Edwards's reputation as a philosopher by finding him to be essentially a modern mind trapped in an antiquated vocabulary has nevertheless distorted his thought. His brilliance has been allowed to obscure a major aspect of his historicity, and the real-life context and impact of his ideas has been neglected. It is misleading to assume that Edwards's definition of the spiritual problem of the age was the only reasonable one, that the impressive internal coherence of his thought was the only proper response, and that somehow the whole phenomenon of a resurgent Calvinism on the frontier was inevitable. Any set of ideas, however marvelous as a work of art, has a human gestation, a social as well as an intellectual matrix. The most renowned biographer of Edwards, Perry Miller, once wrote that "so absorbed was [Edwards] in this interior logic that it may truthfully be said that his external biography was virtually an adjunct to his subjective."[5] But that is at best a partial truth—and Edwards himself repeatedly denied the isolation of the subjective life from the external reality.

Part of this ahistorical distortion of Edwards's thought has derived from our forgetting that Edwards was not a thinker by profession: the vocation and social role of Intellectual had not really been invented yet. Edwards was a *pastor:* he had made a profound commitment to serve God through his daily labors, and his vocation was to persuade others to share his vision of divine glory. How he worked out a definition of Truth in his own mind has been studied in detail; less well analyzed has been his communication of that insight to his congregation. It was their souls he intended to save—not just their minds he wanted to fill with ideas. The traditional approaches to Edwards's theology leave unanswered many important questions about his significance in his own time and place. What was *heard* when Edwards preached? When we ask why Edwards's congregation were "awakened," it is not enough to describe his ideas as "logical," for the same ideas had left his congregation unmoved for years and would later evoke apathy or outright hostility.

When we revere Edwards as the Great Philosopher, we often minimize a major event in his career, his dismissal by his congregation fifteen years after his first success as a revivalist. It is true that his doctrinal pronouncements had changed slightly in language by 1750, but his ideas and public statements had progressed with a clear logic. We must look more deeply to see if that logic was the only one available, to ask why Edwards took one path if there were other possibilities, and to ask why his congregation refused to follow. If we suspend judgment about whether Edwards was right, we don't have to accuse him of being wrong; but we are relieved of having to label his congregation as merely stupid, as has so often been implied, and we can focus on the more important question of why he failed to persuade them to share his views. We can inquire about the sources of the change of mind in the church, and we can recover a necessary appreciation of how much a matter of give and take, on intellectual and emotional wavelengths, was the relationship of pastor and congregation. If we believe Edwards's own assertion that the whole congregation turned against him, and find it supported by available evidence, we can then avoid the dead end of blaming Edwards's pastoral tragedy on the machinations of one man or a handful of evil men, heirs of an apocryphal family feud, proto-entrepreneurs who disliked Edwards's supposed "Puritan" attitude toward business, or democrats who cut their political teeth on Edwards in preparation for the revolution they would lead two decades later.[6] It was really not that simple, or that rationalistic. Perhaps we can best proceed by assuming that the disputants understood the issues and meant what they were saying. In fact, we might start with the tested assumption that it really *was* theology they were arguing about—from that base, we can reexamine the meaning of that theology for minister and layman.

Of course, it was Edwards's dismissal from Northampton that gave him the time—never actively sought—to pursue his work in philosophy, and that work progressed with greater speed and precision when redefinitions of the relationship between God and man did not have to be tested continually against the intractable realities of the ordinary parishioner. Lacking other vocational options, Edwards became missionary to an Indian settlement on the western frontier of Massachusetts at Stockbridge, which also contained a small white congregation who never gave any evidence of caring for the preaching or the counsel of the Reverend Mr. Edwards. On an emotional level, he seems to have abandoned the essence of his true vocation, the cure of souls: he became an Intellectual by default. Devoting himself to the systematic theological treatises for which he is now most famous, Edwards labored in his study for eight years, until he was called to the presidency of what is now Princeton University in 1758 and died suddenly from a smallpox inoculation shortly thereafter. He still concerned himself with the perennial problem of the sinfulness of men, and their confrontation with their God, but it was no longer specific human souls that concerned him. His commitment was to the ideas he refined: he wrote magnificent treatises on the freedom of the will, original sin, the nature of true virtue, and a "history of the Work of Redemption," an analytical narrative of the world from Creation to prove that all human activities were really shadows of the determining hand of God. In the world of Edwards's mind, God grew ever larger in importance until He filled the whole space. Man became more nearly abstract. One wonders how Edwards would have coped with the very real and troublesome students of Princeton if he had lived to take up his new pastorate as their president.

Ultimately, Jonathan Edwards's career should be viewed in the broad context of the evolving nature of the church in colonial New England. He is usually seen as appearing at a critical juncture in the evolution of the New England Way from its Calvinist-communitarian foundations in the seventeenth century to its defeat by the materialism and cosmic optimism of the late eighteenth century.[7] When the intense personal faith of the revolutionary exiles who had formed the core of the "city upon a hill" in 1630 was not inherited by their children, the harshness of Calvinist dogma had to be compromised. Most ministers still held to the formal propositions that God's grace was entirely arbitrary, unearned by even the best works of man; and yet to persuade men to behave well, clergymen tended to put greater emphasis on good behavior as a sign of inner regeneration. On the other hand, although the gift of the Spirit did not depend on the merit of man's prayers, so theoretically there was little man could *do* to gain salvation, evangelical ministers found themselves obliged to preach that man *must* seek and that his earnest seeking (through prayer and various forms of worship) would likely be rewarded.

As new generations came to adulthood in New England without having the conversion experiences that were the price of full membership in most churches and the condition of having one's children baptized (without which they would go straight to hell forever when they died[8]), the church as a social institution also had to be redesigned. In 1662 a Synod of Congregationalist clergy recommended to the individual churches for their adoption a new form of church polity, which came to be known as the Half-Way Covenant. Baptized adults without a discernible "work of the Spirit" in their hearts would be allowed to have their children baptized (although the adults could still not vote for a minister or new admissions in the church, nor partake of the Lord's Supper) if they would "own the covenant," which meant professing an intellectual belief in the basic tenets of Reformed Christianity and formally submitting to the moral discipline of the church.[9] In many towns this process became a rite of passage to adulthood, and it was hoped that a conversion experience would eventually follow and lead to full membership. Even if this never happened, as was usually the case, successive generations would not be entirely shut out of the churches.

This evolution of New England church polity has been labeled by Edmund Morgan a growing "tribalism"—a concern for the children of saints and a concomitant neglect of those who did not have parents or grandparents already in the church.[10] (For example, there is little ministerial writing on the qualifications for baptism for an adult without church-member parents.) But the tribe was also enlarged to include all the descendants of church members—a large majority of the inhabitants of New England for generations to come. Despite the maintenance of the exclusive and socially desirable status of full member, the Half-Way Covenant brought a subtle but profound change in the relationship of the Congregational church to the rest of the community: the pre-1662 assumption that the church covenant was but an outward and social manifestation of the covenant between each regenerate person and God was transformed into a vision of the whole community (the town, the colony—eventually the region and even the nation) in a covenant with God quite independent of individual piety. Few of these implications were faced by those who advocated the *Propositions* of the Synod of 1662, but in retrospect we can see how thoroughly the ground was prepared for those who would go even further in subsequent decades toward opening the church to the masses and not just the presumably elect few. One of the most radical of these extenders of the compromise of the 1660s would be the Reverend Solomon Stoddard, pastor of the church at Northampton on the western frontier.[11]

Stoddard attacked the late-seventeenth-century ecclesiastical consensus in New England at its weakest point by charging that the continued attempt to judge the truth of conversion experiences was nonsensical. Conducting a long doctrinal debate with the Reverend Increase Mather of Boston, spokesman for the Congregational "establishment," Stoddard advocated giving up a pretense of discerning the sheep in the midst of all the goats. Commonly known as a pastor who gave in to the waywardness of a frontier congregation (this part of his reputation especially deserves reexamination), Stoddard opened all the ordinances of his Northampton church, even the

Lord's Supper, to all with a "historical" faith (an intellectual knowledge of the basics of Christianity). This was the same criterion that had long been used for "half-way" membership; and defying the custom that led people to seek membership only when they became parents, Stoddard encouraged people as young as fourteen to become full participants in the church and to partake of the Lord's Supper, which he called a "converting" ordinance. Outspokenly critical of the traditional power of the full members in the church, Stoddard asserted the principles of ministerial power and interchurch government by clerical synods. Yet his writings also showed a sincere sympathy for Christians suffering spiritual doubts, and his preaching of Calvinist doctrines aroused his flock to a number of revivals of piety (which he called "harvests") that were regarded with envy by other ministers and successfully imitated in a number of other towns in the Connecticut Valley. Losing almost entirely the original Puritan conception of an exclusivist "gathered" church in the process, Stoddard took the evolution of New England Congregationalism about as far as it could go in one direction.

It was Stoddard's grandson and successor in the Northampton pulpit, Jonathan Edwards, who came to be regarded as the major force in returning New England to the essence of the Calvinist faith of its fathers, at least temporarily. But here, too, our modern appreciation of Edwards as a philosopher has clouded our understanding of the continuities in both theology and church practice between Stoddard and his heir. When Edwards's success was at its height in 1735, he insisted that his congregation's "awakening" was the same kind of revival that had occurred in Stoddard's day. And fifteen years later, when Edwards was dismissed by his church, Stoddard was again the standard of measurement. In the debates of 1749–50, each side (the pastor versus an almost unanimous church) focused on the expected results of Edwards's doctrines for the relationship between church and community as it had been established by Solomon Stoddard: each side claimed to represent the real Stoddardeanism. Twenty-one years after Stoddard's death, his presence remained with his flock. He, and not his grandson Edwards, was still the Patriarch. Edwards's career was a drama played out—in his own mind and that of his congregation—on the stage of Solomon Stoddard's Northampton. And so that is where the story must begin.

CHAPTER ONE

Inheritance

FEBRUARY 16, 1729. A cold Sabbath morning. Twenty-five-year-old Jonathan Edwards mounted the steps of the pulpit in the Northampton meetinghouse and faced the congregation who were now his flock. He was not unprepared for this responsibility, for he had received an excellent academic training and had over six years of preaching experience, two of them in this very community. But in all his previous engagements he had been temporary, provisional, or subordinate. Now he was alone, and now he had committed his whole life to saving the souls of this particular group of Connecticut Valley farmers who sat on the benches before him. The bond between them was as intimate as each man's concern for his own salvation and as public as the worship service that each man was legally compelled to attend. The relationship between Edwards and the Northampton inhabitants was, in fact, a mutual definition: without his presence, they could not really be a church; without their agreement, he could not be a pastor. Such was the rule by which Congregational churches in New England were organized, and such was the institutional structure within which Edwards, evangelist and philosopher, would live his life.

Only three days earlier, Edwards and the Northampton congregation had suffered together through a melancholy experience that reflected the lifelong commitment of a pastor to his flock. On February 13 they had buried the mortal remains of the beloved Reverend Solomon Stoddard, Edwards's grandfather, his predecessor and colleague for two years in the Northampton pulpit. Stoddard, who died on February 11, must have seemed an indispensible component of life in the community: there were few persons in Northampton who had been born before he became the pastor of the only church in that Puritan village. For sixty years, every aspect of daily life had been the subject of his watchful care and his thundering Sabbath sermons. He had been their intellectual and moral leader, their Patriarch in the Old Testament style he deliberately adopted as a model of church polity and community ethics. But Stoddard's stature transcended even the leadership of a small town on the frontier a hundred miles from Boston, for he had in fact been for many decades one of the most influential clergymen in all of New England.

On the day of Stoddard's burial, the funeral sermon was given by the Reverend William Williams of Hatfield, the next town to the north, who was the most eminent of all of Stoddard's six sons-in-law and one son in the ministry. Williams's sermon, soon thereafter published under the title *The Death of a Prophet Lamented and Improved,* took its text from the Book of Zechariah, taught the lesson that even prophets must eventually die, and yet conveyed the sense of desolation which Stoddard's death had brought to his family, the church, and the whole Valley. Williams himself had lost not only a father but also a revered mentor in theology and pastoral concerns whose counsel had always been "grave, but delightful and very profitable." And so he spoke from the depth of his personal bereavement when he warned those gathered at Northampton "not to idolize men, even the best, the ablest and wisest of men, by raising too great expectations from them, or placing too much dependence on them." The temptation was great, Williams acknowledged, because "there are sometimes men [to] whom it pleases God to impart so much of His wisdom and grace, that under God they are accounted as shields of the Earth, the strength and glory of the places where they live. . . ."[1] There was no greater compliment to be given in New England. An echo of this idolatry came two decades later, when Jonathan Edwards wrote of what was then his own congregation that they still revered "Mr. Stoddard's memory, such that many looked on him almost as a sort of deity."[2]

In the audience on this sad occasion were probably many of those most inclined to remember Stoddard as a giant among men, including a major part of the local civic and religious elite, most of whom were related to Stoddard by blood or marriage. Many of the minis-

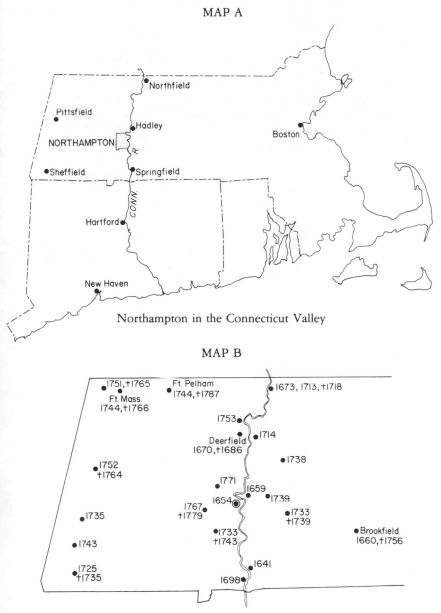

MAP A

Northfield

Pittsfield

Hadley

NORTHAMPTON

Boston

Sheffield

Springfield

Hartford

New Haven

Northampton in the Connecticut Valley

MAP B

1751, †1765

Ft. Mass.
1744, †1766

Ft. Pelham
1744, †1787

1673, 1713, †1718

1753

1714

Deerfield
1670, †1686

1738

1752
†1764

1771

1659

1654

1739

1767
†1779

1735

1733
†1739

1743

1733
†1743

Brookfield
1660, †1756

1725
†1735

1641

1698

The Western Massachusetts Frontier
(Cross indicates church founding, if much later than settlement)

MAP C

Compiled from old maps in the collection at Forbes Library, Northampton, and antiquarian lore from various sources.

Shaded area indicates extent of residential settlement before 1670s. Meetinghouse location indicated (now intersection of Routes 9 and 5, still the center of town). Solomon Stoddard lived on the east slope of Round Hill (house still standing, on Prospect Street); Jonathan Edwards lived on King Street, marked ★ (house gone).

Swampy and hilly areas are indicated. The fields along the river are only a little above the water level in normal times and are frequently flooded. They were the first used, divided as a common field by 1661, were extremely fertile, and remained the most expensive lands in Northampton. The areas marked "inner commons" and the land in what became Southampton and Easthampton were probably not intensively farmed until the mid-nineteenth century. The varying qualities of the land were reflected in the prices registered in deeds, from which the following chart has been drawn. (All prices are in Old Tenor currency.)

PRICES PER ACRE

Date	Old Rainbow	Mountain Div.	Long Div.
1706–12	£6 to £9		
ca. 1720		£0.13.0	£0.5.0
1730–36	£30 to £36	£22.4.5	£0.5.0
1741	£70		
1745		£10	
1749–50	£100		£0.16.4

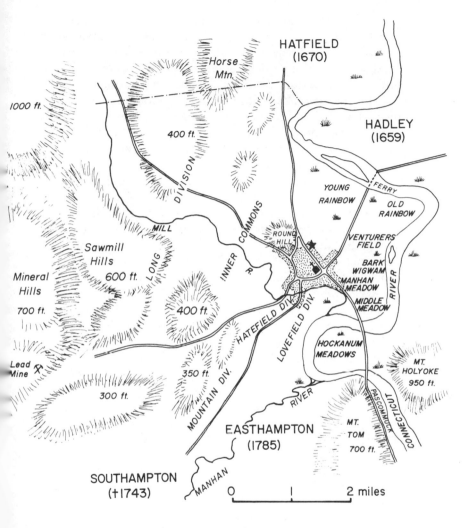

Northampton, 1654–1750s

ters of central New England were undoubtedly there—including Stoddard's oldest son, Anthony, pastor at Woodbury, Connecticut, and his sons-in-law who were ministers at Farmington, Wethersfield, and East Windsor, Connecticut, and Weston and Deerfield, Massachusetts. Another son-in-law, merchant and lawyer Joseph Hawley, lived in Northampton and sat in the meetinghouse near his wife's brother John, Stoddard's only other living son. Colonel John, as he was known, was the military and political leader of all of western Massachusetts; he may have shared a pew with his nephew and protégé, Israel Williams, son of Hatfield's pastor. Israel's cousin Stephen Williams came from his parsonage in Longmeadow, perhaps riding up from Springfield with distantly related magistrate John Pynchon. This distinguished group—Stoddard, Israel Williams, Pynchon—would soon be known colloquially in Boston as the "River Gods," for among themselves they controlled the political, military, and commercial life of the Valley towns and therefore spoke with masterly authority for the region in the General Court.[3] The only man who would have received more automatic reverence in this still-deferential society was the now-deceased Solomon Stoddard, the Patriarch to whom they were paying their last respects.

In the ritual of farewell to the pastor whose career had been longer than most people's lives, the man on whom all eyes must have rested with great curiosity was Stoddard's young successor, Jonathan Edwards, who played a surprisingly small role in the proceedings. He did not preach the funeral sermon, because it was William Williams who was the obvious heir to Stoddard in influence among the community of clergymen in the Valley. Edwards was decidedly a junior colleague.

His relative youth and professional obscurity were again evident a few weeks later, when the great Stoddard was eulogized by one of Boston's most influential divines, the Reverend Doctor Benjamin Colman of the Brattle Street Church. Colman used the occasion of a ceremonial public lecture to lament the loss of a beloved colleague from the west who was "a Prophet and a Father not only to the neighboring churches of his own county, but also to those of the whole land." Colman was conscious of speaking to and for the entire colony, for he knew that his sermon—titled *The Faithful Ministers of Christ Mindful of their own Death. . . . upon the Death of the Learned and*

Venerable Solomon Stoddard—would soon be published and widely distributed.[4] Colman began by noting the most obvious of Stoddard's distinctions, that "for some years" he had been "the most aged minister in the Province." But even in this society which tended to equate age with wisdom, living to fourscore years and six was not the most important source of Stoddard's venerability. He had been famous for "a laborious, burning ministry" and to his fellow clergymen had exemplified the "gifts and graces of the Holy Spirit." Until "near his eightieth year," which was 1723, Stoddard had journeyed almost annually to Boston to attend the Harvard College commencement and then preach the public lecture on the day following, the one time when almost every minister in the colony (most of them Harvard alumni) was sure to be present. It was the most formal of professional occasions, and to have had the honor so regularly signified the height of Stoddard's reputation for both theology and preaching.[5] Colman reported that "both ministers and people received his annual visits with a peculiar reverence and pleasure." He was regarded as "a Peter here among the Disciples . . . very much our Primate . . . among the first for light and integrity, for knowledge and great judgment, for faith and love which is in Christ Jesus, and for zeal and boldness in the cause of Truth and Holiness." Although Stoddard carried himself with an engaging humility in the clerical community, there was "none more diligent and laborious in his studies; none more lively, fervent and unwearied in the Pulpit."

Appended to the published version of Colman's sermon was a copy of the obituary which had appeared in Boston's *Weekly News-Letter* on February 20. "Too eminent a person to be suffered to slip into his grave in silence," Stoddard was described as the very model of the Puritan Patriarch. "His natural powers were quick and strong, and by the blessing of God on his hard studies, he was furnished with that learning which is requisite to make a divine of the first rank." But scholarship alone was not his glory, for he had won many converts to true piety. "He was favoured with a more than ordinary presence of God in his work, and many seals of his ministry, in the course of which there were three remarkable seasons, in which the Spirit of God so moved upon the hearts of his people, that it became almost a general cry of the place, 'What must I do to be saved?' " Stoddard had preached with vigor until the winter of his death, although in his last two years "he had had the satisfaction" of being assisted by his grandson, Jonathan Edwards, as colleague and designated successor. The obituary writer, who was from Northampton but otherwise unidentified, conveyed his sense of the transition in the pulpit by wishing for young Mr. Edwards "that the mantle of Elijah may rest upon Elisha."

But again, we see the young Elisha regarded by others as something of a corollary of the great Stoddard. He preached no public sermon as a memorial to his grandfather, and he did not even write the obituary notice for the Boston newspaper. From the historical record we must assume that he simply took the pulpit by himself on the following Sabbath, after two years of sharing the preaching duties, and finally faced the awesome and lonely challenge of following in Stoddard's footsteps. Because the surviving notes for Edwards's early sermons are not individually dated, we cannot even be sure what his sermon was on that momentous day. But there are three written shortly after that time which refer to Northampton's loss of a special blessing in the ministry of Solomon Stoddard—"him that was as it were Father of the People . . . [who] brought you up most of you from your cradles. . . ." For himself, Edwards asked "that God would be with him that he hath placed here in the work of the ministry, that he would instruct him and give him much of his spirit and grace and give him success in his administrations that he may yet see much of the goodness of God to this people."[6]

These were the hopes of a young man who might well have felt somewhat tense and insecure, a young man who suffered a collapse the following summer which may have been partly emotional. After a long and troubled period of trying to find a place for himself in the professional world, Jonathan Edwards had finally committed himself to a pastoral career in a particular situation in which anything less than astounding success would look like comparative failure. He was stepping into the shoes of the man who had been called the "Congregational Pope" of the Connecticut Valley.[7]

The town to which Solomon Stoddard came as a ministerial candidate in 1669 was still a rude frontier outpost in attitude as well as physical appearance. Northampton had been settled fifteen years earlier, for economic rather than religious reasons, and the early settlers' delay in pursuing the obvious symbols of communal piety distinguished them from the founders of most other Valley towns, who in this era usually migrated as a gathered church with their minister (often after having quarreled with former neighbors over religion).[8] The land-hungry men from Hartford, Windsor, and Springfield downriver who purchased the broad alluvial meadows at Nonotuck from the Indians in 1653 had already been founders of at least one town (some had done it twice), but it took them almost a decade to settle down into the community organization we have come to regard as typically Puritan. Not until 1658 did they hire a preacher, and not until June 1661 was a church officially gathered and the minister officially ordained. In the interval, land had been distributed and cleared and plowed, and civil government was established, but the community had also been disturbed a number of times with quarrels over officeholding and even a period of charges of witchcraft and countercharges of slander.[9]

The decision in 1658 to invite a ministerial candidate and the gathering of a church three years later indicated the town's voluntary transition at last into a settled and orderly Puritan community. The minister was Eleazar Mather (son of the Reverend Richard Mather of Dorchester), and with him he brought six men who were specially invited (with bounties of land) by the town of Northampton and who became its "pillars," not a special party but leaders in church and town government. Whatever the influence of these men, Northampton took on no specially religious character. During the eight years of Mather's pastorate, the members of his church represented only about half the households in town. His influence with even these "saints" was limited, for over his opposition the church endorsed the Half-Way Covenant in October 1668.

Northampton was one of the first churches in the colony to adopt the new polity, which was only recommended to the individual churches by the General Court, and which seemed to meet with more lay than clerical resistance in the first decade after its promulgation. Unlike the church members in many other towns, the Northampton "saints" apparently did not fear diluting their own influence within the church by admitting new members, and the town also showed its liberality by having its representatives vote for the side favoring the new system when the General Court had to arbitrate a controversy over the Half-Way Covenant within Boston's First Church.[10]

When Eleazar Mather died in early 1669, his church hired a successor who was more in accord with their expressed views. Twenty-six-year-old Solomon Stoddard had been a student at Harvard when the Synod of 1662 was meeting there, and—perhaps influenced more by Tutor Jonathan Mitchell than conservative President Charles Chauncy—he emerged as an advocate of the Half-Way Covenant.[11] That position was not, of course, his only qualification for the Northampton pulpit. By 1669 he had taken two degrees at Harvard, served as the college's first librarian, and preached in Barbados for a short time. To this good education and practical experience were added exemplary social credentials. His father, Anthony Stoddard, was a wealthy Boston merchant and a pillar of First Church (a leader, oddly enough, of the conservative faction there).[12] Solomon's mother, his father's second wife, was a daughter of the influential merchant Emmanuel Downing and a niece of Governor John Winthrop. All his life, even when Northampton was no longer really frontier in the social sense, Solomon Stoddard would be the most educated and most cosmopolitan man in the community, as well as one of the richest.

There is no record of the negotiations between Stoddard and his new congregation, but there seems to have been no question of his being settled despite the three-year "trial of his gifts" which was becoming customary in the Connecticut Valley churches. Shortly after his arrival, Stoddard was given a generous gift of land from the town, salary arrangements were made, and within a year he had married his predecessor's widow, Esther Warham Mather. For almost fifteen years he would live in the house which the town had built for her first husband, and he was as devoted a father to the three Mather children as to his own nine offspring.[13]

Stoddard was finally ordained on September 11, 1672, and two months later he and the church signified their agreement to implement fully the recommendations of the Synod of 1662. They established a new category of membership for those "owning the covenant," which they called a "state of education," by voting that

from year to year such as grow up to adult age in the church shall present
themselves to the Elders, and if they be found to understand and assent
unto the doctrine of faith, not to be scandalous in life, and willing to
subject themselves to the government of Christ in this church [they] shall
publickly own the Covenant and be acknowledged members of this
church.

Presumably, the test for admission to full membership (clearly remaining a separate category) was still the relation of an "experimental work of faith," and the judges were "the Elders," the pastor (or
"preaching elder") and the one lay (or "ruling") elder elected by
the church.[14] Although this "half-way" status was the liberal trend
of the era, the direction of change was clearly toward greater ministerial power, since the traditional Congregational role of the brethren as judges of new communicants was silently discarded.

These reforms in church polity indicate the expectation of a dynamic continuum from baptism through "owning the covenant" to
full membership, but the church's hopes for spiritual growth were
not rewarded. Although 105 persons owned the covenant in 1672
and six more did so by 1679, only fourteen of them had become full
members of the church by the later year.[15] Thereafter, the presence
of certain records and the absence of others indicate the further shift
of power to the pastor as a result of this apathy. After 1677 Stoddard
stopped distinguishing in his records between degrees of membership and kept only a running list of members "in full communion."[16]
This was done, however, without any formal enactment by the
church. Stoddard's records, the only official ones, were a de facto
elimination of categories, but the best piece of contemporary evidence suggests that the church adhered at least nominally to its
previous gradations of membership. Only in 1690 did the church
officially agree to the position Stoddard had been advocating from
the pulpit for over a decade, that the Lord's Supper was rightfully
available to all those with "a knowledge of principles of religion and
not scandalous by open sinful living." Significantly, this approval of
open communion was not recorded in the Northampton church
book. A neighboring clergyman was shocked enough to record the
event in his diary for posterity to read, but Stoddard himself deemed
it to be of little importance, since it merely ratified the position he

had already espoused.[17] What he did record was just the names of those who were in full communion because satisfactory to *him* in their understanding of the principles of Christianity and in their behavior. (According to Jonathan Edwards, Stoddard exercised a veto on church admissions.[18]) During the rest of his ministry, almost every adult in Northampton was entered on Stoddard's list—perhaps as early in life as age fourteen—and therefore gathered into the fold of church discipline, in which the most effective authority was that of the pastor.

As he neglected explanations in his church record book, Solomon Stoddard turned to a wider audience through a different medium. In a series of vigorous treatises on church polity and discipline, he presented a coherent doctrinal platform for his innovations in practice. Almost all his writings were focused on the pragmatic issues of church government, the functions of the sacraments, and pastoral technique. Avoiding the polemicist's usual defensiveness, he rarely cited any clerical or philosophical predecessor as an authority but instead he used straightforward exegesis of Scripture, with emphatic language that never hesitated to explore the most far-reaching implications of classic Reformed doctrines.

Stoddard's tracts intensified in acerbity of tone and in depth of critique of the "New England Way" as it had evolved, but his underlying positions remained the same from first (1687) to last (1723). Two principles were the foundation of all his theology. The first was an essentially Calvinist emphasis on the inscrutability and immeasurable glory of God, with its necessary corollaries of man's relative smallness and his inability to earn salvation in any way. As manifestations of His essential justice and mercy, God had sent His son to be man's Redeemer; by definition, therefore, Christ's righteousness was perfect and sufficient for the salvation of all men, who had only to believe in the truth of Gospel promises. (By "all" men was meant, of course, those whom God had preelected for eternal life.) Good works might earn a saint additional glory in heaven, but entrance to that realm was gained only through faith. The second principle of Stoddard's theology was that God had commanded that He be worshipped by all men, even those not elect, who could still use their natural faculties (impaired as they were by Adam's fall) to understand the glory of God and to respond to His majesty with outward and temporal signs of obeisance. This worship, in its broadest meaning, required men to behave morally simply because God so commanded (not because ethics could be deduced from a reasonable or humanistic view of man's relations to other men); and men were reminded of their distance from God because even the best behavior was not sufficient to earn salvation. Although many divines interpreted the New Testament, with its historical elements of early Christian practice, as a total replacement of the Old Testament model, Stoddard insisted that the Mosaic rules were still largely in force—not as the price of salvation, but as requirements of an external covenant even though an inner faith in Christ was the condition for Saving Grace. This double reliance on the fundamental tenets of Reformed Christianity—God's arbitrary dispensation of free grace, and His command of worship—was the basis upon which Stoddard constructed his evolving series of challenges to the "establishment" of New England Congregationalism.

Stoddard's first published treatise appeared in 1687 under the title *The Safety of Appearing at the Day of Judgment in the Righteousness of Christ*, which accurately summarized its message. Emphasizing the effectiveness of Christ's mediation, Stoddard implicitly discarded the "taming" of God that had come about in New England as two generations of Puritan ministers had tried to evade the classic Calvinist dilemmas of enforcing moral behavior when it could not earn salvation and saving men from despair when there was no earthly certainty of being among the elect. What Perry Miller and subsequent historians have called the "federal" theology had increasingly emphasized the likelihood that God would elect those who behaved as though they were saints. They had also enlarged the role of preparation for salvation—the use of means such as prayer, ordinances, sincere moral reform—and had come as close as possible without actually doing so to saying that God would reward those who prepared.[19] In *The Safety of Appearing,* Stoddard was merely reminding his colleagues that God was still utterly arbitrary, and that conversion was a real and discreet event entirely in God's hands, not contained within gradual steps of man's increasing spiritual abilities. So much was well within the bounds of New England orthodoxy, even if the preaching of some ministers had strayed from this strict doctrine.

The Safety of Appearing did, however, contain some disturbing innovations. First of all, in emphasizing the vividness of the inner sense of grace which God gives to his elect in the moment of conversion, Stoddard announced that the truth of this experience is incommunicable. There were some external signs of grace that could lead to a charitable judgment of professions of faith—"their carriage savours of the fear of God, love to God, submission to the will of God, care for the advancement of the glory of God"—but, ultimately, conversion "cannot be made evident by experience to the world, because the world cannot certainly know that those that profess faith in Christ have it in reality." What justification could be drawn, therefore, for the churches' presuming to admit to full membership only those whom they were certain to be saints? And of the benefits of membership, Stoddard had an even more unorthodox opinion. About the Lord's Supper, he wrote:

> *The great design of this ordinance is for the strengthening of faith; therein is offered to us special communion with a crucified saviour. . . . Some when in a discouraged condition are backward to come. . . . But God nowhere requires a faith of assurance in those that partake of that ordinance. . . . And though it must be granted that to partake of it without faith is a sin, and so deserves damnation; and so it does to pray or hear [the Word] without faith.*

Though ambiguous, this language could not disguise the doctrinal foundations being prepared for open communion—for without a certainty of knowledge or the necessity of a "faith of assurance," there was no reason for any man to neglect such spiritual nourishment.[20]

Stoddard was, of course, denying the entire philosophical ground on which the New England churches maintained distinctions between full and "half-way" members, between those with presumed conversion experiences and those who would submit to church discipline by professing only a "historical" faith in the truth of Christian doctrines. *The Safety of Appearing* was a clear and deliberate challenge to the eastern Massachusetts clergy, for whom the major spokesman in the late seventeenth century was the Reverend Increase Mather. For the next twenty years, Stoddard and Mather (aided by his son,

Cotton) would debate the New England Way and its Scriptural underpinnings.[21]

For almost a decade the quarrel just simmered, for the Mathers were busy adjusting their own position and their conception of New England's mission to the consequences of the new Massachusetts charter of 1691, which tended to disestablish the Congregational church by disallowing the requirement of full church membership for the legal status of freeman of the colony (property-holding was substituted). The next sally was Stoddard's, a Boston public lecture in 1698 published under the title *The Tryal of Assurance.* Stoddard there made perfectly clear what had been implied in *The Safety of Appearing,* that men cannot convey any reliable information about their own conversions; therefore, the world cannot judge the professor. This was a position he would maintain for the rest of his career.[22]

By 1690, if not before, Stoddard was preaching that the Lord's Supper was a converting ordinance, but he did not widely advertise such a doctrine until 1700. That year he published in London (perhaps because no Boston printer would abet such unorthodoxy) a treatise called *The Doctrine of Instituted Churches,* by far the most radical of his works. Reiterating the arguments about the lawfulness of participation by the unregenerate, Stoddard then went on to say that the sacrament was a means of regeneration for those already "converted to the Christian religion" (i.e., rationally persuaded of the doctrines of the church).[23] This position might have seemed dangerously close to the Roman Catholic doctrine of effective power in the sacraments, rejected by Protestantism, and Stoddard thereafter was careful to insist that God would undoubtedly only choose the Supper as an occasion on which to convert men who were already proper church members. He emphasized that the Supper was an ordinance much like the others (prayer, preaching, external rituals of obedience); it differed only in being a particularly dramatic enactment of the Word.[24] This definition amounted to a radical devaluation of the sacrament, which had become very special in New England as the last preserve of the elect and therefore the locus of spiritual examination of oneself and others. Stoddard even accused his clerical colleagues of making a superstition of the Supper.[25] But the defensiveness of his tone after *The Doctrine of Instituted*

Churches, and the lack of any public clerical support, show that he had gone too far.

Stoddard was on surer ground when he argued merely for the opening of communion to all because no one could know for sure who was regenerate. In this, he was followed by a number of churches, although not all used his line of justification.[26] When Mather and his supporters insisted on the traditional New England doctrine that the Lord's Supper was a "seal of the covenant," meaning the Covenant of Grace given to man in conversion, Stoddard responded that it *was* a seal of the covenant—but a seal to the external covenant, which included all professors of a historical faith in Christianity. He also described the Supper as a seal in its testimony to the abstract reality of the Covenant of Grace: "Sacraments do not seal up pardon and salvation to all that receive them, but are seals to the truth of the covenant."[27] Stoddard had no patience at all with reverence for tradition, and he didn't scruple to accuse the filiopietistic Mathers of leading the New England churches into an abyss of spiritually arid formalism. He regarded the ecclesiology of the first planters of Massachusetts as an experiment that had not worked, although "some of their posterity" regarded them as "but one degree beneath the Apostles." The hallowed practice of ranked categories of church members was especially pernicious. "The limiting of the Lord's Supper to a small number," he wrote, "has a tendency to nourish carnal confidence in them that are admitted, and to nourish prophaneness in them that are excluded."[28]

Moreover, Stoddard's other radical doctrine turned also on this very point about the carnal confidence of those who passed the tests in the exclusivist churches. *The Doctrine of Instituted Churches* not only defined the Supper as a converting ordinance but also denied any real power to communicants by questioning the entire structure of Congregationalism. Having defined a church as "a society of saints joined together, according to the appointment of Christ for the constant carrying on of his public worship," Stoddard identified that society as the whole community. Individual church covenants were "wholly unscriptural," unnecessary, and "the reason that many among us are shut out of the church, to whom church privileges do belong." The true basis of any church organization was simply in geographic propinquity—God's command that He be worshipped left men to organize in the most efficient way, but their enactments carried no special grace in themselves.[29]

Delivering another blow to Congregational polity, Stoddard defined "visible saints" (traditionally assumed to be persons about whom there was at least a charitable judgment that they were among the elect) as "such as make a serious profession of the true religion, together with those that do descend from them, till rejected of God." They could even be persons who were excommunicated by an individual church. Those under censure could be barred from the Lord's Supper until they repented, but their children were still allowed baptism because the parents remained in the covenant despite rejection by a particular church.[30]

Rendering meaningless the relationship between an individual (even one who was really saved) and the local, covenanted church, Stoddard proceeded to recommend an equally novel form of church government. Although the Cambridge Platform of 1648, still serving as the blueprint for Massachusetts churches, had allowed great powers to the brethren of the church (the lay members in full communion, or at least the males among them), even denying the pastor any power to act without their concurrence, Stoddard insisted that Scripture taught that the "keys" of Christ's kingdom on earth had been given only to church elders. Once elected by the brethren from among "persons fitly qualified," the elders or officers constituted the "Presbytery," which alone had the power of censuring offenders and absolving penitents; with this "the brethren of the church are not to intermeddle." But the "Teaching Officer" or pastor alone "is appointed by Christ to baptize and administer the Lord's Supper, and therefore he is made the Judge by God, what persons those ordinances are to be administered to." There was no role for brethren or lay elders in this judgment: "We never read that the Apostles did advise with the church, whether they should baptize such as offered themselves."[31] By the time Stoddard was writing, in fact, the lay eldership was dying out in New England, so all powers were really left in the hands of the pastor. (The Ruling Elder who served with Stoddard, Ebenezer Strong, was about as old as the ancient pastor and died on the very same day. No one was elected to replace him.)

The autocracy of Stoddard's system was pointed out by the Mathers when they accused their frontier adversary of wanting to be a

"Congregational Pope." But Stoddard's empire would be Presbyterian rather than Roman. The polity he described for an individual congregation would exist within a larger structure which he called the national church and which would be run by authoritative synods of ministers and lay representatives. As usual, he reasoned from Scripture (the subjection of the early Christian churches to the Jewish national church), but he also argued from reason and experience. Local congregational autonomy "is too lordly a principle, it is too ambitious a thing for every small congregation to arrogate such an uncontrollable power, and to be accountable to none on earth; this is neither a probable way for the peace of the churches, nor for the safety of church members. . . ." Synods were not to be seen as infallible, and their recommendations were to be judged by each man against his own conscience. But they would provide necessary courts of appeal for an individual oppressed by his own church, or for persons who wished to complain against others—even church elders—and found their own churches unwilling to hear charges against the accused.[32] Stoddard's contempt for the brethren was elaborated in his 1718 *Examination of the Power of the Fraternity,* which concluded that they should have almost no power. The brethren "have a greater fondness for power than ability to use it . . . the government of the church is given unto the elders . . . the fraternity have no power in binding and loosing." As usual, Scriptural evidence was presented. As usual, the ultimate argument was from experience: "We have no reason to think that Christ would intrust the government of His church with men so uncapable to govern."[33]

This is Stoddard at his most authoritarian. But there was another side to his concern for the church, equally strong in the period during which he wrote these imprecations against the prideful powers of the brethren. This other Stoddard is the evangelist, Stoddard the compassionate guide of souls in the torments of conversion. A link between the two sides of the Patriarch can be found in his preaching technique, which carried the same forceful expression and driving rhythms as did his intellectually stark treatises on ecclesiology. This style has been best described by Wilson H. Kimnach, who notes Stoddard's calculated use of imagery and "pungent, epigrammatic expression" for emotional impact and then concludes:

"In his hands, the traditional Puritan sermon retained the outward form of Ramist logic, but it had become a meticulously prepared instrument of psychological manipulation."[34]

Preaching was central to Stoddard's evangelical technique as outlined most clearly in his *Guide to Christ* (1714) and *Treatise Concerning Conversion* (1719). Preparation for salvation, from the minister's perspective, began with the preaching of terror, to make the consciences of sinners tender. Effective ministers were "Sons of Thunder: men had need have storms in their hearts, before they will betake themselves to Christ for refuge." "The Word is as an Hammer and we should use it to break the Rocky Hearts of Men."[35] A recent survey of Puritan rhetoric has credited Stoddard with "the most powerful—up to that time—preaching of the stark terror of inscrutable judgments and of hell's torments."[36] The master of this technique had many imitators in the Connecticut Valley, and it is largely through Stoddard's influence that the region was peppered with religious revivals in the early eighteenth century. Stoddard himself, according to Jonathan Edwards, had "harvests" in 1679, 1683, 1696, 1712, and 1718, during which "the bigger part of the young people in the town seemed mainly concerned for their eternal salvation."[37] This success was the best propaganda for Stoddardeanism—evangelism within an open church structure—and in the mid-eighteenth century, most of the churches of the upper Connecticut Valley were Stoddardean.[38]

Stoddard's own church was known in the years before the Great Awakening as the nucleus of evangelism in New England, and of course it would become even more famous for that contribution to regional culture during the pastorate of Jonathan Edwards, who derived much of his own preaching technique from his grandfather's tutelage. Edwards described Stoddard's Northampton in his *Faithful Narrative of the Surprising Work of God* as the home of "heart religion," but although that term was used in deliberate opposition to the more common New England style of increasing rationalism, it is a mistake to think of Stoddard as preaching terror in a crude assault on the emotions. From all available evidence, Stoddard and Edwards, and most eighteenth-century evangelists, were very unlike the road-show revivalists so notorious in the nineteenth century. The terror that Stoddard preached was designed to be a very rational exposition of clear and incontrovertible dangers to the person and soul. Hell was a real place, and to describe it in detail was not sensationalism. (Edwards once defended himself against the charge of emotional exploitiveness by saying that it was surely "a reasonable thing to fright a person out of an house on fire."[39])

Stoddard believed that God's Spirit, through the medium of the preached Word, reached man's heart (or "will," in the faculty terminology of the time) through man's understanding, his rational apprehensions. That conduit was not entirely passive, however, and was described thus by Stoddard:

> *God deals with men as with* rational creatures, *and prevails upon their hearts in a way suitable to those natures: though he put forth acts of power yet not* of violence *on the will: but he gains the consent of that by the discovering of those reasons that are of sufficient weight to sway it; indeed the understanding and will in man being faculties of the same soul and really one and the same thing, the same act of God upon the soul that puts light into the understanding, does also suitably incline the will. . . ."*[40]

Decades later, his model of conversion was still the same, and in *Three Sermons Lately Preached at Boston,* published in 1717, he described the will as a "blind faculty" following the understanding. Stoddard was taking one side in a centuries-old debate about whether the Spirit touched the will (the faculty of choice) through the understanding or directly: Stoddard's "intellectualism" put him in the minority among evangelical Protestants.[41] But it is also possible to deduce from Stoddard's writings a definition of conversion as that moment when the understanding and the will are most perfectly integrated. Such a position strongly prefigures the new psychology of conversion that would be outlined by Stoddard's grandson Edwards. Whatever the precise definition of the process in theory, Stoddard did indeed touch people's hearts. In his descriptions of conversion, Stoddard displayed an experiential knowledge that was unrivaled until his grandson Edwards would become the master analyst of the "varieties of religious experience" in the 1730s.

Once terror preaching had broken through man's defenses of intellectual pride and complacency, the wounded soul required skillful encouragement so that it would be receptive to grace. Increasingly intense in Stoddard's writings is a loving sympathy for human beings suffering spiritual anxiety and emotional pain, and he wrote pages and pages of advice to other ministers about dealing gently but firmly with doubts and distresses in converts. His very first treatise, *The Safety of Appearing,* had included a long section with subtly encouraging answers to religious doubts phrased in the first person. Stoddard assumed no divine power to read a heart, but he seemed to possess a rare ability to inspire men to keep striving and keep hoping for God's mercy. His 1714 *Guide to Christ* was a manual for other ministers in guiding souls "through the work of conversion," and he advocated a very austere encouragement to those in spiritual distress. A standard technique was to keep reminding men that their discouragements (especially the temptation of wicked thoughts) were *not* signs that they were not saved.[42] So thorough and sensibly practical was this pastoral guide that it was reprinted and widely sold during the revivals of 1735 and 1742.

The "work of humiliation" was the central tenet in Stoddard's doctrine of conversion. He labeled it a part of preparation and therefore the work of common and not saving grace; here he followed John Norton's *The Orthodox Evangelist* (1657) and differed from the Mathers, who saw the merest spark of spiritual life as a beginning of the principle. Humiliation would sometimes, but not necessarily, be followed by true conversion, which was accomplished in an instant through the understanding and its irresistible power over the will.[43]

Humiliation was particularly important because it represented the ultimate stage to which man could bring himself with the help of the evangelical preacher. Man could and should strive and avoid discouragement—and should even wholeheartedly attempt to use the means that he was told would not work, for Stoddard insisted that God works "particularly, by giving [the elect person] experience of the failing of all means."[44] The word "experience" is crucial to the meaning here. That was the solution, a brilliant one, to the seemingly unavoidable dilemma of Calvinism, the need to mediate between predestination and the necessity to force men to exert themselves. The point Stoddard was making in that marvelous phrase was that men should try their best to save themselves, because *only by having done so would they really understand that it wasn't sufficient.* Any man who didn't try his utmost could always tell himself that a better effort on his part would have conquered his innate sinfulness. Thinking oneself an unregenerate sinner through choice, or some sort of personal volition, was therefore the last bastion of pride. But Stoddard understood. His catalogues of doubts, in the *Guide to Christ* and other works, complement this insight into the nature of experience to make him truly a psychologist of religion. Here lay the source of his unshakable conviction that evangelism within an institutionally open church was the best way to save souls. In Stoddard's church there would be no special status as a refuge for those who could stop short of entire humiliation, complete abasement of self and submission to God. There was no public designation of "sainthood" to shelter the hypocrite: each man was naked before the onslaughts of Stoddard's determination to reach the hearts of his flock. Each man would hear only one message, constantly repeated: the essence of his duty was total trust in God. Then grace would come.

One of the keys to the process was the sensitive spiritual guide, one who could keep men going down in self-esteem until they hit a nadir of pride without letting them develop a self-destructive despair (which was also a kind of pride—thinking that God lacked the power to save you, or mercy enough to cover all your sins—that quintessentially Puritan pride in being the greatest of sinners). And Stoddard became more explicit in the writings of his later years, after he had had revivals of his own, about the qualities needed in a guide of souls. Although he wrote in 1708 that an unconverted man could be the "instrument to convert others," in 1714 he wrote of a "need for experimental knowledge in a minister," and in 1723 he explicitly stated that "experience best fits men to teach others."[45] Once again, experience was the telling concept.

These thoughts on the role of the pastor as spiritual guide through a process so hard to describe, and the centrality of the conversion experience in all of Stoddard's theology, may be explained by the possibility—supported by family tradition—that he himself was converted *after* his entrance into the ministry. It is possible that his ordination was delayed because of his unconverted state, and there is indeed no record of his having joined any church in full communion until he became a member in Northampton in April 1672, three years after his arrival. One version of the story even suggests that it was while distributing the bread of the Lord's Supper to his congregation that Stoddard was visited by the Spirit.[46]

Stoddard's personal spiritual history is one of the many important things that we need to know and probably can never know. Another is exactly what his practice was in his own church. We know that he used the sermon both in Northampton and in public lectures in Boston to preach thundering denunciations of sin.[47] We know that he advocated preaching terror, and a few examples of his vivid descriptions of hell torments do survive.[48] There is reliable testimony that he had religious "harvests." That is really all that we do know. From his doctrines, we might assume that he was a complete autocrat in the Northampton church, and Jonathan Edwards said that Stoddard had a veto, but church records are silent on any changes in polity after 1672. If communion was opened in 1690 or even earlier, it is entirely plausible that Stoddard used more informal means of controlling the community—in fact, he must have done so, because it is just impossible to believe that he tolerated anarchy in his congregation. We know from *The Doctrine of Instituted Churches* that he did not use denial of baptism for infants as a means of controlling the parents, since even children of excommunicated parents were defined as being within the covenant. It is easy to see Stoddard nevertheless denying access to the communion table to particular persons on particular occasions, and acting as sole judge in the matter, for in *Instituted Churches* he described eligible communicants as only those of blameless behavior. He also wrote that only those under censure could be barred from the table—but during his ministry only two admonitions and three excommunications were recorded in the Northampton church book, so there must have been less formalized processes of censure.[49] The Patriarch who did not bother to mark the "new covenanting" of 1690 in his church records might well have dispensed with official indictments of those he disciplined, since—like faithful Christians before their God—their submission to authority would bring complete forgiveness.

Given the heat with which Stoddard and the Mathers argued about the requirements for full communion, it is interesting to note that each would have admitted the same persons. (Mather's preface to Stoddard's *Guide to Christ,* a formal mending of the breach between them to serve the common goal of evangelism, even suggested that Stoddard was too stringent a judge of communicants.) But they would have called them by different names: Stoddard would have admitted men undergoing preparation while calling them still unconverted; to Mather, they would have been admissible because undergoing the first stages of conversion. (In Cotton Mather's 1690 *Companion for Communicants,* and in Boston's Second Church, whose ministry he shared with his father, those with only a hope of or desire for conversion were admitted to full privileges.[50]) One advantage of Stoddardeanism was, therefore, that it maintained this negative definition of most church members and thereby preserved for the minister a stick with which to beat them spiritually—when thundered at from the pulpit, the most arrogant laymen would at least not have the complacency of a publicly certified sainthood.

Real sainthood was not lost in the process, or so Stoddard insisted. If we see his doctrines as separating the social from the spiritual covenants—the church or national covenant from the individual covenant of grace—we must acknowledge that his intent was thereby to liberate the covenant of grace from the tests man would impose on it to avoid the shaping of the experience of true grace to that which man could measure. Nothing hindered true conversions in Northampton. Stoddard's evangelical writings testify to their possibility, and Jonathan Edwards's writings attest to their actuality. (In describing the revival of 1734–35, Edwards noted that the ultimate test of its being truly a work of the Spirit was the favorable verdict by "a considerable number that my grandfather thought to be savingly converted in [his] time."[51]) The great achievement of Stoddard's system was that it kept church discipline separate from evangelical efforts—and vice versa. If there were episodes of bad behavior, one did not have to suspect that the foundations were rotting. Whole nations were in covenant with God, and individual conditions were more private matters. On the other hand, good behavior wasn't allowed to become a source of complacency. Surely it was when his congregation were behaving most morally that Stoddard hammered at them most inexhaustibly about their unregenerate state. In either case, each side of the professional role of pastor

—the disciplinarian and the evangelist—was kept stronger by being functionally separate. Historians who have felt forced to choose one side or the other as the real Stoddard have overlooked the point he made about the interdependence of true piety and good order, as well as the advantages illustrated in his career of keeping the two roles theoretically distinct.[52]

We must return to the question of how the church related to the wider community—particularly, what social structures were assumed in the various models of church polity advanced in colonial New England. There was undoubtedly something peculiar to the Connecticut Valley in Connecticut and Massachusetts that made presbyterian forms of church organization popular, for the Stoddardean churches were in the majority in the upper Valley, and the openness of sacraments in a number of Connecticut churches was complemented by the colony's official recommendation of the presbyterial Saybrook Platform in 1708.[53] But outside the orbit of Stoddard's personal charisma, there were many anti-presbyterial churches downriver, and so it is impossible to discern any real pattern until more communities are studied in detail.

It has often been speculated or even assumed that somehow the Stoddardean system was particularly suited to the frontier condition of Northampton: the dominant interpretation of Stoddard by historians is as an innovator of pragmatic responses to the frontier environment. Perry Miller labeled Stoddard a realist who extended the compromises of the essentially medieval Puritans until the logic of doctrine fit the facts of the West; countering previous assumptions that Stoddard must have been a frontier democrat because he opposed the Mathers, Miller insisted that Stoddard sided with the aristocrats against the leveling tendencies of the frontier.[54] Stoddard was indeed a pragmatist, his major concerns were ecclesiology and psychology rather than the more abstract branches of theology, and there is no doubt that he defended the traditional power of church and clergy against the social trend toward secularization. But it is not so easy to identify Stoddard's enemy and the socioeconomic qualities of his domain.

One of the few scholars to address directly the question of the popularity of Stoddard's doctrines with the laity, the eventual acceptance of open communion by his church (which is avoided by the Stoddard-as-anti-democrat school of thought), has described open communion as especially useful in the isolated Connecticut Valley settlements, which "strongly felt the need to cohere around the church" because they lacked other forms of association.[55] These theories, however, ignore the tendency of true frontier churches in the Valley to be purist about the Lord's Supper, as Northampton itself was until 1690, and they build upon the mistaken assumption that Northampton was still a frontier town in social organization when communion was opened and Stoddard denounced the fundamentals of Congregationalism.[56] On the contrary, a rather different connection between doctrine and social environment in Northampton is suggested by the timing of the changes in church practice and Stoddard's declarations of hostility toward the brethren. Let us look briefly at the social structure of Solomon Stoddard's Northampton.

By the last decade of the seventeenth century, Northampton was forty years old, still in danger from Indian attacks, but no longer socially primitive. The town had grown from fifty-five families in 1661 to about a hundred families in 1675; there would be two hundred families by the time Stoddard died.[57] Although too few pertinent documents have survived for us to evaluate in any detail the economic changes which took place in the Stoddardean era, it is possible to construct a large-scale profile of landholding in Northampton, and the distribution of this most fundamental form of wealth provides a place to look for leveling. The relevant information comes from the list of land given out in the first division in 1661, a 1676 tax list (with most property undoubtedly being in land), and a 1700 list of all land already given to each man that was the basis for the third (and last major) division, later that year.[58] A comparison of these three profiles shows a strikingly similar distribution of land from the earliest to the latest. The richest ten percent of men consistently held about one quarter of all the land; the poorest ten percent of men held no more than two percent of the land. The men on the top and bottom in 1700 were generally the sons of men in similar positions in 1661. By this measure, there was no leveling going on: men were not moving far from the position in the agricultural hierarchy which their families had held in 1661. But the similarity of the profiles of acres or values is somewhat misleading, for this was real property that had an income-producing value of greater variability than its market (sale or rental) value: each acre of land produced a crop which could, if plentiful, contribute to a higher material standard of living or provide capital toward the acquisition of more property. The profit from more acreage was greater than the difference in numbers of acres; the trend was clearly toward a greater distinction between rich and poor families, although anything a social scientist would call class stratification was only just beginning in Northampton in 1700.

This pattern of increasing distance between richer and poorer men in a third-generation agricultural community is by now a common finding of New England town studies,[59] and it was a very gradual process, perhaps less visible to the participants than were certain other markers of social change, small but symbolically important adjustments in the way that community life was organized, which cluster remarkably around the turn of the eighteenth century. About 1700, for example, home lots began to be claimed outside the mile-by-mile-and-a-half nucleated village which had housed two generations. (Map C, on page 17, shows the village and fields.) There also came the first appearance of a spirit of improvement regarding land: when the third division, called the Long Division, was planned, what were to have been four separate ranges were made into two (each man therefore getting twice as much acreage in each of two plots) so that "men might be in better capacity to improve their land."[60] Until this point, land allotments had always been scattered in small parcels in the meadows with names such as Bark Wigwam and Walnut Trees and Old Rainbow, so that the inequalities of productivity might be spread out more evenly. But around the turn of the century, men were starting to consolidate larger holdings, and the deeds registered with the county show an increase in the number of purchases where one specified boundary is land already owned by the grantee.[61] Until some unknown date in the eighteenth century (probably around 1745) the Northampton meadows were cultivated in common: the land was cleared, fenced, plowed, harvested, and opened in winter to grazing animals, all by common labor and common decision. But these commons were the rich alluvial lands first divided in the 1660s, east of the town center; the areas to the west developed after the second division in 1684 were worked by individual families.

After 1700 there seems to have been a serious land problem for the community as a corporate entity and for individuals. There was, first of all, a decline in productivity in the heretofore wondrously fertile flood-plain land which had been used intensively since the 1650s. Not for another century, however, would the Valley adopt the scientific agriculture using legumes, crop rotation, and systematic manuring.[62] To cope with this deficiency, in about 1700 the farmers of the Northampton area began to specialize in fattening cattle for the Boston market, where the "victuallers" were eager for beef; but cattle grazing was profitable only for those who had extensive acreage. Even the clearing of former wastelands would soon not provide enough land for all men to engage in any type of agriculture with the hope of profit.[63]

In 1701 there appeared a formal group made up of the hereditary Proprietors of town land, as distinguished from the Town as a legal body. (They did not list their names, so it is uncertain precisely who was included.) These were the descendants of the founders and those who settled through the 1660s and were admitted to proprietary rights. The Town had always performed the functions of land custodian through its public meetings or selectmen, but in 1701 the official Proprietors reserved to themselves the use of the valuable pine trees on the commons (all men could still cut other wood for limited household use, but the trade in pitch and turpentine was too profitable to share), and in March 1703 the Proprietors formally recorded their confirmation of all previous land grants made by the Town—as though to preface their assumption of this prerogative.[64] There was, nonetheless, so little land left that was worth granting that the Proprietors never really *did* much. Then in 1715 a group of men, whose names have been excised from the records as if deliberately to frustrate the historian, challenged the very legality of all previous land divisions, which were based on the shares granted in 1661. This group tried to get the land divisions overthrown by legal process, but an arbitration committee of prominent Connecticut citizens decided against them, and the matter seemed to die.[65] Until the mid-1750s there remained a constant tension between the Proprietors and those excluded from hereditary shares, although all that was left to fight over were the rocky woodlands, and the records are the typically laconic Yankee accounts that simply say that meeting after meeting was held—not what was said, or who spoke up.[66] Once again, what we would most like to know is probably lost forever.

A major turning point in the town's economic and political history came in March 1703, when the last large-scale granting of home lots was made. As far as can be determined, most of the adult males in town by this time had been given a home lot (usually four acres). Only a very few more home lots were given out after that date, those only to the sons of the more powerful and already land-rich Proprietors, and none after 1731.[67] All the usable meadow lands convenient to the village had long been parceled out. Northampton never self-consciously declared that it had no more land to give, but in retrospect the end of free grants was a major change in the accustomed function of the town.

The town as a corporate body also relinquished almost all its other economic functions in the early eighteenth century. It could no longer (after 1676) give out extra land to rescue men from accidental disaster, such as the destruction of homes in an Indian raid. No longer were rates set for "public utilities" such as mills.[68] The old-fashioned economics of subsistence farming in close-knit Puritan communities were giving way to the forces of competition—though competition between families more than between individuals. This change can be seen in the method by which it was decided what nonagricultural occupations would be practiced in Northampton. In the frontier years of the first generation, the town could only support one man in each craft, but a number of crafts were necessary; the town therefore used bounties of common land to attract men with specific skills—a tanner, a cooper, a blacksmith—and to encourage capital investments such as mill building. But this practice was abandoned after the turn of the eighteenth century.[69] Thereafter, the decisions were made by family units, as illustrated in the history of the Pomeroy family, who were blacksmiths. In the 1660s the town secured the services of Medad Pomeroy (or Pumry, as he spelled it and probably pronounced it), who had recently arrived from Windsor, with the gift of a set of blacksmith tools and a promise of all the town's work and a large parcel of land, on condition that he would stay in town and be their smith. Medad's son Ebenezer and his sons Seth and Ebenezer, Jr., succeeded in the family trade, which was a local monopoly. When Seth's second son was born in 1739, the baby was named Quartus—not because he was the fourth child or the fourth son, but because (declared his father's will a few years later) he was intended to be the fourth blacksmith in a direct line.[70] The family and the market (which did not yet guarantee enough business for another smithy), not any communal decision of the town, determined that Quartus would be a blacksmith. And he was. The Pomeroys were also among the richest families in Northampton in real estate, because the initial advantage of Medad's generous Proprietor's grants was increased by judicious marriages and purchases, and the consolidation of holdings was facilitated by the capital for investment available to successful artisans.

As the traditional economic resources of land and trade monopolies became scarce after 1700, there occurred a number of events that indicated the increasing psychological distance between richer and poorer members of the community. In 1705, six years after first electing "overseers of the poor," the town voted to build a poorhouse. Significantly, there is little evidence from other records that there were many poor people in Northampton, certainly not enough to warrant an asylum. But somehow they were *perceived* to exist, and the vote to build a poorhouse—though never put into effect—is a vote of no-confidence in the older system of poor relief by which people without means were boarded by private charity or with town funds in the homes of more well-off citizens.[71] Perhaps it was becoming harder to get the successful farmers to take in the indigent. The residents of Northampton, on the other hand, seemed equally reluctant to exercise the Christian watch over their neighbors' behavior that had been a mainstay of the Puritan community on the frontier: in 1699 it was voted to pay cash rewards to those who informed on crimes. Payment was now also a necessary incentive to get men to serve as town constable. Other services once required of citizens became tasks for special economic categories of men: as late as 1699, each man had to work a few days per year repairing roads, but in 1722 it was voted to hire laborers with town taxes.[72] Hard physical work, that greatest of equalizers among the men who first settled Northampton, was now to be avoided by those who didn't need to do it for cash. This provides a useful sign of the passing of the frontier and all that it had meant socially.

Unless Northampton was different from every other New England town which has been studied in recent years, there should have been developing some perceptible social classes by the time a third generation of settlers was coming to maturity. By the standards of the nineteenth and twentieth centuries, the distance between richest and poorest was still small, but the absence of a developed market economy also made it very difficult for any man to amass great wealth on his own. It was becoming more likely that a man would spend his life in the economic station to which he had been born, and that was something of a change from the opportunities offered to the first settlers of the frontier town, for some of the richest men in early Northampton had once been poor.

Perhaps in parallel development, rather than as a direct reflection of a tightening of economic resources, the community's self-expression through what is usually called town politics became notably less harmonious after about 1690. (The absence in the records of explicit mention of disorder is, of course, no sure sign of the existence of harmony; but we can at least note the occurrence of disorder so extreme that it reached the public records.) As might be expected, as the community had first organized itself into a working system, there had been some "tumults" in the early town meetings and occasional charges of voting irregularities. The next period of disorder did not come until 1679, when there was "much discourse and agitation" about the town's grant of working capital to men trying to start a lead mine. (The mine fizzled, and the problem disappeared.) Men quite regularly came to the town meeting in the following years to request pieces of land or privileges to dam waterways and rearrange roads so as to start mills, and their requests were always granted. But in 1692, in a rather un-Puritan and un-communal show of self-interest, a number of men (who seem not to have had young children) dissented openly when the majority voted that the schoolmaster be paid from common funds rather than by the students' families. The dissenters were relatively rich men, and so open was their disregard for the conventions of quiet consensus that they ordered their names recorded in the town book as opposing the majority in two separate votes.[73]

There was no other recorded disturbance of the public peace until the "anonymous" challenge to the land divisions, mentioned earlier, which received only a surprisingly oblique mention in the town-meeting records. But James Russell Trumbull's *History of Northampton* contains letters revealing a bitter feud between two groups of candidates for militia offices in 1689.[74] Neither group can be identified as a party in any other context (they were all among the richer men in town, as were most militia officers), and there seems to be no connection with the politics of the province as the much-hated administration of Governor Andros was deposed when news came from England of the Glorious Revolution against his patron, the equally repugnant King James II. Perhaps these Northampton soldiers were just men who wanted the glory of higher office, and they were willing to engage in a public contention to gain personal advantage. Somehow the feud was settled, and in a telling commentary on the degree to which this behavior had *not* been considered proper by the community as a whole, in February 1690 the town recorded the following vote with regard to fortifying the town:

> *Whereas the concurrence and agreement as one of any Society in public concerns is the strength and (under God) the Safety and Preservation of the same and that the consideration that a condescending spirit one to another in matters of public affairs wherein both the Honor of God and our own safety is advanced, we therefore do agree and bind ourselves to this viz. that the major[ity] vote of the town shall determine in or as to making of fortification on our defence against the [Indian] enemy that though we as to our own apprehensions [and] judgments are of another persuasion, yet notwithstanding we will acquiesce and rest satisfied with the determination of the major vote of the town and readily to the utmost of our power do and perform each of us our parts of the same. Voted unanimously or very fully. . . .[75]*

Some historians would read this statement as simply an expression of the consensus that was so highly prized in early New England towns; but it also acknowledges the struggle by which consensus was reached. The very identification of a majority was unusual in this period, and there would have been no need for such a formal agreement except as a way to force the cooperation of a grudgingly acquiescent minority. The self-conscious "condescending spirit" apparently so valued was a transition between real commonality of aims and means and a recognition of the effective power of mere majoritarianism—the aggregate of individual self-interests. But even this condescension was coming to an end in Northampton by the turn of the eighteenth century.

The newly obvious show of men's self-interest, producing community tensions which occasionally flared into open contention, was the kind of behavior which Solomon Stoddard saw growing in Northampton as his pastoral care of the town extended into its third and fourth and fifth decades. Although Northampton in its frontier state was hardly an egalitarian democracy, there was no leveling by the end of the seventeenth century. Rather, it is probable that there was some disturbingly transparent social climbing by the few men who moved up the economic ladder. Stoddard had no patience with status seeking. He was tireless in denouncing the fashions of a would-be leisure class, especially wigs and extravagant clothing: he even supported the prosecution of wealthy Elder John Strong's two daughters for wearing silk in a "flaunting" manner. (Their friend Hannah Lyman, an incorrigible hussy, wore her fancy dress to court!)[76] Perhaps the increasing display of status symbols was coming to include marks of spiritual superiority; and when Stoddard denounced arrogant men for using their "sainthood" as a weapon against others, weren't the offenders more likely to be richer rather than poorer? There is a tantalizing clue left us in a letter by Jonathan Edwards: in portraying Northampton as a habitually contentious town, he wrote that in Stoddard's era there were "some mighty contests and controversies among them," a great deal of pride and much "heat and violence." There were even "some great quarrels in the Church, wherein Mr. Stoddard, great as his authority was, knew not what to do with them." So bitter did the argument between "two parties" in the church become that "a member of one party met the head of the opposite party, and assaulted him, and beat him unmercifully." (Edwards even suggested that this contentiousness was enhanced by the imitation of Stoddard's own "dogmatical temper" by some of his congregation.) Edwards also commented that since the early eighteenth century there had been *a sort of settled division of the people into two parties, somewhat like the Court and Country party in England, (if I may compare small things with great). There have been some of the chief men in the town, of chief authority and wealth, that have been great proprietors of their lands, who have had one party with them. And the other party, which has commonly been the greatest, have been of those, who have been jealous of them, apt to envy them, and afraid of their having too much power and influence in town and church.*

There is no real evidence in any other documents for this partisan division, and the stars of the drama are hard to identify. If these parties did exist, we can guess that Solomon Stoddard's son Colonel John (richest man in town, Tory in colony politics, one of the largest landowners in Massachusetts) was the center of the Court party. But the Country party were not necessarily have-nots: the best candidate for leadership of that group is Joseph Parsons, Colonel John's chief opponent in the only documented political fight in Northampton, and the sixth richest man in town in 1700. Each of these leaders probably had followers scattered down the economic ladder, but the problem (as in the English political model) was really one of competing elites.[77]

Solomon Stoddard *does* seem to have been an aristocrat by temperament, and he was himself close to the top of the economic hierarchy. He was the thirteenth largest landowner (of 103) in 1700; and, probably reflecting a considerable inheritance from his father, Stoddard left an estate of 78 acres of land (not assessed) plus £1126 in personal property and perhaps "several hundred pounds more" (mostly in money—cash, bills of credit, mortgages), as well as 462 books and 491 unbound pamphlets. Nor was he a Puritan about business matters—for many years he had owned a share in a sawmill (with the above-mentioned Joseph Parsons), and he had once advised a legislative committee that the building of a church in a frontier town not only would keep the children there from becoming "ignorant and heathenish," but also "much good land that is now unprofitable would soon be brought into improvement."[78] He understood the "real world" and dealt with it as best he could. But he kept the church as far out of the business of social-status-seeking as possible. He didn't need to use it himself for social control, since

he had an effective secular deputy in his son Colonel John, undisput-
edly the major political figure in Northampton until his death in
1748. No one else, nevertheless, would be able to use the church
for spiritual certification that could be translated into civic power.
There was no pressure on Stoddard to recognize large numbers of
people as saved. Those about whom he felt certainty could be privately identified (as he advocated in the *Guide to Christ*); the others
would have no political grounds for quarrel with the church. Furthermore, Stoddard could keep the disciplinary role of the pastor
separate from the evangelical role: public order could be insisted
upon even in times of evangelical languor; a "harvest" which might
prove temporarily effective would not interfere with enforced obedience to the moral code. In a region distinguished by its bitter
church controversies, there was never recorded (except in that ultimately self-serving letter of Jonathan Edwards) any challenge to
Solomon Stoddard—and that can be said of few ministers in the
Connecticut Valley.

But let us look at Stoddard's practices from one more angle, to
suggest another aspect of the social context in which he opened
communion. If the notebook entries of Edward Taylor are at all
accurate, and it was the older generation of church members who
resisted Stoddard's innovations until their deaths in the 1680s, we
can perhaps derive a bit more information from that than just a
confirmation of the truism that the older generation always dislikes
new ideas. Perhaps, we might conjecture, the older men were clinging to a notion of community surviving from the true frontier years,
and had not really lost their faith in the centripetal forces of communalism to temper the self-seeking of their neighbors. On the other
hand, it is possible that their resistance was a way of clinging to their
own power as patriarchs, for church membership was also an event
in the life of a family. Were the elders too severe as judges of the
spirituality of their children? Were they pressuring their children to
achieve conversion experiences as a way of proving that they were
truly grown up and ready to begin adult economic lives?[79] As the
seventeenth century drew to a close, there were important changes
in family relationships focusing on rites of passage to adulthood.
There was no more unallocated land good for tillage in Northampton, and from then on a young man would acquire his farm either

by inheritance from his father (or other relative) or by purchase (usually with his father's financial backing). After 1705, he could not even get a symbolic start in community life as an adult out of the common resources of the community, for no more home lots were given out. This changing relationship of land and a protracted state of adolescence will be explored more fully in Chapter 4, since the documentation for the Edwards years is much fuller than that for the Stoddard years. But we can at least mark the beginning of the trend, and we can correlate that beginning with Stoddard's opening of the church to all persons over the age of fourteen and his "harvests" among the young people. Perhaps by making the relationships among the brethren within the church more democratic, he showed sympathy for the plight of the young people whose elders were becoming too authoritarian. Solomon Stoddard established himself as the chief patriarchal figure in town, perhaps an alternative authority figure as a court of appeal for those who would not rise if the community were left to replicate its secular power relationships within the covenanted church.

For the last three centuries, it is the appellation "Patriarch" (with its variant, "Pope") that has stuck to Stoddard. If there seems to be a paradox between the stern behavioral judgment and gentle emotional support, they can be seen to combine in the role of a *father*. Sereno Dwight, writing in the early nineteenth century, called Stoddard "a loved and venerated parent" to Northampton; and a recent analyst of ministerial problems in the Connecticut Valley has written that "of all the ministers of the time, he came closest to re-creating the aura of the first generation."[80] His congregation were his children—relatively unfit to govern, of course, but beloved and tenderly comforted when obedient, encouraged but also disciplined.

On an even wider scale, the patriarchal style of Solomon Stoddard found expression in the Hampshire Association, founded by Stoddard and five neighboring churches in 1714. Soon joined by most of the churches in the upper Valley, the Association's purpose was to offer advice to heal inter- and intracongregational problems of all sorts. Most importantly, they took on the responsibility to discipline all inhabitants of their towns *as though* they had all "owned the covenant." The founding enactment is unfortunately the only Association record that survives before 1731, so the actual early functioning of the group is unknown.[81] It is safe to assume that Stoddard was not satisfied with this limited presbyterianism and with the results of efforts at discipline, since the sins against which the Association gathered their forces did continue to multiply.

Even within his own congregation, as the early eighteenth century progressed, Solomon Stoddard faced implicit, if not explicit, challenges to the role he had designed for himself as the Patriarch. Although his great-great-grandson Timothy Dwight asserted that Stoddard had "possessed probably more influence than any other clergyman in the province during a period of thirty years," there were increasing limits to clerical authority.[82] A seventy-year-old community of prosperous farmers and growing numbers of tradesmen and professionals, filled with a sense of temporal security, was quite different from the small band of men and women who braved the wilderness. Eighteenth-century men seemed to feel less need for an oracular figure to interpret their emotions and their surroundings for them, although from the minister's point of view they were much more in need of pious exhortation and discipline than their Puritan grandfathers had been. As communal enterprises designed for basic survival evolved into clan- and family-centered units of production and consumption, men were less willing to have their economic lives directed by a central figure whose ethical ideal formed the basis of his judgment. Men and women still joined the church, and Stoddard's evangelism enjoyed the reputation of striking success in the context of a regional decline in religiosity, but joining the church was an experience probably less central to everyday life than any minister would wish.

Northampton's respect and love for Stoddard were something that greatly impressed his grandson Jonathan Edwards, our only literary witness to Stoddard's last years. Edwards, who had grown up in a Connecticut parsonage pervaded by the anxieties of a minister who constantly fought his church and never won, was especially sensitive to problems of church discipline; he found Northampton in the mid-1720s respecting Stoddard, even revering him, but not really obeying him in daily affairs. In the portrait of Northampton with which Edwards began his *Faithful Narrative* of the revival of 1735, he described the townspeople as "very insensible of the things of religion," though Stoddard had hopes that a handful might be "savingly converted." The young people, Stoddard's special concern and Edwards's own preoccupation, even had the effrontery to be "indecent in their carriage at meeting" under the dimming eyes of their ancient pastor.[83] On the other hand, the adolescents did not reform their behavior when scrutinized by the clear-sighted Mr. Edwards. The challenges of his pastorate were beginning to reveal their dimensions.

Especially because so many of the important questions about Solomon Stoddard's career have to be left to speculation, we really would like to know what words he used as he passed the mantle of Elijah onto young Elisha. How did he evaluate his own incredibly long and dramatic career—did he still believe in the truth of the conversions that came during his "harvests?" Did he warn his grandson about the character of the people of Northampton, or the unavoidable dilemmas of an evangelical Congregationalist pastorate? Did he appreciate, and did he convey to Edwards, the degree to which so much of his success as a disciplinarian and as a revivalist may have been due to his personal charisma and could not be assumed an automatic legacy to the new religious leader of Northampton?

All that we know is that Edwards inherited the pulpit of a man who was called a "Congregational Pope," a preacher who was famous for bringing his flock to renown for both "good order" and "heart religion." Edwards would love and revere his grandfather even when, decades later, he had to endure the pain of publicly condemning Stoddardeanism. The high points of Stoddard's success, as a polemicist and as a pastor, would always provide a standard against which Jonathan Edwards would measure his own achievements.

CHAPTER TWO

Preparation

IN APRIL 1725 the town of Northampton voted to find an assistant and successor to their eighty-three-year-old pastor, Solomon Stoddard. This newly created position, sharing such a distinguished pulpit, was one of the best opportunities in New England for a young minister, and finding the right man was not easy. The Northampton committee took over a year to solicit suggestions and interview clergymen in Boston and Hartford. In the winter of 1725–26 the town temporarily hired Mr. Israel Chauncy, a recent Harvard graduate and son of the pastor at Hadley. Finally, in August 1726, an offer was made to Stoddard's grandson Jonathan Edwards, then a tutor at Yale College. The financial settlement offered to Edwards and recorded in November was generous, and he was ordained on February 15, 1727.[1]

It is easy to assume that Stoddard deliberately chose his grandson to be his successor, but there were other available grandsons besides Jonathan, so family connection alone cannot account for his good fortune. There is no evidence that he had ever been especially close to his grandfather or had previously spent time in Northampton.[2] But if the church and town were to choose a young man who had recently finished his studies, as was the custom, then it is hard to imagine that many better candidates than Edwards were available. In the words of his early biographer, Sereno Dwight, Edwards "had passed through the successive periods of childhood, youth, and early manhood, not only without reproach, but in such a manner, as to secure the high esteem of all who knew him." He was "a young man of uncommon promise."[3]

Only the barest outline of Jonathan's youth is known. Born in 1703, he was the only son (out of eleven children) of Stoddard's daughter Esther, who had married the young Northampton schoolmaster who then became pastor at East Windsor, Connecticut.[4] Timothy Edwards had turned away from the wealth of his merchant family to enter the prestigious but unremunerative calling of country parson, and his alliance with the Stoddards enhanced the social advantages of his chosen profession. (In later years, his journeys to Boston included visits with the aristocratic Stoddard clan there.) In many religious families, the first son was pushed toward the ministry; with such a family heritage, there could have been no doubt that the only son of Timothy and Esther Edwards was destined to be a clergyman.

Jonathan's intellectual gifts were prodigious, and his father, who trained many Connecticut boys for college, must have given his best efforts to preparing his son. When away from home in Jonathan's seventh summer, Timothy Edwards wrote to his wife to carry on his program: Jonathan was to learn "above two sides of *propria quae moribus* [Latin exercises] by heart" in addition to his regular reading and writing. Esther was also to "take special care of Jonathan that he dont learn to be rude &c of which thee and I have lately discoursed."[5] By his eleventh or twelfth year the precocious Jonathan had been reading Newton's *Optics* and was employing his skills as a naturalist to gather information on the habits of the rainbow and flying spiders; the results included short essays using these natural phenomena to illustrate the "goodness" and "wisdom" of the Creator.[6]

Shortly before his thirteenth birthday, Jonathan began collegiate studies in formal preparation for the ministry. Through the turbulent years of Yale College's early history he studied with his cousin, Tutor Elisha Williams, minister at Wethersfield, and then with President Timothy Cutler when the college finally gathered and settled in New Haven.[7] He earned Cutler's praise for his "promising abilitys and advances in learning" and graduated at the top of his class in September 1720. Three more years of theological study at Yale led to an M.A. degree, and the next step in his career was clearly a pastoral position of distinction.[8] Edwards, in fact, went to New York for a year to preach before he took his M.A. in 1723, and then accepted an appointment in Bolton, Connecticut, which for some unknown reason lasted only a short time. He returned to Yale as a tutor for a year and in the summer of 1726 was called to Northampton.[9]

It is possible that the Northampton pastorate had long been an ambition of Jonathan's, or at least his family's desire for him. Timothy Edwards made a note in early 1723 in his memorandum book that the Northampton church had made an offer to Solomon Williams, son of William Williams of Hatfield and Stoddard's daughter Christian. What is most interesting about Timothy's note on the Northampton situation is that there is no record of any such offer in the Northampton records, and Williams had been ordained in Lebanon, Connecticut, in December of 1722 after preaching there for ten months—and so Timothy's information may have been a fantasy of his own fear. The possibility that Jonathan also sensed a rivalry with his cousin is hinted in a letter he wrote to his sister Mary in December of 1721, when Mary was staying with the Williams family: Jonathan asked for "particular information concerning cousin Solo. whether he is like to settle or no." At about the same time that Timothy was noting Solomon Williams's reputed success, Jonathan wrote in his diary a long reproof to himself for envying others which concluded with a vow "always to rejoice in everyone's prosperity . . . and to expect no happiness of that nature, as long as I live."[10] Fortunately, he did achieve the happiness of being summoned to succeed his grandfather in Northampton.

As the story is usually told, Jonathan Edwards's life progressed smoothly from a precocious youth to a distinguished adulthood; in retrospect, there is an inevitability about his call to Northampton. But these early years are usually described simply as the formative years of the Great Philosopher, and intellectual promise (which there was, of course, in great measure) is all that is considered important. If we are concerned with Edwards's career as a pastor, however, these early years deserve a closer examination, for they contain stresses and attempts at resolutions that portend Edwards's professional future. Among the personal baggage that Edwards carried with him to Northampton were a very difficult adolescence and some personal problems in accepting the pastorate as a career. Edwards's early life provides clues to what would become his special preoccupations in later years—particularly his real sympathy with the problems of the young people in his congregation, but also his special sensitivity to their challenges to his authority—and clues to his predispositions toward certain ways of defining his role as a minister.

Because it is so common for biographers to describe Jonathan Edwards as fortunate, in some unspecified way, to be the son of a minister, we should begin by asking what benefit really accrued to the son of Timothy Edwards. Any other father, after all, might have encouraged his son to be a clergyman and might have provided the necessary liberal education. What Timothy Edwards provided in addition was a close-range view of the realities of the profession as a daily experience. The particular lesson that Jonathan learned in the East Windsor parsonage was, in fact, that although the ministry was the most honorable of professions it could easily be a martyr's vocation. From his father's career, Jonathan may have taken the lesson that a minister must wage constant warfare with his congregation for even the minimum respect and authority that God had intended him to have.

The beginnings of Timothy Edwards's career are similar in outline to the early life of his illustrious father-in-law. Timothy, born in 1669, was the eldest son of a prosperous Hartford merchant-cooper. His Harvard education was interrupted by a dismissal for some now obscure misbehavior, and after studying for a while with the pastor at Springfield and then teaching school for a few months in Northampton, he took both Bachelor's and Master's degrees at Harvard in September 1694. Two months later he married Esther Stoddard and immediately began a trial period as a preacher in what was then the second church in Windsor, Connecticut.[11] The original Windsor township grant straddled the Connecticut River, and although the east-side lands had been farmed since the 1640s and a village had grown gradually, Timothy Edwards was the first preacher hired by East Windsor. The community, like Northampton in its frontier years, gave no evidence of particular religiosity. Symbolically, there was not even a meetinghouse there until the spring of 1698, when Timothy was ordained. For the rest of his eighty-nine years he devoted himself to an ideal of the Christian community, with the church at its center of consciousness and the minister as the chief guardian of moral order. His career was marked with some success: although his surviving sermons are painfully boring expositions of Old Testament texts about obedience, his congregation did share in the religious revivals which periodically spread through the Connecticut Valley in the first half of the eighteenth century.[12]

In his everyday relations with his congregation, however, Timothy Edwards endured chronic frustration. He was obsessed with pastoral authority—or, rather, his lack of it. There was frequent open conflict in East Windsor over the pastor's salary—a matter of practical importance and a symbol of respect that bedeviled many clergymen—and over the pastor's right to absolute control within the church.

Compared with ministers in other rural towns, Edwards received a stipend that was about average. Around 1717, however, when his son Jonathan was beginning college, he felt so underpaid that he threatened to leave East Windsor, and the quarrels over money persisted for at least another thirty years. Compulsively seeking comparisons, Edwards filled his memorandum books with the rumored salaries of other ministers, and they were always more than his own.[13] His father-in-law Stoddard was wealthy, his own father and brothers and many of his friends were rich merchants, and so unhappy comparisons came to mind frequently. A characteristic diary entry reads, in part: "Major Talcott ye Dep Gov'r told me that he spent above £200 a year in his family [and was] very sensible that ministers could never live on their salaries &c."[14] Edwards also recorded detailed analyses of the rising costs of living and the demeaning uncertainties of the "country pay" in which he received his wages: amid the bushels of grain and odd squashes and firkins of butter, all given according to the donor's surplus and not Edwards's need, were occasional bad bills of credit or green corn that quickly shrank by one-sixth of its volume. Somehow, he managed to feed his family and to educate his son. He apparently endured stinging symbolic insults.[15] He had even more serious challenges to ponder, and in matters of ministerial prerogative within the church he was not inclined to be passive.

For the first decade of his tenure, Timothy Edwards and his congregation seem to have agreed at least on the fundamentals of religion. The fight which was to last through the rest of his career became open in 1708, when Edwards enthusiastically endorsed the Saybrook Platform. The East Windsor church, like many others, refused to accept this new Presbyterian form of church government with powerful regional councils overriding local autonomy and pervasive ministerial authoritarianism. Over the next three decades there were a number of clashes in East Windsor over the minister's prerogatives; in the open warfare of 1735–41 between pastor and flock, Edwards demanded an absolute veto on admission and discipline and even complete control of the choice of issues to be discussed by the church at their meetings. The church, of course, refused. Three councils of neighboring ministers and laymen failed to effect a compromise, and so bitter was the fight that the Lord's Supper was suspended for three years. The last entry in the narrative of these troubles, written by the leader of the anti-Edwards party (by then including all but two of the church members), shows that both sides were still angry in 1741.[16]

As recent studies have shown, Timothy Edwards was not the only early-eighteenth-century minister to have what he believed to be an inadequate salary or the only one to fight his church over clerical perquisites.[17] But in his case, as presumably in others, temperament was important; for each pastor, certain types of incidents triggered the venting of underlying tensions. Timothy Edwards was especially sensitive about the discipline of young people (young women who married without parental consent were the catalysts for the two major episodes of intrachurch war), and he demanded, as a personal disciplinary tool, the power to veto church admissions. He displayed a need for deference that had no chance for fulfillment in his parish, he demanded powers far exceeding those of most Congregational ministers, and he absolutely refused to compromise. These aspects of his personality might be attributed to an emotionally turbulent adolescence (his father divorced his mother for adultery, she was violent and perhaps insane, and Timothy was forced to testify against her).[18] His rigidities might also stem from a disappointed ambition to hold a more important pulpit in a more urbane community where ministers were treated as gentlemen, or from attempted emulation of his father-in-law Stoddard, who was reputed to wield absolute authority over his own church. Whatever the causes, Timothy's demands exacerbated the anti-clerical prejudices of his congregation, and their assertiveness only fueled his obstinacy.

This was the atmosphere in which Jonathan Edwards grew up; this was the personal model for the pastor-church relationship that he carried with him as he studied for the ministry. Later in his own career there would be echoes of his father's concerns with salary and its symbolism, immoral young people, and ministerial control of church admission and discipline. This family background, as well as the more obvious gifts of intelligence and formal education that he received from his parents, was an important part of Jonathan Edwards's preparation for his pastorate.

Despite Timothy Edwards's unhappy experiences as a pastor, there could be no question that his only son would follow him in the Lord's work, for the ministry was still the only occupation in colonial New England that demanded a trained intellect.[19] Even as a child, Jonathan showed great intelligence, which his father carefully nurtured; perhaps it occurred to him that the life of the mind might be some compensation for whatever frustrations Jonathan would encounter in the pastoral side of his ministry. The elder Edwards has left us no evidence of any real interest in abstract theological speculation or science, but his son's precocious essays testify to Timothy's encouragement. While he was at Yale, Jonathan's interest in contemporary philosophy flowered, and some historians have regarded his attempts to reinterpret Calvinist dogma in light of current science as the most important aspect of his life.[20] But those leanings toward philosophy were not really very good preparation for the pastoral side of the career Edwards undertook. While it cannot be said that a love of abstraction materially interfered with his more mundane encounters with ministerial duty, the satisfactions of intellectual excitement shown to him in his early years perhaps made more intense the frustrations of pastoral endeavor—progress could be made so much more quickly with difficult ideas than with stubborn human beings. Edwards, who later confessed to being "by nature very unfit for secular business," was cut out to be a thinker; but the social role of professional intellectual, as separate from the pastorate, was impossible for a man with no private income. Even college teachers were usually young men in transition from their own post-graduate studies to the ministry.[21] Edwards gladly returned to Yale as a tutor in 1724, indicating a preference for the cloistered life after his short preaching appointments in New York and Bolton, but he had no permanent role in the college. Tutors were transient and were primarily disciplinarians, responsible only for elementary instruction; even college presidents, who guided more advanced studies, were recruited not from among the tutors but from among distinguished clergymen (as Princeton would call Edwards in 1758).

The intellectual side of Edwards's preparation for the ministry was therefore an ambiguous portent for his pastorate. He was well trained in the classic curriculum, but that course of study had contributed little in the way of *practical* skills: there had been no courses on homiletics (beyond study of the early Puritan divines), nor any instruction in pastoral politics. (These were the things to be learned by the apprentice as he lived with a mature minister, before or after his college training. The lessons Jonathan Edwards might have learned in East Windsor have been indicated.) The degree to which the development of his theological knowledge and literary skills would affect the pastoral side of his career is very difficult to determine, and the question can at least be postponed until we scrutinize the specific interaction of Edwards as spiritual guide with his Northampton congregation.

A classical education and intellectual encouragement were not the only products of Jonathan Edwards's youth in New Haven. Equally important for his later life was the other desirable side of preparation for the ministry—a personal religious conversion. Because so much of his later effort as a pastor and theologian was concerned with encouraging and defining true conversion experiences, Edwards's own conversion is a matter of great historical importance. Once again, surviving evidence suggests a more complicated and less purely positive experience than is part of the usual narrative of Edwards's early years.

Most biographical accounts have followed Edwards's own version written about 1740, commonly known as the "Personal Narrative."[22] In this short autobiography, Edwards states that his religious growth began in childhood during the small revivals that frequently swept through the Connecticut Valley. As a boy, he "was abundant in duties," especially private prayer. But not until the time of his graduation from Yale, when he underwent the first of the physical/emotional collapses that came throughout his life after periods of extreme stress (God "brought me nigh to the grave, and shook me over the pit of hell"), was he able to abandon "all ways of known outward sin." More important, he finally overcame his inner objections to the "horrible" doctrine of God's absolute sovereignty. When his "reason apprehended the justice and reasonableness of it," at last, his "mind rested in it." Jonathan found his soul "diffused" with a "sense of the glory of the Divine Being; a new sense, quite different from anything I ever experienced before." During the next year he was filled with a "sweet . . . sense of the glorious majesty and grace of God" and would "sing forth my contemplations." There were some ups and downs of his spirit thereafter; but after he settled at Northampton in 1726, he found his sense of the "glorious and lovely Being" growing stronger.

Or so Edwards remembered his conversion, and so he described it in an elegant essay written around 1740. There is, however, no confirmation of this retrospective view from the documents—a diary, a set of "Resolutions," family letters—which survive from the years in question. Letters from and about Jonathan discuss his physical health but not his spiritual state. Despite the attribution in the "Personal Narrative" of the turning point to the year after his 1720 college graduation, Edwards's "Resolutions" begun in the fall of 1722 imply no feeling of being saved. The surviving part of his diary begins in December of that year with a questioning that his preparatory work was not sufficiently inward—a seemingly inappropriate anxiety for one who had felt the aesthetic raptures described in the "Personal Narrative."[23] The following August he was worried, on the other hand, that his experience did not follow the "particular steps" outlined in English and New England models for conversion.[24] Both diary and resolutions for 1722 and 1723 record a mood of depression alternating with desperate resolves to control his behavior and to focus his attention on things spiritual. It is difficult to imagine the man who wrote those diary entries being able to "sing forth his contemplations," as—twenty years later—he remembered doing. Although as early as January 1723 he had recognized that the Calvinist cliché of man's inability to take any actions for his own salvation did apply also to his own particular case, he was not *at the time* able to "rest" in the "sweet sense of the glorious majesty and grace of God" but was overcome with a compulsion to take some steps (even if ultimately ineffective ones) toward an appearance of holiness, to perform rituals that would ease his mind. Although he had suffered from serious bouts of illness and frequent periods of weakness, Edwards pursued a rigidly ascetic course of physical self-denial, with which he tried to create psychological stability.

On January 12, 1723, Edwards wrote in his diary: "I have this day, solemnly renewed my baptismal covenant and self-dedication, which I renewed, when I was taken into the communion of the church." This sentence is then followed by a rambling statement of the submission of self to God that morning, and this formal dedication has often been interpreted as contemporary confirmation of the conversion later described in the "Personal Narrative." The phrase "baptismal covenant" clearly indicates, however, that he was either joining the church in "half-way" status or participating in a community ritual of covenant renewal, neither of which implied personal regeneration. The emotional tone of the complete January 12 diary entry also argues against any contemporary perception of a resolution to his emotional torments.[25] Three days later he was "decaying," he wrote, and two days after that he was "overwhelmed with melancholy." In less than a month he was ill again: "I think that I stretched myself farther than I could bear, and so broke." But repeatedly he drove himself beyond physical endurance. If he felt himself to be regenerated, why did he still need to struggle for the comfort he said he found only "after the greatest mortifications"? As late as May 1725 Edwards confessed that, "whether I am now converted or not," he was unable to do more for his own condition, and in September 1726 he wrote that he had been in a "low, sunk estate" for about three years.[26]

There is, in sum, strong reason to believe that the conversion as described by Edwards in his 1740 "Personal Narrative" was not really experienced in the same terms as it was later described with the ups and downs smoothed out. Whatever experience he had in 1723, only *later* did he have the confidence to call it Saving Grace —only after the passage of time had supplied a new perspective on those emotional torments, after he had observed the conversions of many other persons during the revival of 1735, and after he had found his professional role of encourager to the spiritual experiences of others. In helping them, he came to terms with what had happened to himself. The translation of the subjective experience into an objective description of a psychological process would necessarily involve seeing the steps along the way as contributing to an accomplished end: in retrospect, the emotional highs and lows were put in their proper relation to each other, almost as waves in a dynamic movement toward the fusion of subjective and objective grace. The process of preaching, like the writing of a self-conscious autobiography, may also have evoked a translation of experiential truth into an objectified form that accentuated the positive aspects. Among the undated sermon manuscripts which have now been reliably attributed to the New York years of Edwards's career, there are a number of poetic passages expressing the delights of spiritual exaltation and therein foreshadowing the tone of the "Personal Narrative."[27] And the very first entry in Edwards's theological notebooks, called the "Miscellanies," begun before Edwards went to New York in the fall of 1722, captures the same aesthetic sense of conversion. "Holiness," Edwards wrote, is "of a sweet, pleasant, charming, lovely, amiable, delightful, serene, calm and still nature. . . . like a delightful field or garden planted by God . . . that is all pleasant and delightful, undisturbed, free from all the noise of man and beast, enjoying a sweet calm, and the bright, calm, and gently vivifying beams of the sun forever more."[28] The repetition of key phrases in this private writing gives it the quality of a meditation—and yet the very insistence on serenity and freedom from disturbance still hints that this is a state of being that was desired rather than achieved. Edwards clearly knew what feelings he *wanted* conversion to include, but in the early 1720s he does not yet convey a sense of having achieved that blissful state of serenity.

In Calvinist doctrine, of course, men were never supposed to be sure of their being saved; but Edwards had *experienced* that uncertainty in the most vivid way, and as we shall see, his awakening-era definitions of what a conversion experience should be took full account of the existential truth of both the doctrines he had rebelled against as horrible in his youth and the plateaus of aesthetic rapture which could be the gift of grace. The effectiveness of Edwards's preaching and spiritual counsel later in his career may have derived in part from the intensity of his own experience, which—as Solomon Stoddard was writing, about the same time as Edwards was being tormented—"best fits men to teach others."

It is also interesting to speculate on the particular purpose which may have colored the "Personal Narrative," for it may have been written to encourage another young man who had been having a spiritual crisis. We know from internal evidence that the "Narrative" was written after January 1739. There exists a letter of March 1741 to Edwards from his future son-in-law, young minister Aaron Burr of Newark, New Jersey, in which Burr thanked Edwards for a letter of December 14 describing Edwards's "experiences"; Burr responded with a description of his own conversion. The original Edwards letter to Burr has not been found, but what has survived as the "Personal Narrative" is probably a draft.[29]

What may be the strongest link between this later-crafted autobiography and the contemporary documents is provided by a description that Jonathan wrote in 1723 of his future wife, Sarah Pierrepont.[30] She was a child (only thirteen years old) obviously "beloved of that Great Being," caring for little "except to meditate on Him. She is of a wonderful sweetness, calmness and universal benevolence of mind. . . . She loves to be alone, walking the fields and groves, and seems to have someone invisible always conversing with her." Sarah was a vivid model of the enveloping sweetness of true piety, and such a blissful state was to be envied. Her spiritual peace was a condition that Jonathan only later attributed to his younger self. It is even possible that Sarah's manifest holiness contributed to his self-doubts in the early 1720s.[31] After their marriage in July 1727, Sarah continued to be an exemplar of the purest piety; and in *Some Thoughts Concerning the Present Revival of Religion,* Edwards's 1743 attempt to define the essence of the work of God's Spirit, he would use Sarah's experiences as a model of the conversions toward which he was trying to lead all of New England.

Whatever the specific content and *contemporaneous* self-definition of Jonathan Edwards's conversion, we should not leave this turning point in his adolescent life without considering the effect of this experience on Edwards's vocation as a pastor. This relationship has been illuminated by Richard L. Bushman's fascinating analysis of

Jonathan's youth and family life. Using Edwards as a case study in the Puritan consciousness, Bushman has pointed out the prominence of Oedipal themes ("man's lowliness, God's power, and the necessity of submission") in the description of the conversion experience in both the 1722–23 diary and the "Personal Narrative." The climax of Edwards's conversion, like those of so many other Calvinists, was complete abasement before a father-like God and subsequent peace: "Only when utterly humble was he confident of divine approval."[32] But Jonathan found it difficult to be humble, as witness his "Personal Narrative" description of the long-enduring inner objections to the "horrible" doctrine of God's sovereignty. He was indeed being pulled in two directions—his remarkable intellectual abilities were themselves temptations, for where did one draw the line between ambition and sinful pride? Bushman has described the way in which Jonathan's Oedipal crisis can be seen to be intertwined with and exacerbated by his professional ambitions and those of his parents for him. His mother may have played a crucial role in this drama: perhaps in competition with her sisters to produce the most fitting heir to their famous father, Esther Stoddard Edwards prized learning and may have urged her son to compete (unconsciously?) with his father.[33]

Even if one feels uncomfortable using the term "Oedipal crisis" because of the sexual connotations, it is possible to follow Bushman's formulations to their conclusion by seeing Edwards's turmoil as a more straightforward problem of becoming an adult man in a Puritan culture where secular ambition and any classically masculine assertions of will were not quite legitimate unless subsumed within a profound obeisance before the great Father.[34] The conversion experience could provide an apparent resolution of the guilt that came with self-assertion, and the modern literature on the psychology of conversion is full of references to such a function of the classic late-adolescent spiritual crisis.[35] Exactly *how* this works, however, is so far as inexplicable in the psychoanalytic idiom as in the theological. Solomon Stoddard might have been able to explain it thus: man must use the means and talents that God has given him, and must do his best with the real world as God has designed it; but man should constantly remind himself that in cosmic perspective his highest achievements were of minuscule importance compared to the smallest manifestation of God's glory. There could be no real competition. It was safe for man to be willful if he knew his will was only a fleeting whimper in the cosmic drama.

For a young man whose spiritual crisis had involved a difficult adjustment to maturity in the face of higher authority, as Bushman clearly points out, the ministry was an eminently suitable vocation. Edwards's "office permitted him to talk freely of God's wrath, of human defilement, and of the exquisite joys of grace. . . . Even the disposition to chide and rebuke [which is frequently revealed in Edwards's diary] was dignified to a duty," and "the whole was sanctified and purged of pride because done for God and not for self."[36] Sometime during 1723, probably in the summer, while he waited in his parents' home between his temporary preaching jobs at New York City and Bolton, Connecticut, Edwards meditated on the role of the minister and wrote the following in his "Miscellanies":

> *Without doubt, ministers are to administer the sacraments to Christians, and they are to administer them only to such as they think Christ would have them administer them. Without doubt, ministers are to teach men what Christ would have them to do, and to teach them who doth these things and who doth them not, that is, who are Christians and who are not; and the people are to hear them as much in this as in other things; and so far forth as the people are obliged to hear what I teach them, so great is my pastoral, or ministerial, or teaching power. And this is all the difference of power there is amongst ministers, whether apostles or whatever.*
>
> *Thus if I in a right manner am become the teacher of a people, so far as they ought to hear what I teach them, so much power I have. Thus if they are obliged to hear me only because they themselves have chosen me to guide them, and therein declared that they thought me sufficiently instructed in the mind of Christ to teach them, and because I have the other requisites of being their teacher, then I have power as other ministers have in these days. But if it was plain to them that I was under the infallible guidance of Christ, then I should have more power. And if it was plain to all the world of Christians that I was under the infallible guidance of Christ, and I was sent forth to teach the world*

the will of Christ, then I should have power in all the world. I should have power to teach them what they ought to do, and they would be obliged to hear me; I should have power to teach them who were Christians and who not, and in this likewise they would be obliged to hear me. [37]

The shift near the end of the first paragraph from the third person to the first, as well as the explicitness of Edwards's desire for "infallible guidance" as a means to "power in all the world," testifies to the potential satisfactions of a pastoral career. On the other hand, the unlikelihood that Edwards would ever receive "infallible guidance" or that such a gift would be plain to his congregation makes this meditation a fantasy. There is a strong possibility that at this very time the East Windsor parsonage was filled with tension over pastor Timothy Edwards's unsuccessful attempts to use the church as a means of disciplining the man who had seduced his niece; and so we can again see Jonathan taking lessons in the practical realities of the ministerial profession, perhaps finding solace in dreams of unlimited power.[38]

The vocation to the pastorate was not, therefore, an easily attained safety valve for the frustrations of learning to deal with temporal and cosmic authority figures. The ministry is not, after all, just a job: a minister must believe that he understands a complex and subtle truth (and for one with Edwards's intellect, in the era of the Enlightenment, that truth was not simple to grasp), he must have full confidence in his ability to receive messages from an infallible guide, and he must ultimately persuade others to share his vision. Without that last step, the ability to harness personal faith and knowledge into a communication of the Word that produced conversions, a man's holy vocation would become mere self-absorbed contemplation. Therefore, the tension between intellect, emotion, and received doctrine which is so clearly evident in Edwards's diary and "Resolutions" would have to be resolved *before* the formal role of minister could become an identity for him. That tension was *not* entirely resolved before Edwards arrived in Northampton, and its persistence and its after-shocks had an important effect on Edwards's definitions of the conversions he guided in others and of the minister's role in the community.

One more aspect of Edwards's years of preparation for the Northampton pastorate deserves reexamination, and may serve to link the important personal aspects of his early-1720s spiritual crisis with the long-range resolution of that crisis in the new self-image he achieved (by the time he wrote the "Personal Narrative") in Northampton. Between his Yale graduation and his call to his grandfather's pulpit, Edwards undertook a pair of short preaching trials which together help mark his progress from childhood to adulthood. They were, in fact, a rite of passage to adult competency as it was culturally defined, but that transition was neither smooth nor automatic.

Edwards's first preaching call was to a small congregation which had split off from a Presbyterian church in New York City. (The line between Presbyterianism and Congregationalism had become rather unimportant in Connecticut by this time.) We know little about his short tenure (September 1722 to April 1723) in the city: Jonathan did not record in his diary either the invitation (which may have come through his father's influence) or the reason why he left.[39] Although it has usually been assumed that Edwards could not stay because the church was insolvent, a letter from a member of that congregation to a friend followed a comment on their sorrow to lose the "much respected Mr. Edwards" with a description of the extremely accomplished candidate (by implication, more polished than Edwards) they were hoping to hire.[40] It appears that by late 1722 Timothy Edwards had decided that Bolton, Connecticut (not far from East Windsor), was a better place for his son than New York.

By early December, Jonathan was reluctantly negotiating with the church committee at Bolton: he wrote to them that his present circumstances and his father's inclination indicated that he would probably leave New York the following spring, but he refused to promise anything and postponed final consideration of the Bolton offer. His tone was negative, almost rude, and the flowery compliments which close the letter sound insincere. Timothy Edwards nevertheless wrote to Bolton in a letter covering his son's that *he* found nothing "discouraging to the motion [to invite Jonathan] you have made."[41] Although his reasons for wanting Jonathan to go to Bolton remain a mystery, Timothy's intent was very clear.

In his diary, Jonathan described his parting from New York as melancholy and reported that whenever he was in a new state of life he found the "troubles and difficulties of that state were greater than those of any other state that I proposed to be in . . . [or] those that I left last." He prayed to be cured of worldly attachments. Early in May, after he had been at home in East Windsor only a few days, he wrote in his diary that he had somewhat "subdued a disposition to chide and fret" but was still too quick "to manifest my own dislike and scorn." There is no direct reference to the source of his discomfort within his father's parsonage, but the next day he resolved "never to allow the least measure of any fretting or uneasiness at my father and mother" to effect "the least alteration of speech, or motion of my eye; and to be especially careful of it with respect to any of our family." But two weeks later he again had to remind himself of "what great obligations I am under to love and honour my parents." Many resolutions to replace his "air of dislike, anger and fretfulness" with an "appearance of love, cheerfulness, and benignity" had to be repeated in July. But by August he had again "sinned in not being careful enough to please my parents."[42]

"To please his parents" probably meant accepting the call to Bolton, and he clearly did not want to go. (It was at this time that he penned the meditation on infallible guidance and ministerial power.) Was he hoping to avoid any serious entanglements while waiting for that desired call to his grandfather's pulpit? He may also have been reluctant to locate himself so close to his father's parish and thereby render himself a perpetual junior in the local circle of clergymen. He might have been unenthusiastic about the pastorate of such a country backwater, where he would have so little opportunity to exercise his intellectual prowess. Whatever the cause of his reluctance and his unhappiness, in the fall he at last gave in and went to Bolton to preach on trial, signed a settlement agreement in the town record book on November 11—and sometime shortly thereafter left Bolton.[43] Significantly, he never mentioned Bolton at all in his diary or later correspondence, and the whole episode might be easy to overlook were it not for that signed contract. After some months of waiting at home, in May 1724 Jonathan was invited to be a tutor at Yale.[44] He unhesitatingly turned his back on the pastoral role with which he had experimented; the lure of the academic community was a strong and positive contrast.

Ironically, there was also a pastoral aspect to that role—the discipline as well as the instruction of rowdy undergraduates—and it caused Jonathan "despondencies, fears, perplexities," and "distraction of mind."[45] Even while he was a student himself, he had felt only disgust at the normal student pranks, and he had once found it important enough to write to his father that "no new quarrels [have] broke out between me and any of the scholars."[46] He was, simply, not good at getting along with people in their everyday impieties. And his position as tutor in a college without a president (Rector Timothy Cutler's defection to Anglicanism so shocked the Congregational community that no replacement was found for three years) demanded an effective authoritarianism not backed by full official sanction. The physical, intellectual, and emotional burdens on Jonathan, not long since a mere student himself, were very great. By September 1725 he had been serving for about a year; then, just as some of the responsibility was lifted from his shoulders by the appointment of his former mentor, Elisha Williams, as rector, Edwards suffered a total collapse. Gravely ill, he lay at the home of a friend for almost three months before he could travel to East Windsor for a long convalescence.[47] Although he did not officially resign his office for another year, it is not certain that he ever returned to his duties at Yale before leaving Connecticut for Northampton. When he arrived to take up this permanent post, he must have had mixed feelings about his abilities to perform pastoral duties with greater success than he had heretofore known.

Of course there is no doubt that Jonathan Edwards was happy and honored to be chosen to succeed his grandfather Stoddard in the Northampton pulpit. And he was as well fitted for that position as he could have been, under the circumstances. He had gone through all the motions of a successful preparation for a distinguished career —sound academic development of innate intellectual skills, the requisite conversion experience, practice appointments as a minister— but he does not seem to have found any lasting emotional satisfaction at any stage of that growth. With the ivory-tower pleasures of the cloistered life of the professional thinker as a suggested contrast, he had learned vicariously and personally that the pastoral life could be intensely frustrating. There were, however, no alternatives. And so he took up his duties as the pastor of the Church of Christ in Northampton. We have already explored some of the important requirements of that position as Edwards inherited it from Solomon Stoddard. Let us now watch him shape the future of his congregation and his own career out of his personal resources and the challenges he would face as the evangelical and moral center of the Northampton community.

CHAPTER THREE

Strategies

THE CLOSEST that Jonathan Edwards ever came to describing directly his early-1730s perceptions about Northampton, its church, and his role as their minister, is the document he wrote in late 1735 to explain the wonderful revival that had recently come to the town. As a prelude to the chronicle of his own pastorate, he began his *Faithful Narrative of the Surprising Work of God* with a listing of the excellencies of the town during his grandfather's era—Edwards was, in fact, the most effective promoter of the myth of Northampton's golden Stoddardean age. The people were "sober, and orderly, and good," free from "error and variety of sects and opinions," because they were at a "distance from seaports" and therefore uncorrupted by the mainstream of civilization. Stoddard's firm control had enforced "purity of doctrine," and Northampton was therefore "the freest of any part of the land from unhappy divisions and quarrels in our ecclesiastical and religious affairs." His congregation had grown "rational and understanding"; many of those he counseled were "remarkable for their distinct knowledge of things that relate to heart religion and Christian experience, and their great regards thereto," and their piety had been manifest in the five famous seasons of "harvest."[1] As the writer of Stoddard's obituary in the *Boston Weekly News-Letter* had observed of the Patriarch, "his being our pastor gave a name and reputation to the town."

That reputation itself had a profound influence on Stoddard's grandson. Edwards had spent little if any time in Northampton before he became a candidate for the pulpit, and what he knew of Stoddard was primarily a boy's larger-than-life image of a grandsire

71

who was called the "Congregational Pope" of the Connecticut Valley by the most powerful ministers in Boston. It was because of Stoddard's reputation that Edwards felt such surprise when he arrived in Northampton in 1726. His shock at finding the community less than utopian is reflected in his little history of Northampton in the *Faithful Narrative,* for after four paragraphs on the saintliness of the town, as quoted above, Edwards abruptly begins an indictment of their degeneracy in the late 1720s—just the time he had become an eyewitness. He reinforced the image of his grandfather's power by attributing the rise of spiritual apathy and political contentiousness to the inevitable relaxing of discipline in Stoddard's ninth decade of life. But clearly the town was not living up to what Edwards had assumed to be its pious heritage.

"Just after my grandfather's death," he wrote, "it seemed to be a time of extraordinary dullness in religion; licentiousness for some years prevailed among the youth of the town. . . . There had also long prevailed in the town a spirit of contention between two parties, into which they had for many years been divided . . . they were prepared to oppose one another in all public affairs," and were beginning to do so in open disregard for the customs of consensus in the Puritan village.[2] As any other minister would have done, Edwards interpreted both types of misbehavior as arising from a single source, lack of piety. After recovering from the emotional prostration that made him unable to deal with his congregation for several months in the summer of 1729, Jonathan Edwards began his real work in Northampton. In the years 1730–35, what might be termed Edwards's strategies as a pastor showed the impact of the model provided by Stoddard's successful evangelism, as well as the clear challenge presented by the community's most obvious symptom of social decay, the disrespect for authority shown by its young people.

As Edwards continued the family line in the Northampton pulpit, he had many reasons to continue the theology and pastoral practice of his grandfather. His experience in East Windsor had shown him the desirability of strong ministerial authority and presbyterian church government—causes espoused but not achieved by Timothy Edwards—and the obstinacy of the brethren of the East Windsor church in fighting their pastor was a deep lesson in the disorders that could arise when a minister lost control of the situation. In theology, Jonathan had been trained by Calvinist conservatives, including his father; his Yale tutor, and his experience as a tutor himself, had encouraged him to fight the liberalism which Stoddard had denounced.[3] Stoddard's system of doctrine and church practice had worked well in Northampton for generations, and Edwards certainly had had little practical experience in which to develop new techniques to command piety and morality. He therefore took on the Stoddardean methods which seemed to come with the pulpit. Decades were to pass before the patriarchalism underlying that system was itself openly questioned, and Edwards later confessed that he had been too young and inexperienced to foresee ill consequences in the Stoddardeanism he embraced in the late 1720s.[4]

To appreciate both Edwards's later innovations and his eventual failure as a pastor, it is necessary to comprehend that his initial positions on church sacraments and conversion were thoroughly Stoddardean. For Edwards, as for Stoddard, the key to the entire system was the doctrine of open communion, the admission of those without Saving Grace to the Lord's Supper and full privileges. In hindsight, Edwards came to regard that as the most pernicious of church practices, but in the early 1730s he wrote a number of sermons which showed full approval. In a January 1733 sermon he described the Supper as a "most solemn renewal of the covenant" between God and man. This covenant, however, was made at baptism, not at the time of adult conversion; and the invitation to the Supper was "universal," without any "hard terms." To those who showed "contempt" for the Supper and "pretended" to stay away because unfit, Edwards admitted that all men *were* unworthy of the Sacrament or God's mercy, but "if your unworthiness be what you acknowledge and lament and deplore you are one that is evangelically fit."[5] This notion of "evangelical fitness" is essentially the same as Stoddard's doctrine that a minister could not deny the Sacrament to those with hope but without assurance, because the minister's knowledge of another's heart was imperfect.

About one year later Edwards preached a series of sermons on the works of preparation for conversion which man might undertake with only God's "common assistance." Man lacking Saving Grace could not fully control the sinful "inclinations" of his heart, but he could control the "outward gratifications of his lusts." Man must use the means available to him (good behavior, prayer, attendance on all church ordinances) although "there is no natural efficacy in them"—simply because God so commanded. And it seemed no paradox to Edwards to preach also that men were largely at fault for their own unconverted state: "If you had done what you could for your salvation[,] in all probability you might have been converted long ago."[6] The people of Northampton were obviously not seizing every opportunity, for a sermon on the Lord's Supper preached in June 1733 accused the congregation of ignoring Christ's invitation to dine at his table: "You are so in love with sin and with the world that rather than part with those you will reject this glorious privilege and happiness." This appeal to a calculation of ultimate (as opposed to short-term and illusory) self-interest was followed a year later with an explanation of the "unreasonableness" of being "unresolved" in religious duties. Man *could* determine the truth of religious doctrines, wrote Edwards, and God had provided many aids to the clear choice between sin and God. "Those who live under the Gospel and thus continue undetermined about religion, are more abominable to God than the heathen," and it would be entirely just for God to give man no further chances to prepare himself.[7]

This emphasis on preparation was clearly in the tradition of Stoddard's doctrine that man had to do what he could in order to know that his efforts were truly in vain; Edwards once preached that human exertions were God's "ordinary means" of acquainting men with their own "helplessness." Usually, however, the usefulness of activity was treated more ambiguously, and men who did not keep the basic tenets of Calvinism clearly in mind might have received the impression that they *could* help themselves to heaven. (Did they remember that they must only strive to receive the *gift* of belief, and that there was no "merit of congruity" or "true" proportion between their seeking and that gift?)[8] Such ambiguity was more than merely a borrowed convention, for it was also one logical response to the dwindling piety of the Northampton congregation, a response no less appropriate because used by many other ministers faced with similar "declension" over the previous fifty years. A little semi-intentional confusion in preaching Reformed doctrine was, in essence, a *pastoral* strategy suited to the circumstances of the times in New England.[9] When men ceased to respond to the challenging requirements of experiential grace for church membership, preaching about steps they could take was a tactic to encourage piety and a way of enforcing at least a minimum of community morality.

Edwards's sermons prepared for more learned audiences, on the other hand, were much more precisely orthodox. When he lectured in Boston during Harvard's Commencement Week in July 1731, and when he wrote a sermon for publication in 1734, Edwards was much less equivocal about the powers of natural man to take any action toward his own salvation. Rather, he emphasized the absolute power of God. The 1731 lecture, published almost immediately as *God Glorified in the Work of Redemption, by the Greatness of Man's Dependence upon Him in the Whole of It,* contained a repeated insistence that Faith (not man's merit) was the only true means to salvation. "Faith is a sensibleness of what is real in the work of redemption," and that is the "absolute and universal" dependence of fallen man on God. In the face of Boston's increasingly liberal divines, Edwards asserted that "those doctrines and schemes of divinity that are in any respect opposite to such an absolute and universal dependence on God . . . thwart the design of our redemption."[10] This sentence was not in the original sermon as preached in Northampton, and is only one example of the way that Edwards's writing becomes "more erudite and radical in its argument" when aimed at a Boston audience, as Wilson H. Kimnach has discussed in one of his many articles on Edwards's artistry as a preacher. Kimnach summarizes the differences very nicely by writing that "Edwards was an evangelical pastor in Northampton; in Boston he was an eloquent interpreter presenting his understanding of a portion of the Word for the consideration of fellow-inquirers."[11]

In the treatise published in 1734, entitled *A Divine and Supernatural Light, Immediately Imparted to the Soul by the Spirit of God, Shown to be both a Scriptural and Rational Doctrine,* Edwards restated God's power and defined the conversion experience as the reception of divine light from the Holy Spirit. Man's role in salvation was not earning merit through his activities but preparing himself through humiliation for a new sensibility. (An appropriate analogy might be washing the windows of the soul: removing the grime would facilitate a perception of the sunlight, although it would not be the cause of the sun's shining, nor would a neglect of such cleaning keep the sun's rays from heating up the room even imperceptibly.) The result was a "true sense of the divine excellency of the things revealed in the Word of God, and a conviction of the truth and reality of them thence arising. . . . a sense of the loveliness of God's holiness. . . . not a speculative thing, but . . . [a] sense of the heart. . . . above all others sweet and joyful." Only this divine light "will bring the soul to a saving close with Christ" and bear fruit in "an universal holiness of life."[12]

Although Edwards as a professional theologian could develop for a learned audience an elegant fusion of the old Calvinist doctrines of man's absolute dependence on God with the new language of sensibility so appealing to "enlightened" thinkers, as a country pastor he needed to stress a different aspect of conversion—the observable end product, a holiness of life, that more tangible acting out of the influence of grace. Faced with the inevitable Puritan dilemma of maintaining community discipline while exhorting his flock to vivid inner piety, Edwards seems to have saved his dissection of the subtleties of holy sensations for a sophisticated Boston audience, and to have used his Northampton sermons for more practical directions to those who were actively seeking the consolations of conversion, or who still wallowed in the complacency of sin. The tension between Edwards's doctrine of the absolute power of God and his parallel emphasis on man's doing all within his capability was not a contradiction but a different stress on two parts of one argument, depending on the role which Edwards played. His mind was exploring ideas which he did not yet know how to synthesize with the full range of pastoral responsibilities. The work of the Spirit in actual conversion, which Edwards *described* so beautifully for those who could appreciate the art of theological hair-splitting, was something that he nevertheless could not *effect*. He could only preach obedience and striving toward God, and hope that the Spirit would descend on the members of his congregation who were responsive to the Word.

Most of Edwards's early sermons which survive in manuscript are conventional exhortations to reform behavior while there is still time. Sinners were reminded not to expect God to perform miracles to awaken them. Life was likened to a pilgrimage toward heaven:

"How ill do they improve their lives, that spend them in traveling towards hell!" The manuscript sermons from this period rarely contain the new images or the impressive logical constructions of the published works; many were the thoroughly predictable ritualized entreaty to spiritually sluggish congregations. Equally conventional were Edwards's complaints that his advice was not received enthusiastically. The doctrine of one sermon read: "If the business of ministers was the further gratification of men's lusts, they would be much better received by men than they are now." It is easy to imagine the Northampton congregation drowsing through still another sermon explaining why "time is precious" and perhaps stirring only to watch their neighbors' faces when Edwards charged that there were persons so guilty of corrupting others that "it would have been better for the town where they live, to have been at the charge of maintaining them in doing nothing," if that would have kept them in a state of inactivity. (The specter of "public charge" was probably the most frightening part of that sermon.) Even when Edwards tried to instill the common ethics of charity and honesty in business and politics, to persuade Northampton men that seeking self-interest in disregard of the needs of others was "of the same nature as theft or robbery," he met with little positive response. It was, as he wrote in the *Faithful Narrative,* a time when his people were "very insensible of the things of religion."[13]

Through 1733 Edwards seems to have followed the Stoddardean pastoral tradition of open communion and attempts to discipline public behavior. He met with little success, and by this time he was writing entries in his private theological notebooks that reflected a frustration with the lack of effective disciplinary powers in the church and that played with the idea of reintroducing exclusivity in the church as a means of social control.[14] These thoughts would not be brought to fruition in an open statement of changed principles for about fifteen years, for practical success intervened and kept Edwards from despairing of his effectiveness in his calling. Some time in 1733, Edwards began to develop a technique that would make him a true shepherd to his flock. The technique, which would eventually encompass a variety of tones of voice, was to direct sermons and advice specifically to the adolescents in the community. (Stoddard had recorded his concern for this group, but there is no evidence that he dealt with them separately.) Edwards had appealed to the parents to save their children from damnation—challenging them as early as 1729 to dare to instruct their offspring properly and thereby guarantee "great outpourings of God's spirit in the town" —but had produced no appreciable results.[15] In 1733 he preached at least one sermon with a very long Application focused on disharmony within the family, especially ineffectiveness in its government, and the parents were again warned about the probable results of their lax discipline. "Family government is in a great measure extinct," Edwards wrote. "By neglect in this particular, parents bring the guilt of their children's sins upon their own souls, and the blood of their children will be required at their hands."[16] When even this horrible threat failed, Edwards began to speak directly to the children and young people in terms they would understand clearly.

In the first phase of this new technique, Edwards portrayed the advantages of salvation in concepts calculated to interest the youngsters. He maintained that God gave extra help to early seekers by giving them leisure and impressibility of heart. In a sermon in May 1734 the doctrine used was "the directest way that young people can take to spend their youth pleasantly is to walk in the ways of virtue and piety." The Application of this sermon shows clearly the tone that Edwards was taking with the young people, who had begun to be tractable. "Let me intreat you to continue in that reformation which I hope many of you have begun in these particulars. I hope you are generally convinced of the reasonableness of it and that experience has or will convince you that there is no great difficulty in it and that there is no danger of your sustaining any loss by it or that your youth will be the less pleasant for it." In August 1734 he exhorted the young people to "consider how exceedingly it will be for the comfort and pleasure of your life, if you are converted. . . . you will gain unspeakably by it, while in this world." On the other hand, Edwards maintained in a sermon on the "ruinous pleasure" of "sinful mirth," young people who sinned and neglected opportunities for religious strivings would find their later lives filled with bitterness and guilt and the consciousness of a hardened heart.[17] The evolution of Edwards's rhetoric is illustrated by the contrast between this sermon and one preached eighteen months earlier "to the young people at a private meeting." Then, on the doctrine that "many persons never get rid of the guilt of the sins of their youth," Edwards had stressed the eternal punishment for these sins, and guilt was still the objective condition of deserving punishment. In the later sermon on sinful mirth, however, guilt was a psychological condition, an inner shame that made men unhappy.[18] The newer style of sermon was probably more successful, for Edwards continued the emphasis on internalized guilt and unhappiness in this life. Repeated stress on pleasure and pain in this world was apparently effective since, according to Edwards's *Faithful Narrative,* it was at the time he preached these sermons that the adolescents began to lead the town in "religious concern." They showed a "thorough reformation" of their former scandalous behavior.[19]

But if Edwards was pleased by the increased religiosity of a part of his congregation, forces from the outside world intruded to alarm "the friends of vital piety" in Northampton and to remind Edwards that promising earthly rewards and the consciousness of conversion (the corollary of internalized guilt for sin) was dangerously close to the Arminian tendency to emphasize God's dealings with man in terms of human capabilities. In late 1734 and 1735 Hampshire County was filled with a "great noise" about the suspected Arminianism of ministers William Rand of Sunderland and Robert Breck of Springfield. The anti-Arminian forces were led by Jonathan Edwards's uncle, William Williams of Hatfield, the patriarch of the Hampshire clergy after Stoddard's death, and Edwards was active within the Hampshire Association of Ministers as it coaxed Rand back to orthodoxy and stood firm in opposing Breck.[20] Although he was concerned about the invasion of the Valley by dangerous liberal ideas, even more upsetting to Edwards was the doctrinal confusion aroused in his own congregation.[21] Chagrined that they should be unsure of the correct views after six years of his ministry, Edwards responded with his best weapon, pulpit oratory. In this head-on confrontation with Arminianism, the doctrines of Edwards the theologian and the advice of Edwards the pastor fused into a powerful statement of religious principle that appeared to have enormous effect on the town of Northampton.

In the winter of 1734–35 Edwards preached a series of discourses on "Justification by Faith Alone," which he later felt "was most evidently attended with a very remarkable blessing of heaven to the souls of the people in this town," and which was shortly followed by the descent of the Spirit in the full-scale revival described in the *Faithful Narrative.* [22] What made these sermons so effective was their clarity. In contrast to Edwards's earlier assertions of both man's dependence on God and the necessity for man to be active in pursuing his own conversion, the doctrine of justification by faith alone was explicated with a luminous logic that left no room for doubt about the relative activities of man and God in the scheme of salvation. Edwards described his aim as showing that any works of man were insufficient to merit salvation, but that faith in Christ was sufficient, and he disclaimed any attempt to define faith more precisely than simply "the soul's active uniting with Christ." Man had no claim to heaven except as united to Christ—because "the evil and demerit of sin is infinitely great," only union with Christ enabled man to fulfill the condition of perfect obedience to God, man's sufficiency would derogate from the glory of free grace and the honor of its giver, and it would detract from "the honor of the Mediator." The acts of a Christian life were necessary after conversion only as expressions of faith, not as means to salvation. Those accepted as "heirs of glory" were thereafter commanded by God to perform certain acts as preparation for their heavenly rewards as "vessels of different sizes." The need for these post-conversion exercises, as obedience to the still-applicable Law, was the answer to those who charged that the doctrine of justification by faith alone tended toward licentiousness. On the contrary, Edwards insisted, any other idea of salvation was "fatal to the soul." [23]

Once Edwards had enlightened his congregation about the lack of logical and Scriptural bases for Arminian doctrines, and after he had so clearly outlined the true and only way to heaven, he received a reward far beyond his expectations: "Then it was, in the latter part of December [1734], that the Spirit of God began extraordinarily to set in, and wonderfully to work amongst us." Soon "a great and earnest concern about the great things of religion and the eternal world became universal in all parts of the town, and among persons of all degrees and all ages." [24]

During the following spring Edwards preached a number of sermons which amplified his doctrine of justification and developed a style of exhortation suitable to an ongoing revival. There are a few sermons that continue the pre-revival theme of the sweet "reason-ableness" of religious truth, with statements such as "God doth not require us to submit contrary to reason, but to submit as seeing the reason and ground of submission."[25] Appeals to man's rationality, however, receded in importance during the revival. The predomi-nant style of Edwards's pulpit oratory, as evidenced by the surviving manuscripts, came to be more emotional, direct, and frightening. After the absolute power of God had been sufficiently described, the corollary of man's infinite sinfulness invited the full play of Ed-wards's dramatic skills. In a sermon on "The Justice of God in the Damnation of Sinners," Edwards described his congregation in an indictment so harsh and multi-faceted that a great number of persons in his audience must have seen at last that trust in their own righ-teousness was indeed "fatal to the soul." The Application of this sermon is worth quoting at length because it is the *weight* of the attack which best illustrates the power of Edwards's preaching.

Let eternal damnation be never so dreadful, yet it is just. . . . Look over your past life. . . . How manifold have been the abominations of your life! . . . After what manner have many of you kept God's holy day. . . . How have you not only not attended to the worship, but have in the mean time been feasting your lusts, and wallowing yourself in abominable uncleanness! . . . When you on sabbath-days have got along with your wicked companions, how has holy time been treated among you? What kind of conversation has there been! Yea, how have some of you, by a very indecent carriage, openly dishonoured and cast con-tempt on the sacred services of God's house, and holy day! And what a trade have many of you made of absenting yourselves from the worship of the families you belong to, for the sake of vain company! . . . What wicked carriage have some of you been guilty of towards your parents! . . . Have you not even harboured ill-will and malice towards them? And when they have displeased you, have [you] wished evil to them? Have not some of you often disobeyed your parents, yea, and refused to be subject to them? . . . What revenge and malice have you been guilty of towards your neighbours! . . . For the world you have envied and hated your neighbour; for the world you have cast God, and Christ, and heaven, behind your back; for the world you have sold your own soul. . . . How much of a spirit of pride has appeared in you, which is in a peculiar manner the spirit and condemnation of the devil! How have some of you vaunted yourselves in your apparel! Others in their riches! Others in their knowledge and abilities! . . . How sensual have you been! Are there not some here that have debased themselves below the dignity of human nature, by wallowing in sensual filthiness, as swine in the mire, or as filthy vermin feeding with delight on rotten carrion? What intemperance have some of you been guilty of! How much of your precious time have you spent away at the tavern, and in drinking companies, when you ought to have been at home seeking God and your salvation in your families and closets! . . . And what abominable lasciviousness have some of you been guilty of! How have you indulged yourself from day to day, and from night to night, in all manner of unclean imaginations! Has not your soul been filled with them, till it has become a hold of foul spirits, and a cage of every unclean and hateful bird? What foul-mouthed persons have some of you been, often in lewd and lascivious talk and unclean songs, wherein were things not fit to be spoken! . . . God and your own consciences know what abominable lasciviousness you have practised in things not fit to be named, when you have been alone; when you ought to have been reading, or meditating, or on your knees before God in secret prayer. And how have you corrupted others, as well as polluted yourselves! . . . What lying have some of you been guilty of, especially in your childhood! . . . And how have some of you behaved yourselves in your family relations! . . . How have some of you attended that sacred ordinance of the Lord's Supper without any manner of serious preparation, and in a careless slighty frame of spirits, and chiefly to comply with custom! . . . What stupidity and sottishness has attended your course of wickedness; which has appeared in your obstinacy. . . . [26]

Surely there was no unconverted person in the congregation who had not at least once behaved badly during religious services, or in his or her family, or envied a neighbor or indulged in pride, or allowed unclean imaginings—or worse. This was a direct indictment unclouded by Biblical similes, unencumbered with parables that the guilty could misinterpret. This was not a traditional jeremiad in which the Scriptural motif dominated the contemporary application.[27] The combination of specificity of sins with the universality of probable guilt was the technique which seemed to bring the

Northampton congregation to a pitch of fervor in that spring of 1735. When Edwards continued the sermon by asking the congregation, "Now, can you think when you have thus behaved yourself, that God is *obliged* to show you mercy?" few in his audience could have answered affirmatively. Rather, they had to assent to Edwards's direction "to consider, if God should eternally reject and destroy you, what an agreeableness and exact mutual answerableness there would be between God so dealing with you, and your spirit and behavior."

The printed page cannot adequately convey the emotional impact which Edwards's revival sermons had on his flock. His delivery was supposedly "easy, natural, and very solemn," and his voice was low and very distinct. "His words often discovered [revealed] a great degree of inward fervor, without much noise of external emotion, and fell with great weight on the minds of his hearers. He made but little motion of his head or hands in the desk." Although he has the reputation for staring at the bell rope at the back of the meeting-house while he preached, it is hard to imagine Edwards *not* fixing his eyes on the faces of his congregation while he read the accusation quoted above. If delivered as printed, the whole passage from which the excerpt was taken must have lasted at least half an hour, perhaps more; if it was delivered in a solemn tone with dramatic pauses, it must have been terrifying. A Northampton man later recalled that when he was ten years old and heard Edwards give some similar sermons, he had been deeply disappointed when Edwards's "awful scene" of judgment did not, in fact, take place outside the Northampton meetinghouse on that very day.[28] But the revival sermons in themselves could not have produced such a great response in Edwards's flock without the cumulative effects of twice-weekly indictments, prayer meetings, children's deaths and conversions, and constant reminders that God was about to punish the whole world for its sins—building tensions that Edwards carefully cultivated from the fall of 1734 through the spring of 1735.[29]

Although Edwards manipulated the fears of his flock, he stopped short of the extremes of terror. He closed the sermon on "The Justice of God in the Damnation of Sinners" by cautioning his flock "not to improve the doctrine to discouragement. For though it would be righteous in God for ever to cast you off, and destroy you, yet it would also be just in God to save you, in and through Christ."[30] And one major way of fighting depression, implied Edwards's sermons, was Christian activity. In a February 1735 sermon titled "Pressing into the Kingdom of God," Edwards recommended "an engagedness and earnestness, that is directly about that business of getting into the kingdom of God."[31] Such exertions would lead to humiliation, as Stoddard had told his flock long ago and as his grandson now reminded them; and this humiliation was the antithesis of despair. To despair was to assume that because man could not save himself, God could not or would not rescue him; humiliation was seeing one's own inability as it contrasted with the unlimited power and mercy of God.

In the spring of 1735, confident that his flock would remember that salvation was God's free gift to those with true faith, Edwards fanned the flames of revival by preaching that it was a time of exceptional opportunity for the community to escape from the damnation of the temporal world. It was God's "most extraordinary" appearance ever in New England, and man's persevering was perhaps to be rewarded under the special dispensation being granted to Northampton. In the excitement of the moment, Edwards preached that men could "take" heaven almost "as it were by violence." The sense of urgency was also increased by his constant reminders that the extraordinary times might portend imminent doom. "It has been God's manner before he casts off a visible people, or brings some great and destroying judgments upon them, first to gather in his elect, that they may be secure." Especially great punishments might follow such unusual opportunities to seek salvation, if they were not taken.[32] Those who heeded the Gospel message in time would, however, be safe for all eternity.

Another impetus behind Edwards's particular style of preaching strenuous activity within an atmosphere of impending disaster was his intimate experience with the emotions he tried to arouse in his audience. When he spoke from the pulpit of the inability of man to earn salvation by his own merits, he drew on personal experience: human exercises did indeed serve only for humiliation. When he taught that man must nevertheless be active to the limits of his ability, he spoke in echo of his own "Resolutions" to do better and to live more ascetically, which were the urgent gropings of a depressed man toward some sense of emotional stability. When he spoke of the beauty of God's majesty, of the joyful psychological relief that could come from submission to that divine power, was he not sharing with his audience an experience from his own youth? Or was it even, perhaps, an experience that he was *having* in those very months, in that very pulpit? Was submission to the will of God, so difficult in his youth but clearly achieved by the time he would write his "Personal Narrative" around 1740, now possible because he could see the workings of the Spirit in others more clearly than he could ever discern regeneration in himself? What was once a "horrible" doctrine of God's sovereignty was indeed beautiful in its manifestation in Northampton. Was a part of Edwards's effectiveness in preaching Calvinist doctrine—which was not, after all, a new set of ideas in Northampton—derived from this young man's true empathy with the seekers in his flock, his truly sharing their search while he tried to describe it in the limited vocabulary of mortal men? Could there have been this special link between Edwards and the young people who responded so ardently to his exhortations in 1734–35?

The appeal of Edwards's definition of faith, certainly, had to have a broader foundation than the charisma of the preacher. And the compulsion of intellectual logic alone cannot account for the sudden mass responsiveness to what were familiar doctrines. There was clearly an emotional predisposition in the congregation which had previously been missing, or which had been less widely present in the entire community. The whole upper Connecticut Valley, in fact, was inflamed by Edwards and his followers and imitators in 1734–35 and again in 1740–42, although the indigenous tradition of revivalism had hitherto been experienced as sparks geographically scattered and widely spaced in time. What was new in the 1730s?

One clue to the revitalizing effectiveness of Calvinist doctrine may lie in its essential devaluation of the world: no effective means to eternal life were to be found in material Creation. While forbidding escape from the world into the monastic life of contemplation, and continually invoking the sense of "calling" to engage men's wills with the never ending fight against temporal sin, good Calvinist preachers encouraged an emotional distance from temporal satisfactions. To be in the world but not of it, one had to renounce any ultimate attachment to things, persons, and pride in one's own abilities. In this sense, "justification by faith alone" was a psychological as well as an intellectual antithesis of Arminianism, which commended the profitable use of the human faculties and worldly goods which God had given. (In exemplary Arminian fashion, Ben Franklin was proud of his humility; and when he wrote his will in 1750, he thanked the God he usually addressed as "Powerful Goodness" for both "such a mind, with moderate passions, or so much of His gracious assistance in governing them," and "such a competency of this world's goods as might make a reasonable mind easy."[33]) Calvinists, on the other hand, were engaged in the Sisyphean task of fighting their own inherently sinful natures, and only grace could rescue them from inevitable perdition. Without a secure sense of the work of the Spirit in one's soul, no reasonable mind could ever be easy in counting temporal blessings as signs of favor. On the other hand, the Calvinist had to beware of that contrary temptation to neglect strivings after true grace while contemplating one's temporal state in a negative frame of mind—worrying about a lack of worldly success was perhaps even more sinful than being satisfied with its achievement. The only proper attitude was that it didn't matter.

Edwards's use of the language of sensibility to describe conversion facilitated the escapist potential of his doctrines. What was a sense, after all, but an idea that was not a matter of the understanding's rational judgment or the merely animal emotions of fear or satisfaction? Regeneration was a free gift from God, which would produce a feeling of ultimate security, independent of the unfortunate circumstances of everyday life. Edwards's audience might have inferred that since all men are powerless before God, a relative lack of power among men is unimportant; any particular set of social credentials was no barrier to God's arbitrary election and the gift of a reborn sensibility. For those who had real doubts about what future the world had to offer them, or who could not escape the burden of inner guilt for previous transgressions of the Puritan ethical code, the promise of being able to feel securely chosen by God must have been difficult to resist.

The phenomenon of religious awakening shows that something in Edwards's Calvinist vision was answering the emotional needs of the people of the Valley in the 1730s more fully than did the Arminianism which was gradually becoming dominant in New England.[34] Edwards was appealing to insecurities in the community that could be expressed in his pulpit rhetoric as a discovery that worldly ambitions were mere delusions and that temporal success brought no lasting satisfaction. Too few communities have had their revivals dissected by historians to permit more than conjecture, but the location of the most intense Awakening—the Connecticut Valley and eastern Connecticut—suggests that an important social component of the response was the stage of economic and social development which distinguished the region, as well as the town of Northampton.

Many communities in the area were making the difficult adjustments from the plentiful resources of frontier settlements to the scarcities and competition of established agricultural towns, and from the overwhelming agrarian emphasis of seventeenth-century Valley society to a more elaborated social and economic diversity. Progress—population growth and economic development—was fast eroding the pertinence of the old Puritan norms of behavior, without providing any suitable replacement.[35] To men still inclined, as most were, to see at least the shadow of God's hand in temporal events, the eastern New England earthquake of late 1727 and the epidemic of "throat distemper" (diphtheria) which killed thousands of children in New England in the mid-1730s were signs that God was displeased with his covenanted people.[36] Even for those of more secular outlook, those disasters were reminders that there were strict limits to man's ability to control his world beyond the superficial prosperity of tidy farms or to gain real security in a competitive society with growing distinctions between winners and losers.

As we shall explore in greater detail in the next chapter, those most responsive to Awakening doctrines in Northampton and other communities were young people, especially young men aged eighteen to twenty-six.[37] They were the group most critically affected by the rapidly changing socioeconomic conditions. We can never really know what it was about evangelical Calvinist doctrines that touched their hearts, but the model we can derive from Jonathan Edwards's own conversion provides a workable interpretation for the experiences of youth in Northampton in the 1730s. The important features of Edwards's conversion were the catalyst of temporal problems in forming an adult identity (with its problematic vocational component and its confrontation with parental authority), and the way that absolute submission to God seemed to ease the emotional burden of finding that delicate line between proper deference to parents and necessary self-assertion as an adult. In Northampton and elsewhere in the slower-developing parts of New England which experienced revivals in 1735 and 1740–42 (as the influence of evangelicalism was apparently superficial in the urban and eastern-rural parts of Massachusetts), changing circumstances of practical life were bringing young men more and more into conflict with their fathers. Their "wild" behavior, as commented upon by Edwards and others, signified both their own assertions of independence and the difficulties that their parents were having in asserting and enforcing their own authority. When the advice that an older generation could give no longer seemed to fit present social realities, and when parents could no longer use economic rewards to govern their children, there was indeed a decline in traditional family government.

Much of the modern psychoanalytical literature on conversion experiences points to the commonness of a crisis in late adolescence, as the individual must make a transition between the social status of child and that of adult by accepting certain economic responsibilities and by finding a comfortable new position vis-à-vis parental authority. Empirical research done in the late nineteenth century found a strong pattern of adolescent conversion, and most twentieth-century psychological theory accepts the universality of a crisis in adolescence. Although we do not know how much of that turmoil was present in pre-industrial societies, the frequency with which contemporaries remarked on the importance of adolescent constituencies for revival preachers in the 1730s and 1740s tells us that there was a crisis of adolescence in that era, also.[38] It was at this time in much of New England that young people first had to confront the necessity of making a choice about what vocation to follow, or even what town to live in, for the rest of their lives. Socioeconomic change was cutting them off from the moorings of traditional concepts of work and community life, and Calvinist doctrines may have eased the tension of facing a new world.

In Northampton, at least, the psychological usefulness of Calvinism and conversion would fade as the young people found adult ways to deal with practical problems; Edwards's followers quickly lapsed back into sinful behavior and would eventually reject their once-beloved pastor entirely. But for a few years, for young people and their parents, publicly assertive sainthood provided a sense of security to those experiencing the transition between the old social order established by a Puritan God and a chaotic new world that was less obviously designed by a wise hand. In those years between 1734 and 1742, the restatement of old doctrines of an authoritarian God and a necessarily submissive man penetrated through what had come to seem a very secularized Yankee sensibility, touched the hearts of a significant number of people, and transformed Northampton into a facsimile of the pious and well-disciplined community that it may once have been.

CHAPTER FOUR

Constituency

"I HAVE ever had a peculiar concern for the souls of the young people," Jonathan Edwards reminded his congregation in his 1750 farewell sermon, "and a desire that religion might flourish among them; and I have especially exerted myself in order to it. . . . This is what I longed for; and it has been exceedingly grievous to me, when I have heard of vice, vanity and disorder, among our youth."[1] Edwards's career *was* particularly closely intertwined with the lives of the young people in Northampton: when they followed his advice, he achieved authority over the whole community, and when they rejected his leadership, his pastoral vocation itself was endangered. From another perspective, however, Edwards was merely sharing a ministerial focus on the youth of New England that had been growing in intensity since the late seventeenth century.

In 1705 Solomon Stoddard had voiced the frustrations of two generations of ministers by citing the failure to convert the young people as the chief cause and sign of New England's growing sinfulness. Many sermons and treatises published from about the time of King Philip's War into the eighteenth century reflected the clergy's preoccupation with the role of the "rising generation" in the perceptible decline from an already-idealized Puritan (stable, hierarchical, and godly) society.[2] It was the behavior of the young people which was the most obvious symptom of the decay of communalism. On the brink of adulthood, but not yet established in the social functions of maturity, adolescents were most affected by the social and economic changes that were generating a widening array of careers, opportunities for wealth, and dangers of poverty. Being free from

91

most adult responsibilities, they were also freer to act out the tensions that they shared with their parents. In Northampton this acting out was recorded by the censorious Jonathan Edwards as tavern frequenting, night walking (unsupervised courtship), and boisterousness during religious services.[3] Their "frolicking" can be summarized as an unwillingness to obey the authority of parents and a lack of proper deference to the authority of the minister as an agent of God and family. From the clerical viewpoint, the youthful misbehavior was an exaggeration of the more general community disinclination to fashion all its conduct on the Biblical model of primitive Christians so much extolled in the earliest years of New England. That model had worked well in the early, Puritan years—or had *seemed* to because the patterns of behavior found appropriate for practical reasons were closely parallel to the conduct prescribed for the "city upon a hill."[4] But as a scheme of social organization, Puritan communitarianism rarely survived the transition from frontier conditions to stable agricultural subsistence.

Northampton, founded in 1653 and no longer frontier in socioeconomic character or attitudes by 1700, was probably typical of many inland Massachusetts communities as they evolved. By the end of its first half century, the town began to look prosperous. The inhabitants enjoyed more and better houses, even a few luxury items such as sugar, raisins, rum, and cloth, ribbons, and even furniture imported from Boston. They had enough income to make their minister the best-paid clergyman outside Boston.[5] Prosperity tended to bring competition, however, and progress inevitably brought many changes that increased the potential for serious social tensions not easily resolved. Even if we avoid romanticizing traditional society, we must acknowledge an important indication of the satisfactions of life organized around a simple and communal enterprise: the formerly Puritan colonies of Connecticut and Massachusetts clung to the communitarian *model* of social life until the mid-eighteenth century, even while the behavior of most people was much more modern and individualistic and their ambitions much more materialistic.[6] Not until the Revolutionary era would an ideology arise that effectively legitimized the behavior of a man who grasped the best worldly opportunities. During Edwards's pastorate, however, young people coming to maturity were caught in a dilemma. When the fourth Northampton generation approached adulthood and began to plan their future lives, economic circumstances had changed in many important ways, but the ideals of behavior invoked were still those of the Puritan frontier community. Meanwhile, lessons that could be learned from authority figures—parents and ministers—were becoming inappropriate guides to the many choices which the rising generation had to make. Young people faced a different world than that mastered—or endured—by their grandparents.

Jonathan Edwards has left us some important clues for examining this social evolution in terms of the changing relation of the individual to the community. Edwards's *Faithful Narrative* emphasizes the decline in harmony in public affairs and the failure of family government, although in retrospect it is impossible to discern any major change in the *structure* of community and familial institutions. The public affairs still centered on a town meeting that governed land grants, roads, public buildings, and the care of the few local poor; a few men represented the town at the county and province levels where disputes were adjudicated, taxes demanded, and military decisions made. The family was still dominantly the husband-wife-unmarried-children nuclear residential unit surrounded by a complex network of kin. Family and community, however, depended for their *functional* style on the character of Northampton as a simple agricultural village. Institutionally as well as physically, land underlay the social arrangements of the community. As the population grew and pressures on the available land increased, the functions of political and familial structures changed. The town meeting ceased to be the almost automatic provider of the means of sustenance and became the arena of competition for scarce resources. The family unit, often living at greater geographical distance from its kin and neighbors, had to adapt itself to declining agricultural opportunities by preparing the young to endure prolonged dependence or to grasp new kinds of opportunities in a very individualistic fashion.[7]

These changes, so small in scale compared to the dramatic changes between the condition of the colonies in 1650 and America in the nineteenth century, are extremely difficult to measure quantitatively. To analyze the Northampton situation as clearly as is possible, we can use a ready-made sampling of people whose life histories can be traced in some detail: this group is actually self-selected, for they are the men who joined the Northampton church during the ministerial tenure of Jonathan Edwards. (It is, of course, our broader interest in their lives, and their responsiveness to Edwards's preaching, that underlies this brief digression from the main narrative of Edwards's career. And it is our need to draw information from relatively public documents—especially various property transfers—that necessitates a concentration on young men, although the young women were undoubtedly facing parallel problems.) Most of these men were in their late teens or early twenties when they joined the church between 1727 and 1746.[8] They are not really a random sample, for the group includes almost all the young men who can be located in the community during the Edwards years, and so their lives provide an aggregate picture of the changes in the community from about 1725 to 1750. We will focus on a number of rituals of coming-of-age, highly symbolic customs which signaled the achievement of adulthood, rituals which were particularly susceptible to change as economic conditions developed and which can be analyzed from surviving documents.

Before we turn to the lives of these Edwards converts, however, it will be useful to digress briefly for a survey of one potential measure of dissatisfaction with Northampton as the town developed, the level of emigration, which was rather low until the 1760s because of the Indian threat to the north and west. (As late as 1748, Southampton, on the southwest edge of Northampton and only nine miles west of the Connecticut River, had to be abandoned over the winter because of Indian raids.) Among the first generation of settlers, a number of men who came to Northampton moved on to found other towns; for some of these hardy pioneers, Northampton was but one of three or four towns which they would help to establish.[9] Other men moved away over the next eighty years in small numbers to scattered locations, at a rate of thirteen to twenty-nine men per decade, with a peak in the 1730s and 1740s. The 1740s had the highest (approximate) total number for one decade, twenty-nine men, and even this figure represents only one male emigrant for each eight established households in town. (Only men who moved after age sixteen have been counted.) Most men seemed to move in their thirties. Emigrants often left with some other relative, or went to a town where another Northampton man had recently settled, but rarely did more than three families move together at one time.[10] (The group who establish a new village within the Northampton bounds, discussed below, are not counted in these emigration statistics.) Few men of the pre-Revolutionary age were acting like the archetypical pioneer who wanted "elbow room." People wanted land, but they wanted family and neighbors as well: even when there was no immediate Indian threat, the desire for community was a cultural heritage that clearly kept its hold on men's ideals long after it had become difficult to practice.[11]

Such a relatively low level of emigration is testimony to the fact that the land problem was not really desperate during the Edwards years. Men were worried, however, about what further changes the future would bring, what further erosions of the old community spirit would take place. The preferred way of coping with a need for more land for sons coming of age in the first three decades of the eighteenth century was itself a statement of faith in a traditional pattern of communal organization. Before the young men could organize themselves and cause trouble in town politics, as occurred in other communities short of land, some fathers provided for their sons by arranging an exceptionally orderly march to the closest part of the frontier. (This action was almost the last statement of communal policy to be made without recorded controversy.)

In 1730 the Northampton Proprietors, with the concurrence of the Town, agreed to divide the mountainous southwestern corner of the original Northampton land grant, about 14,000 acres in all.[12] They thereby created a new town, about eight miles from the center of Northampton, soon named Southampton. The village land was given only to owners by inheritance of Northampton Proprietors' shares, and of them only to those "who shall undertake to bring forward a speedy settlement." The emphasis was on founding a community and alleviating a particular problem, not on promoting individualism and opportunism; there would be no speculation allowed, and substitutes were found for those who would not move. Thirty shares, of up to ninety acres each (including twenty-acre home lots), were laid out. A few men had already farmed lands in the Southampton tract, and by 1735 there were about twenty households established, most of them clustered in an old-fashioned nucleated village. Southampton organized its own church in 1743 and in 1753 became a district (a separate town with all rights except separate representation in the too populous General Court). Both stages of separation were accomplished with Northampton's blessing; probably because of the poor quality of the land, Southampton did not become prosperous enough for its loss to have a major effect on Northampton tax revenues.[13] The new community was settled by relatively young men (the residents who petitioned for their own church in 1741 averaged only 33.5 years of age in that year), and they were all descended from original Northampton Proprietors. They were taking advantage of a safety valve arranged for them by their powerful grandfathers and great-grandfathers. Significantly, the grantees of 1730 were already an elite group in the community, they had to be given decidedly inferior farmland, and it was the last open land available. After 1730 there was no hope that Northampton as a corporate enterprise could provide adequate land for those coming of age.

If we add the Southampton settlers to the estimated emigrants of the 1730s, twenty-five in number, we find a total of forty-five or more men who were willing to brave the Indian danger and move far away from families and friends to search for individual opportunities. If we came across this piece of information before we knew there was a large religious revival in Northampton in the 1730s, we might well look for some sign of unusual tension in the religious or political aspects of community life. Even men who did not choose to leave had problems, and there were economic causes for tensions between the generations that might have resulted in implicit or explicit challenges to the traditional system of family government which the Northampton minister labeled as the mainstay of social order.

For men unwilling to risk the dangers of the frontier, or unwilling to start from scratch in another town, there were two primary ways of acquiring land. One was by inheritance. A major disadvantage of this was the decreasing productivity of the land: those acquiring land in the 1730s and 1740s were the third or fourth or even fifth generation to use Northampton's good tilling plots, and complaints about its depletion had been voiced since 1715.[14] Another disadvantage of inheritance was the further subdivision of parcels, perhaps into smaller than useful lots, or the necessity of joint ownership with brothers or cousins. Then there was the problem of timing: not all fathers could be counted on to distribute their property (by deed or death) at the time when the son or sons first became eager to own land.

The other major method of acquiring land was by purchase. But few men in the area could afford to extend credit, and cash was always in short supply. Purchase was also growing very expensive in relative terms: in the 1730s a laborer earned two to five shillings a day, from which he had to pay for his own housing and food; the best land in town (the river plains) cost four hundred to eight hundred days' labor per acre, and inferior land cost forty to eighty days' work per acre.[15] Since the local economy had not developed to the point where there was much demand for labor beyond that supplied by a property owner's own family, the young man in Northampton would find few opportunities to hire out his labor for many days a year; he would be old before he could save enough to buy an adequate farm.

Searching for a livelihood, a young man might consider becoming an artisan or merchant. After the 1740s, as Northampton became a trading center for villages springing up to the north and west (Northampton was just north of the end of navigability for barges on the Connecticut River), and as the economy within Northampton itself developed, a group of merchants and craftsmen achieved wealth and political power, in spite of the mistrust of commercial activity as harmful to the interdependent society.[16] Through the 1730s, nevertheless, there was little demand for specialized services; one or two blacksmiths, one tanner, one hatmaker, and one general store were sufficient. Before the period of revival, few men can be identified whose primary economic activity was not farming. Most young men coming of age in that era could neither amass the capital necessary to set up shop nor expect to earn a livelihood by non-agricultural labor.

Whether emigration or an innovative occupation was chosen to meet the problem for one or more sons, there would be tensions within the family which were likely to be new in quantity if not in quality. Through the late seventeenth century, most young men coming to adulthood had simply followed in the steps of their fathers, taking on a part of the father's extensive acreage, or getting their own grant from the town meeting, perhaps continuing a family tradition of a part-time craft. Surely there were problems within families over which son would get which piece of land, or when the transfer from one generation to another would be made, but there is no reason to suspect a widespread and systematic incidence of intergenerational tensions until the eighteenth century. Then, even the most obvious solutions to the land shortage involved making explicit the difference between father and son. The son of a farmer who chose to go into trade was rejecting his father's way of life; the son who emigrated was usually asking his father to make a major capital investment that he would not be able to supervise. Once there were choices to be made before adulthood was attained, there was enormous possibility for discord between father and son and between brothers, who might also be in competition for scarce family resources.

The best place to look for a measurable change in the rituals of coming to adulthood in Northampton in the early eighteenth century is in the complicated process of household formation. Marrying and moving into a house separate from parents (which might not happen at the same time) were the primary rites of passage into the social category of adult; and the age of marriage and residential independence, as well as the process by which a homestead was acquired, is a much more sensitive index of economic competency than are any available statistics on acreage owned. Because most Northampton men were farmers, setting up a new household was also the only important ritual of transition, since few men went through the formal education and trade apprenticeship that mark intermediate steps between childhood and adulthood.[17] (In Northampton in the Stoddard era, even joining the church probably ceased to be a major ritual of adulthood, since the system of open communion was so fluid and may have allowed persons as young as fourteen to enjoy full privileges.) S. N. Eisenstadt's classic work, *From Generation to Generation: Age Groups and Social Structure,* emphasizes that among the many age categories that could be deemed special, most societies designate the right to establish a family as the crucial turning point in life. Peter Laslett has asserted that the most important demographic variable in the modeling of the history of the family "seems to be age at the time of succession to headship of household." In a rural, agricultural community, this undertaking of adult responsibilities was almost wholly dependent on land acquisition. In County Clare, Ireland, for example, even in the twentieth century a man who might himself be a grandfather was still referred to as a boy until his father ("the old fellow") surrendered control of his farm, which could usually support just one married son. Northampton in the eighteenth century was hardly so extreme a case, yet there can be no doubt that a man without land of his own and a wife was regarded as less than a full and independent member of society.[18]

Let us now see how the Edwards converts became adults in socio-economic terms in Northampton. Their experiences can be contrasted with those of their own fathers and grandfathers—surely the comparison that would have made the most sense to them—and in the history of three generations we can see at least the shadow of the broad changes in the community from the late seventeenth to the mid-eighteenth century.

All possible information has been gathered on the 268 men who joined the Northampton church between 1727 and 1746. Of these Edwards converts, 236 (88%) were born to parents who resided in Northampton, and most were descendants of families who settled in the town's early years. Information on their fathers and paternal grandfathers has also been collected, although available economic data for the seventeenth century are extremely limited. In a comparison of these three generations, the degree of economic change in Northampton is apparent and the direction of change is unmistakable.[19]

Of the 268 Edwards converts, 226 shared 69 paternal grandfathers who were Northampton residents. Since most of these grandfathers had been adults eligible for town land grants in the frontier years before 1700, it is not surprising that 64 of the 68 received town grants (many of them were original Proprietors and so shared in a number of land divisions). The crucial change in Northampton land policies discussed in Chapter 1, the end of town land grants around 1705, is evident in the lives of these grandfathers as contrasted with those of their sons, the fathers of the Edwards converts. The fathers who lived in Northampton numbered 121, and only 58 of them (48%) received Northampton land grants. Of these 58, three were Proprietors, four had home lots granted to their fathers *for* them, and the rest received a home lot or specified acreage in their own names. Most of the grants were made in the 1690s. The ages at grant are known for 51 of these fathers: the average is 30.4 years, the median is 27 years.[20] The home-lot grants were obviously intended for residential purposes, and they were so used: there is no evidence of any speculation in home lots in Northampton, and most of the grants to older men may have been intended for their teenage sons. About three-fifths of these fathers are known to have been married when they received the home-lot grant, but most had been married only a few years.

Almost all their sons, the young men who came of age in the Edwards era, would go through a rite of passage to adulthood that was quite different from Northampton's traditional pattern of house-hold formation. Although 94% of the eligible grandfathers had received land grants, and 48% of the eligible fathers did so, only 1.3% (3 men of 236) of the native-born Edwards converts were given land by the town. Rather than receiving a symbolic stake in the community out of communal resources, signifying the inter-dependence of individual economic fate with the good of the whole society, and the reciprocal extension of an individual's responsibility to provide for his sons into the wider community's ability to sustain its members, the young men of the 1720s and 1730s had to await inheritance from their long-lived fathers, find ways to buy their own homesteads, or emigrate in search of greater opportunities.

Information on the process by which these young men obtained their homesteads has been drawn from deeds, wills, tax lists, and a variety of Northampton antiquarian collections. Useful information is available for 161 cases (68% of the 236 native-born Edwards converts).[21] Six were proprietors of the Southampton tract and moved there; three received home-lot grants in Northampton itself. Eight men were educated at Yale and became merchants or ministers in other towns. Fourteen men seem to have purchased their own homesteads; and since only the young man was named in the deed, we cannot know if his father was supplying the purchase price. About 55% of these young men, 130 of 236, are known to have acquired their homesteads through gift or inheritance from their fathers, and this transfer of property often came when the son was well past thirty.[22] Property could be transferred from father to son in a variety of ways, but the data suggest the generally prolonged dependence of adult sons. Illustrative, if not typical, was the plight of the Clark "boys," Ebenezer, Jr., and Ezra: when their father, Lieutenant Ebenezer, died and relinquished his title to the homesteads his sons had long inhabited, they were sixty-seven and sixty-five years old, respectively.[23] Unfortunately, the Hampshire County court records lack the kind of family-controversy documents which Philip J. Greven, Jr., used so effectively to study similar dependency in Essex County.[24] Since these records also contain an amazingly small number of criminal and civil suits, given the size of the population, it seems safe to assume that a lack of evidence is not negative evidence. The Northampton material does, nevertheless, suggest a number of dimensions of dependency that are worth consideration.

Lacking evidence to the contrary, we must assume that the father had the initiative in the timing of any transfer before death. We must also assume that young men wanted to have their own homes by their mid-twenties, and there is some contemporary support for such an assumption. Eliakim Clark, who joined the church shortly after Edwards became pastor, in his will gave a special reward to his eldest son, Hadiah, "for living with me two or three years after he arrived to the age of 21."[25] Homestead acquisition by "own purchase" provides a significant index to the desirability of prolonged co-residence with parents: although the accumulation of the purchase price would rarely have been easy, the men who were able to buy their own homesteads did so at a younger average age than other men acquired land by gift or inheritance from a father. If the father actually financed the purchase, as may often have happened, then the son showed a willingness to be in debt rather than remain in the parental home.

The eighteenth-century dependence of a young-adult son on his father was certainly nothing new, and the short frontier period had been unique in providing an opportunity for a young man to acquire property with only his muscles (and perhaps his piety) for capital. In the perception of eighteenth-century Northampton residents, however, the period could be taken as a norm from which change was measured. One measure available to historians, and often used as an index to economic conditions, is age at first marriage. As Jared Eliot wrote in *Essays upon Field Husbandry* in the 1750s, "when people have a clear prospect of support for a family, they will marry young."[26] Men in Northampton married almost three years later in the eighteenth century than they had in the last half of the seventeenth. The Edwards converts married at an average age of 28.6 years, almost exactly three years later than their fathers.[27] (There is not enough data on the grandfathers for their inclusion in the comparison.) Furthermore, the marriage age of recipients of land grants and men who acquired homesteads in other ways reinforces tentative conclusions about dependence. The men who achieved independence earliest, by grant in Southampton, married significantly younger than any other group; the other group who acquired their homesteads relatively early, those who purchased, also married at a comparatively young age. The correspondence between land acquisition and marriage age is not perfect, for the statistics given are the barest outline of a complicated process. But a parallel example is provided at the other end of the spectrum, by the men who inherited only a part of their fathers' homesteads. These men, most of whom seem to have shared the parental house with married siblings for some years after inheriting their share, perhaps had long *expected* to have little real privacy even after they married and their parents died. They married latest of all, more than two years later than the average for the Edwards group as a whole (in which average they are included).[28] If sexual desire began in the mid-teen years for most young men, and since premarital sexual gratification was strongly punished by the community, it is difficult to believe that ten to twenty years of celibacy was completely voluntary.[29]

Strains in family ties would have resulted from any inability of parents to provide for their children, for in pre-industrial society the family was the most important agent for placing a child in the occupational structure of his community. The real problem with the dependence of eighteenth-century New England adult sons on their fathers was that the rewards were usually so small. Most fathers, those who were not rich in fertile land, could ultimately give their sons only small lots with rapidly declining productivity. Only those fathers who had advanced beyond the subsistence level had the capital to buy farms for their sons in Northampton or less crowded communities or even on the frontier. Most families could hold back but not push forward. The sons who had to wait for adulthood with so little expectation for success later may have chafed under the restraint. Studies of Andover and Salem Village have indicated the frequency of intrafamily conflict over economic resources.[30] There is scattered similar evidence in Northampton.

Of the approximately 300 Northampton wills read, only a very few break out of the formalized legal jargon to express any individualized attitudes toward the testator's family; but all those which express hope, or design legacies to enforce, that children will live in peace with each other and their widowed mother were written after 1730. By then, many children in Northampton may have felt themselves to be in competition with their siblings. When Jonathan Alvord's sons filed an agreement about real-estate distribution in 1738, to replace the one filed by their mother in 1729 which some of them had disputed, they stated that the need to divide the homestead and meadow into distinct shares was due to their "desire to live in love and peace," a condition hitherto unattained while they shared a home. Lieutenant Joseph King's will of 1734 charged his children to maintain "love and peace" toward each other when dividing the estate. Deacon Stephen Wright of Southampton, father of two of the boys who joined the Northampton church during the 1741–42 revival, left his estate to his wife and children, "desiring they may live in unity with one another in the enjoyment of what I shall devise to them." Ebenezer Miller advised his children in his will "to live in love and peace among themselves and with all men, that the God of Peace may be with them."[31]

These instructions were not a matter of convention; evidently, they were needed. Love and peace seem to have been increasingly elusive in family relationships when provision for the younger generation became difficult. Wealthy families with few sons perhaps found peace easier to maintain, although the smallness of the group of those who explicitly reveal their lack of harmony does not permit emphasis of class differences. There is no evidence from Northampton that families of greater or lesser economic standing followed the supposed Puritan custom of sending their adolescent children to live with other families, which could have been a way of reducing intrafamily tension.[32] Many family problems were probably relieved, although other strains arose, when in the 1730s a sizable number of Northampton's young men joined the groups forming new towns in the Berkshire hills of western Massachusetts. Simply removing the excess population, however, would not return the town to its frontier peace, since all the community institutions were adjusting in fits and starts, and with a great deal of apparent friction, to modern times.

The subtle but important changes in agricultural life that pervaded Northampton in the first half of the eighteenth century cannot be measured by coming-of-age rituals alone, for even after maturity, economic life became increasingly non-traditional. Once a farmer was established, he found himself either with depleted soil or with newly cleared and stony terrain. Through the eighteenth century he was increasingly likely to work consolidated holdings, not common fields. With individual farms the disparities in landholding were no longer disguised, and each man could more easily measure his neighbor's real estate. An increase in availability of consumer goods enabled men to display their wealth more tangibly. As the town grew more populous and agriculture more market-oriented, and especially as Northampton became ringed to the north and west with frontier villages, full-time craftsmen prospered and provided the town with goods, services, and a different style of life as a model for the young. Hat manufacturer Ebenezer Hunt, miller and tavern owner Jonathan Clapp, and lawyer-merchant Joseph Hawley were aggressive entrepreneurs and became rich; they are examples of possible ways out of the dilemma of an overpopulated agricultural village. But each started as the son of a rich father, and those who would follow their example needed to learn the traits of energetic selfishness which had not been fostered by the village of common fields and Puritan communalism. The diversity of economic function that resulted when an innovative few tried to get ahead produced prosperity for the town as a whole, which in turn fostered further diversification. The distance between rich and poor grew larger and harder to traverse for the average man. (The richest men in town in 1759, the best year for estimating wealth, had fathers who were relatively well off or had come to town with capital to invest.) The network of reciprocity that structured this still small market (the husbandman's produce paid for the tanner's leather or as installment on the gentleman's money at interest) was still far different from the cash nexus that would overtake the village in the nineteenth century, but the change from the society envisioned by Northampton founding fathers was too important to ignore. What the community gained in a better standard of living, and a greater variety of life, it lost in a sense of common purpose and Puritan control over the behavior of its people.

Other community institutions besides personal economic activity reflected the change, and the tensions resulting from confrontations with the new and unexpected were increasingly evident in the town's public affairs in the eighteenth century. As economic life became more a setting for competition than cooperation, so the harmony of community government was transformed into the factional contention of town politics. The Southampton land division of 1730 was the last major community policy adopted without a struggle among competing interest groups. Disagreement was of course not new, but it had never been quite legitimate. In the second third of the eighteenth century, the building of a new meetinghouse and its "seating" (the designation of individual seats by social rank), repairs on town highways and bridges, and other public matters frequently caused "considerable debate."[33] Those who are familiar with the records of New England towns know that conflict occurred which was never officially recorded, and that the town record books themselves were frequently edited. Evidences of discord that do surface, therefore, can be interpreted as serious breaches of the village peace. In Northampton, for example, starting in 1735, one major indication of trouble is the frequent use of adjournments during town meeting, probably as devices to cool off tempers or to allow time for "persuasion": a series of negative votes would be followed by an adjournment, and the returning voters would suddenly favor the policy proposed—or they would adjourn again, if necessary, until the issue was settled.[34] Strenuous efforts toward consensus are clearly evidences of disharmony.

The greatest changes came in the 1730s, for after 1733 a special committee was chosen annually to audit town accounts, and after 1734 a moderator was chosen for every town meeting (since 1700 there had been one for the annual election meeting in March). Town meetings grew more frequent and the agenda for each grew longer, as the assembled citizens took back more and more issues from the grasp of the selectmen, whose discretionary powers had grown large since the end of the seventeenth century.[35] Actually, as measured by the number of meetings per year besides the obligatory March election, the periods of intensity of popular concern with politics came at roughly generational intervals. After the flurry of issues to be settled in the first decade of the community's history, greater than normal activity came in the 1670s (partly caused by King Philip's War), 1696–1706, and the late 1730s. Indeed, in politics as well as in agriculture and religion, the late 1730s were a time of turmoil.[36]

By the mid-1730s it was apparent to the people of Northampton that broad changes were underway in many aspects of community life, and they may have sensed an acceleration in the rate of change. Most affected were those coming to adulthood in that period. For them, traditions that had governed the community for sixty years were not a reliable guide to planning a future—a future that would include important changes in agriculture, perhaps taking up a trade, perhaps emigration, and probably participation in town politics, which was now functioning as an arena for conflict among competing interests. We know that adolescents often find adjustment to their adult roles difficult, and their unwillingness to be properly submissive to their parents has been commented upon in all cultures in almost all periods of history. But the 1730s in Northampton were a particularly bad time to be an adolescent, and the young people were acting out their tensions in significant ways. Their chief sin, according to Jonathan Edwards, was staying away from home in late-night "frolics" of boys and girls together. What an interesting mirror image this behavior forms with the desired pattern of good conduct!—seemingly endless work under parental supervision, with independence and legitimate relations with the opposite sex far in the future. The children were obviously not very responsive to their parents' demands for traditional deference when traditional rewards were fewer and fewer.

The nightly gatherings in taverns or other unsupervised spots reflect a decline of tradition in an interesting way, for they may have been one of the few opportunities the young people had for recreation with peers. The end of common-field agriculture probably reduced sharply the number of times and places in which young people could get together. Did the prosperity of the town erode the customs of barn raisings and corn huskings which had been important social occasions on the frontier? Simple daily contact with friends would have been less common for families living on individual farms, as more were doing. Agricultural societies often assign special tasks to children or teenagers; but the recreational gatherings described in Edwards's *Faithful Narrative* resemble much more the age groups which, according to Eisenstadt, appear in modern societies, in which the transition from childhood to adulthood is difficult and prolonged. One might even interpret the frolics as a sign that the socio-psychological stage of adolescence was emerging in rural New England. An interesting parallel is offered by the notoriously destructive "play" of colonial college students, who have been called "the only adolescents in a culture that did not know adolescence."[37] The students underwent a prolonged preparation for adulthood that differed only in degree from that endured even by the sons of agrarian families in an overpopulated village. In Northampton and other towns in the 1730s, adolescence became a problem for families and for the community.

Even if the teenage frolicking differed little in degree from the misbehavior universally attributed to youth, from one perspective, at least, the adolescents were a serious concern. Jonathan Edwards had condemned the carousing of Yale undergraduates, and to him the behavior of the young people of Northampton was even more alarming. It was but a symptom of a profound disturbance in the traditional and proper organization of New England society. Edwards's point of view was more than personal, for he was the spokesman for a strongly held ideal of the older generation which had already become a matter for nostalgia—that golden bygone era when adolescents had no leisure or spare energy for frolicking after their work was done, when they had no spending money with which to patronize the taverns, and when, most important of all, the adults were so united in their standards of good conduct that such behavior would simply not have been allowed. Edwards had a firm criterion for judging the various aspects of his era: "If they be things that come with a decay of religion," he preached in 1738, "that creep in as [piety] decays, we may determine they are things of no good tendency. . . . What is it but darkness that comes in as light withdraws?"[38] The darkness was not only the anti-authoritarian behavior, but also the failure of the community to control it. The authority that had been implicit in the Puritan and frontier period of the town's history, and which might have been effective if parents could still offer impressive rewards for filial obedience, proved inadequate to deal with the circumstances of Northampton in the 1730s.

It was at this stage of Northampton's evolution, when the pressures on families were becoming severe and the obvious cure, emigration, was not an easy choice to make, that Jonathan Edwards arrived. To fill the vacuum of authority that he saw as the result of a failure of family government, he attempted to assert the power of the pastorate as the one survival among the old centralizing institutions in the community. Aiming to re-create the success of "Pope" Stoddard, he directed his best efforts to the young people; and for a time the roles of leader and follower were mutually satisfactory. Edwards's triumph would be eloquent testimony to the nostalgic appeal of the simpler life of a once harmonious society of piety and good order. It would also be a confirmation of the rightness of his youthful decision to devote himself to the pastoral vocation. All his diary vows of disregard for worldly success notwithstanding, the achievement of authority over his congregation was necessary to Edwards's psychological equilibrium, his sense that God was with him. If Edwards *was* converting himself in the very act of converting others, the ability to resign himself to the will of God was enhanced by his knowledge that God was using him as a medium of grace to others. How could he resist the apparent testimony of the Holy Spirit that his preaching was producing conversions in his flock? He measured his success in numbers of converts and in public morality —those distinguishing marks of his grandfather's renowned ministry —and in the spring of 1735 Jonathan Edwards could count himself a success, a true heir to the great Stoddard, an effective leader of a small Christian commonwealth.

CHAPTER FIVE

Awakening

REVIVALS had occurred before at random intervals in scattered parishes in the Connecticut Valley, but the Awakening of 1735 was extraordinary in its effect on all kinds of persons and in the swiftness of its spread from Northampton through the Valley in western Massachusetts and Connecticut. It was also unusual in the amount of publicity it received. Seeking to counter misrepresentations of the events in Northampton, Jonathan Edwards wrote a vividly detailed account of the converts in his congregation which was published in 1737 as *A Faithful Narrative of the Surprising Work of God*. . . .[1] This treatise gave Edwards an international reputation as an evangelist and became a popular handbook for the second tide of revivalism that spread over the northern American colonies in 1741–42. Especially useful for our purposes are its descriptions of community behavior, for the *Narrative* is practically the only firsthand account of the Northampton revival. It is also an intriguing autobiographical document.

The title of the *Narrative* is somewhat ironic, because the conversions were not altogether surprising. Edwards had worked strenuously to revitalize the faith of his flock. He wrote his narrative to convince the world that the Spirit was behind the revival and that he had acted with propriety in encouraging it. Most of the text is description of the conversions he had witnessed, to show that they were genuine and not filled with the manic delusions and widespread hysteria that were being gossiped about among cynics.[2] Edwards's flock were, it seems, acting out the very doctrinal soundness and new sensibilities that he had prescribed in earlier sermons.

Although conversion was a matter of the emotions, the process in Northampton in 1735 was well under the minister's control; and the *Narrative* strives to express a delicate balance between his responsibility and his surprise at the degree of the Spirit's bounty. Lying not far beneath this advertisement of happy accomplishment, however, is a narrative of quite different tone. In many ways the intended self-vindication became a confession of uncertainty, even failure. In historical perspective, the *Narrative* reveals some of the negative implications—for his own future career and for the broader issues of ministerial position in an eighteenth-century community—of the great success Edwards enjoyed in fighting Arminianism and sin during the 1734–35 revival.

Edwards's first accomplishment had been to effect a reform in the hitherto scandalous behavior of the adolescents of Northampton. By the end of 1733 they had showed "a very unusual flexibleness, and yielding to advice." They conceded to the minister a point he regarded as critically important, the "frolics" that had become customary in the evening after the Sabbath lecture.[3] For years, Edwards had admonished parents to keep their children home; he even tried to shame them by citing their "advantage of the honour and the esteem of their children[,] which children[—]*except* they are greatly neglected or mismanaged by their parents[—]ordinarily have." But as if to reinforce with irony their lack of deference to their elders, the young people responded directly to the minister instead of to his advice passed through the parents. When heads of families at last met in neighborhood groups to devise a plan of action against their dependents, they "found little or no occasion for the exercise of government in the case: the young people declared themselves convinced by what they had heard from the pulpit, and were willing of themselves to comply with the counsel that had been given . . . and there was a thorough reformation of these disorders thenceforward."[4]

Edwards's account of this success in the *Narrative* implicitly claims that his new technique of appealing directly to Northampton's adolescents turned the tide of immorality. However exaggerated this description of ministerial effectiveness may have been, it indicates a new kind of relationship between a Congregational pastor and the young people in his flock, one that extracted the children and adolescents from their proper place in the natural hierarchical social order of the traditional community.[5] The problem in Northampton, as Edwards himself defined it in the *Narrative,* was the failure of family government. But while decrying the decline of parental authority, Edwards ironically eroded part of what was left of it by appealing directly to the adolescents and intervening between child and parent in significant ways.

Part of Edwards's success in reforming the young people was undoubtedly due to the pre-1734 technique of proclaiming the temporal rewards of holiness, and part was due to the calculated emotional impact of the Calvinist sermons, to which the young people may have been initially more susceptible than their parents. (Many of the sins Edwards described so clearly in the long passage quoted in Chapter 3 were the special temptations of youth: rebellion against family discipline, unclean imaginings, masturbation.) There was flattery involved in treating the adolescents as adults fully responsible for their own behavior. In fact, the church was the only institution in the community where teenage boys and girls were entitled to the same privileges and punishments as their elders. In 1734–35 they were more than equal to their parents in importance in Northampton.

Edwards further undermined the deference of his special constituents to their parents by gathering them into age-graded groups for prayer and study under his own supervision. To persuade the youngsters "to spend the evenings after lectures in social religion" in neighborhood groups, which the minister visited in rotation, was not the same thing as returning the children to the immediate supervision of their parents.[6] Essentially, the evening frolics became legitimized as "social religion." The Reverend Thomas Shepard of Cambridge, one of the most famous evangelists amonelists among the first-generation Puritan pastors in New England, once commented with timeless skepticism on the link between the urge to worship in company and the urge for mere social contact: "So many young people will go abroad to hear sermons. What is the end of it? It is, that ye may get wives and husbands, many of you."[7]

Edwards also drew children away from their parents to catechize them in his study. In many towns this was a tradition, but there is no evidence that Stoddard did not instruct his people in family groups. The Hampshire Association of Ministers did vote in 1731 that although "personal [pastoral] visitation may in some cases be very expedient or beneficial," it was better to have families catechize their own young.[8] Edwards went against the Association, and probably Valley custom, on both counts: not only did he insist on catechizing the children and young people himself, but he never visited the homes of his parishioners except in emergencies.[9] He could not and would not make small talk, but he was always ready to receive a child or adult in his study and to give private counsel. He was comfortable only in his own domain. Certainly, he taught the children nothing their parents would disapprove, but he also did little to return them to the parental hearth for instruction and discipline—the traditional components of the family government whose decline Edwards lamented.

Edwards may have enlarged another wedge between parents and children by strenuously advocating singing in worship. Ola Elizabeth Winslow has described the great "Singing Quarrel" of 1715–30 in New England as dividing conservative and ritual-fearing parents against their children, who liked this novelty of singing hymns with tunes from books. The children may especially have liked the evening meetings for learning the tunes, or so suggested contemporary observers. Winslow says that the controversy was over in most places by 1730, but it seems to have been alive in Northampton half a dozen years later. Edwards preached sermons in 1734 and 1736 that endorsed singing, against the apparent resistance of the parents, who needed to be told at least twice that it was their Christian duty to allow their children to learn to sing.[10]

When the adolescent reformation blossomed into a full-scale revival in Northampton, it also became the duty of the parents to follow their children's example. The model of the young people's prayer meetings was soon "imitated by elder people," and this was only one symbol of a reversal of the old-fashioned parent-child instructional relationship that pervaded Northampton in the spring of 1735.[11] It was not a coincidence that when he later wrote about the "little awakening" in the *Faithful Narrative,* the models of piety that Edwards presented were a four-year-old girl and a young unmarried woman.[12] In the true Christian community, those usually last in social importance would be first.

Four-year-old Phebe Bartlett, now one of the most famous converts in evangelical literature, illustrates in an only slightly extreme
form many of the characteristics of the revival as seen through the
pastor's eyes. Phebe had a dramatic, emotional conversion that
completely upset normal patterns of deference and discipline in the
Bartlett household. This child exhorted her siblings and parents to
greater concern for their souls, lectured them on the virtue of
charity, and was "exceeding importunate" with her parents for
neglecting their responsibilities. Her family seem to have been
perfectly docile while being bullied by Phebe, even though her
mother's constant questioning of what was the matter with the
child and frequent attempts to ignore her do suggest that the Bart-
letts did not altogether share Phebe's ecstatic piety. One person
who did empathize, obviously, was her pastor. When he returned
from a journey, Phebe joyfully announced to all within hearing,
" 'Mr. Edwards is come home! Mr. Edwards is come home!' " Because of her conversion, the sympathetic link between Edwards
and Phebe appears to have replaced the normal domination of parent over child.[13]

Jonathan Edwards took great pride in the love of his converts. He
could not resist bragging in the *Narrative* that "this work of God [the
revival] had also a good effect to unite the people's affections much
to their minister." The congregation was "eager to drink in the
words of the minister as they came from his mouth" and were often
"in tears while the Word was preached." Perhaps most symbolic of
the total change in the temper of the town was the replacement of
the tavern by the minister's house as the favorite gathering place.
Edwards was proud of the numbers of converts he had made: he
confessed a hope that he had brought "300 souls . . . to Christ in
this town in the space of half a year (how many more I don't guess)."
(These numbers are perhaps exaggerated, since he recorded fewer
than half that many names in the church membership rolls during
that time.) Although the converts included both the very old and the
very young, the following that Edwards created among the adolescents was clearly the most important to him psychologically.[14] It was
their behavior that he returned to again and again in the *Narrative*
as an index of the state of the community. They were his special
constituency. In the difficult years when he had worked so hard to

emulate the patriarchal figure of his grandfather, the community had shown no sign of according him that power until he had touched the hearts of the young people. He had neither the years nor the impressiveness of figure to imitate Stoddard; but perhaps because he was young, almost young enough to seem to empathize sincerely with their problems, the adolescents had responded to his words.

Besides being the first to heed the call, there is another way in which the young people were the epitome of the Northampton revival experience: their conversions became the norm prescribed for others. The classic Puritan morphology of conversion had emphasized its rationalistic elements, and most converts were adults; children, if they were considered converted at all, tended to have more emotional religious experiences. Conversion as described in the *Faithful Narrative* (and in all Edwards's other works), however, was centered in the emotions.

The first stage of conversion, which came gradually or suddenly and through various means, was a new and ever more distressing awareness of one's sinful state. Some suffered for "but a few days, and others for months or years." The varieties of distress were many and sometimes included a "disturbance to animal nature." Some were in terror of sleeping, lest they die in an unconverted state. A common first reaction to these "legal awakenings," repentance for specific sins and resolutions for better behavior, gave way under the influence of true grace to a full conviction of the insufficiency of moral obedience and man's absolute dependence on God's freely given Saving Grace. This new conviction was followed "most frequently, though not always," by a "before-unexpected quietness and composure," then "gracious discoveries" of the sufficiency and mercy of God and Christ, and other comforting apprehensions. Although most knew it not, this "sweet complacence" and "holy repose of soul" was indeed evidence of their conversion. The result of this experience was "an inward firm persuasion of the reality of divine things, such as they don't use to have before their conversion." Saints had "seen and tasted," and "intuitively beheld, and immediately felt" the "divine excellency and glory of the things of Christianity."[15]

Conversion, as witnessed by Jonathan Edwards in Northampton in 1735 (and as he maintained in all his sermons and treatises), was therefore a matter of *sensibility*. He had expressed this definition epigrammatically in a 1733 sermon as the "difference between having a rational judgment that honey is sweet, and having a sense of its sweetness."[16] This sense came only from the Holy Spirit. The strivings recommended to natural man served only to wean his affections from temporal things so that he would be receptive to the experience of God's grace and the Spirit's cultivation of the saint's enhanced senses. The conversion process was really one of developing *consciousness* of these senses—and *awareness* that one tasted and felt often came only through pastoral guidance. "Sweet complacence" was judged reliably only by an expert. Edwards wrote that his special duty was to the "many" persons who were unaware of their own conversion, to be "a guide to lead them to an understanding of what we are taught in the Word of God of the nature of grace, and to help them to apply it to themselves."[17] He would, in effect, give legitimacy to their intuitions.

Edwards was acutely conscious that in this important role a minister was especially vulnerable to criticism, and in mid-narrative his tone becomes openly defensive. He knew that his definition of the self-awareness he encouraged in converts sounded dangerously close to the kind of assurance that a Calvinist could never rightfully have. He had been "much blamed and censured by many," he wrote (not revealing whether his critics were townspeople or other ministers), that he had "signified" to persons his satisfaction about their "good estate." But, he insisted, "[I] have been far from doing this concerning all that I have had some hopes of; and I believe have used much more caution than many have supposed. . . ." He was "sensible the practice would have been safer in the hands of one of a riper judgment and greater experience" (such as his grandfather Stoddard, respected by townspeople and fellow clergy alike). But he had "often" warned his people that no man could see into another's heart, had found them extremely cautious in judging themselves, and therefore had found it an "absolute necessity" to use assurances to restrain some who tended to dangerous despair.[18]

The existence of this despair among the people of Northampton seems to provide a clue to Edwards's defensiveness in the *Faithful Narrative*. More dangerous than any accusation that he gave his congregation too much assurance about the state of their souls was the opposite charge, that his doctrines of men's total depravity drove some of them to self-destruction. Edwards therefore asserted that despair was the work of the Devil, and he confessed in the *Narrative* that Satan had come to Northampton to end the revival.

In March 1735, "a poor weak man . . . in great spiritual trouble" cut his throat but lived to recover from his melancholy and confess the sin of "yielding to temptation." By the end of May, Edwards wrote further, it became very obvious that "the Spirit of God was gradually withdrawing from us" as Satan "raged in a dreadful manner." He was referring to a case of suicide among his flock. One of Northampton's leading citizens, Edwards's uncle Joseph Hawley (husband of Solomon Stoddard's daughter Rebecca), became so discouraged over the state of his soul that he cut his throat and died on June 1, a Sabbath morning. He was described by his nephew as "a gentleman of more than common understanding, of strict morals, religious in his behavior, and an useful honorable person in the town." All these attributes, of course, were as nothing in the scheme of salvation that Edwards had outlined so dramatically from the pulpit. This wealthy merchant and Justice of the Peace felt himself to be without Saving Grace, and "the Devil took advantage, and drove him into despairing thoughts. He was kept awake anights, meditating terror; so that he had scarce any sleep at all, for a long time together. And it was observed at last, that he was scarcely well capable of managing his ordinary business, and was judged delirious by the coroner's inquest." The ultimate point of Edwards's lengthy description of Hawley's mental condition was that this tragedy was beyond ministerial control. The Hawley family was supposedly "exceeding prone to the disease of melancholy, and [Joseph's] mother was killed with it." This disease became so overpowering that Hawley "was in great measure past a capacity of receiving advice, or being reasoned with to any purpose." The implication is that Edwards *did* try in vain to reason with his uncle. He was extremely alarmed when "multitudes in this and other towns" thereafter "seemed to have it strongly suggested to 'em, and pressed upon 'em, to do as this person had done." But even though most were saved from self-destruction, through the summer of 1735 there was a "gradual decline of that general, engaged, lively spirit in religion, which had been before."[19] The Devil had ended the revival. In his funeral sermon for his uncle Hawley, Edwards used the tragedy to illustrate the lesson that only God's intervention keeps men from being easy work for the Devil: only God's mercy has kept all men from "adultery or sodomy or buggery or murder or blasphemy as others have done or [from having] destroyed our own lives." The doctrine of this sermon stated the message succinctly: "We are all in ourselves utterly without any strength or power to help ourselves."[20]

In his need to vindicate himself of suspicions (even his own) of inadvertently aiding the Devil to drive out the Holy Spirit, Edwards made one subtle but important deviation from his generally faithful chronology in the *Narrative*—a deviation which may be testimony to his sense of guilt over the Hawley suicide. That artistic liberty is the particular placement in the narrative of its most dramatic section, the detailed account of the conversions of Abigail Hutchinson and Phebe Bartlett. These experiences are used as examples of the wondrous work of the Spirit at its height, intended as full contrast to the work of the Devil in Hawley—and yet both actually occurred *after* Hawley's suicide on June 1, 1735. Abigail's conversion had begun the previous winter, but it reached a peak only shortly before her death on June 27. Phebe's religious experiences began in early May but she did not find God until late July, and her spiritual crisis continued into the following winter. Edwards is subtle in rearranging the revival's chronology: the dates mentioned above are all given in the text, but they become submerged in the great mass of detail. And the strongest impression is left when immediately *following* Phebe's story, Edwards introduces the rise of Satan with these words: "In the former part of this great work of God amongst us, till it got to its height, we seemed to be wonderfully smiled upon and blessed in all respects. Satan . . . seemed to be unusually restrained. . . . In the latter part of May, it began to be very sensible that the Spirit of God was gradually withdrawing from us. . . ." *Then* comes the Hawley story.[21] The effect is to locate the experiences of Abigail and Phebe in the "former part" of the work, since *they* were not influenced by Satan, and to place the Hawley suicide in the later part, when God and Edwards lost control of Northampton to the Devil. Edwards may simply have remembered things in the order that he wrote them. Whatever the impetus to its artistry, Edwards's *Narra-*

tive conveys the subjective as well as the objective pastoral view of the awakening. When Hawley committed suicide, the happy confidence in the revival was over for Edwards. He was very uncomfortable with the mix of good and evil that had come to the community after the emotions of his flock had been let loose.

The structure of the *Narrative* leaves the reader with the impression that the Devil himself finally lost ground, not to the Spirit, but to the resurgence of worldly concerns. Among the several things that diverted people's minds from the important business of their salvation were the visit to nearby Deerfield of the Governor and his Council, to conclude an Indian treaty; the quarrel among Hampshire clergy and gentry over the Springfield ordination of Robert Breck, a suspected Arminian; and the building of a new meetinghouse in Northampton, which was the occasion of some uncharitable wrangling about seating and taxes. The minister who had promoted the revival did not himself stay aloof from these mundane matters; he watched closely the meetinghouse contention, played host for a week to at least one distinguished Boston official, and took an active role in the Breck controversy.[22] As he turned his attention to fighting Arminianism on a broader scale, Edwards saw the people of Northampton return to what had been normal before the great excitement of the preceding year. Public affairs produced factional bickering, and the church again produced occasional self-doubting, private conversions. In Edwards's eyes, or rather in his published words, the situation was somewhat better than it had been in those turbulent years preceding the revival, for now at least the young people, still his special concern, remained docile. He wrote that he knew of "no one young person in the town that has returned to former ways of looseness and extravagancy in any respect." As if to renege a bit on this rather unbelievable assertion, he continued in a more cautious tone that although he was not "so vain as to imagine that we han't been mistaken" about some converts or that there were no "wolves in sheep's clothing" among his communicants, he nevertheless had hopes that "we still remain a reformed people."[23]

There is a wistfulness in that hope, and Edwards would hardly have wished only for reform at the revival's height, when he had expectations that the whole community would be completely transformed by the universal effects of Saving Grace. There is also an irony in his most basic defense of the revival. After writing that his converts had been "overthrown in many of their former conceits" about the nature of conversion—notions formed under Stoddard's instruction—Edwards went on to describe the revival as "evidently the same that was wrought in my venerable predecessor's days" and to write that none of Stoddard's converts "in the least doubts of its being the same spirit and the same work."[24] The Spirit may have been consistent, but the method of operation showed such variation that Edwards's assertion of continuity between Stoddard's revivals and his own deserves special attention. There is little apparent similarity between the image of patient nurturing and gathering at maturity of the Stoddardean "harvests" and the dramatic Edwardsean conversions which became suspect for excessive emotion. On the other hand, the resulting *community* behavior, which was crucially important to both ministers, *was* similar. The congregation reformed, joined the church, and gave Edwards the public adulation that he imagined to have been accorded to his grandfather at the height of his powers. By the late spring of 1735 Edwards had achieved the kind of control over Northampton that had brought renown to Solomon Stoddard. But by the time he wrote the *Faithful Narrative* eighteen months later, his cautious, defensive tone showed that his confidence in himself and his congregation was already slipping.

Edwards had made a great emotional investment in the awakening of his flock. In the fall of 1735, after the revival had ended and dullness of spirit and contentious behavior resumed, Edwards was forced to take a long journey to recover his health. Like his 1729 weakness, this illness may have been emotional—exhaustion, depression—since again he could not fulfill his pastoral duties even though he could travel very long distances. At the close of the *Narrative* he also mentions an illness in the fall of 1736. His dejection about what he described four years later as still "a sorrowfully dull and dead time with us" is understandable.[25] After the heights of morality and piety of 1735, normality would forever appear bleak.

Contributing to Edwards's discouragement was the knowledge that although he had won a local battle with Arminian temptations in his own congregation, the conservative Calvinists seemed to be losing the war in the Valley, and the unpleasant odor of heterodox opinions would remain perceptible in Northampton. The Hampshire Association of Ministers had fought valiantly since late 1734 to keep a Harvard graduate named Robert Breck from being ordained by Springfield's First Church, because the Reverend Thomas Clap and others from Connecticut had presented evidence that Breck, while a pulpit candidate there, had preached and privately defended Arminian principles. Through the winter of 1735, the Association, led by William Williams of Hatfield, denied Breck the official approval that was the customary precondition for ordination by a particular church. They even encouraged a minority within the Springfield church to fight Breck's ordination; and when Breck had himself certified by a group of liberal Boston ministers, the local controversy became an open fight between eastern and western Massachusetts definitions of orthodoxy. A proposed ordination council gathered both sides to Springfield in early October 1735, and argument turned into near-riot when the anti-Breck faction in Springfield persuaded the Northampton Justices of the Peace (including Colonel John Stoddard) to have Breck arrested and sent back to Connecticut to answer trumped-up charges there. That arrest came to nothing—except disgrace for the cause of clerical and magisterial dignity in the Valley.[26] Breck had himself ordained at last by the Boston ministers in January 1736, and in the following summer successfully fought a court challenge to his orthodoxy. But the breach between himself and the other Hampshire ministers was not healed for some years: he was not admitted to the local Association until October 1741, the first meeting after the implacable William Williams had died.[27]

Although no member of the Hampshire Association was openly Arminian after William Rand's temporary lapse in 1734 (and even Breck himself was only suspect), there was a subtle cleavage within the group. The majority, however, were conservative, and it is significant that Jonathan Edwards was one of them. He was away from home in the fall of 1735, recovering his health, and so was not present for the spectacle at Springfield. But he was the author of the two tracts that constituted the Hampshire side in the bitter pamphlet war that followed Breck's ordination. He and Samuel Hopkins of

West Springfield (who had married Edwards's sister) wrote a *Narrative of the Proceedings* in 1736, which was answered by an anonymous letter defending Breck and his Boston allies; Edwards alone wrote a rejoinder to this pamphlet in 1737. The evolution of the charges and countercharges shows the Hampshire Association, with Edwards as its spokesman, moving beyond its concern with Breck's position on theological fine points toward a conscious defense of their professional status. The crux of the matter, for which Breck himself had been only a catalyst, was control over an individual congregation's affairs by a regional ministerial association—at heart, the question of lay versus clerical authority. By law and custom, the Springfield church had a right to choose its minister, and the majority clearly favored Breck. The Hampshire Association, on the other hand, was keeping the autocratic spirit of Solomon Stoddard alive, although it was on the shakiest ground when it interfered. (The Breck case was indeed the last time, to the end of the surviving records in 1748, that the Association voted against the majority of a church whose problems were submitted for arbitration.) But Edwards and Hopkins had defended the Association's opposition to Springfield's exercise of its rights by asserting that "a heterodox minister settled amongst us" would "destroy the peace of the ministry of the county and the comfort and benefit of mutual society, and to poison our flocks, and to bring our religious state into confusion."[28] There could hardly be a more bald statement of threatened *professional* interest. The orthodox Hampshire clergy very much needed their "peace" and "comfort and benefit of mutual society," for most of them were fighting religious dullness in their congregations with the same lack of success that bedeviled Edwards. The problems Edwards faced in trying to create a permanent, active role for the ministry in the community were also encountered by his fellow clergymen. Like him, they tended to turn to their clerical peers for emotional support as the aftermath of the revival brought increasing tensions between pastor and flock all over the Connecticut Valley.[29]

In the trying times of "declension" between 1735 and 1740, Jonathan Edwards might have found consolation in his new prestige as an author. The simple communication of proud and wondrous excitement that had occasioned Edwards's first letter to Benjamin

Colman in 1735 had led to the publication in London (1737) and Boston (1738) of the *Faithful Narrative.* That tract, which seems to have been a best-seller among Scots Presbyterian and English Dissenting clergymen, was followed in 1738 by Edwards's *Five Discourses on Important Subjects,* which cemented the author's international reputation as an evangelist.[30] Such recognition must have been pleasing to Edwards—but was it not also a painful reminder of how fleeting his pastoral success had been in reality? Now he was famous for being something he no longer *was,* and now any future successes would be measured against an exalted standard.

With the Spirit gone from the Connecticut Valley, Edwards the pastor was essentially faced with the conditions of the pre-revival days he described so sadly at the beginning of the *Faithful Narrative.* Until 1742 he would continue to exhort his people to repent and turn from the world to God; but when a resurgence of piety finally did come, the effect on the community was to be quite different from the love and harmony and deference that Edwards had seen in 1735. Although the vision of a pious society that Edwards had offered his people in 1734–35 had had a temporary appeal to the community, it did not result in a permanent restructuring of Northampton life into patterns of morality among the youth, nonpartisanship in town politics, and continual and complete deference to the will of the minister as the will of God. The story of Edwards's last fifteen years in Northampton might be summed up as his own holding fast to an ideal vision of community life and ministerial influence that seemingly became a reality in 1734–35, while the community continued to grow economically and socially away from the ability or the desire to participate in such a mode of life.

CHAPTER SIX

Reassessment

FOR A DECADE after the 1735 revival in Northampton, Jonathan Edwards was intensely preoccupied with resolving problems that had, ironically, grown from his (and the Spirit's) very triumph. Appalled to find a serious declension following the piety of 1734–35, he fought again to assert the authority of the pastor against the forces of worldliness and sin—but always in the shadow of Northampton as a former "city on a hill" that had identified the will of the minister with the will of God. Sin was becoming indeed more difficult to conquer, for in addition to its old forms of apathy and lust and contention, it took on a new and insidious guise. Masquerading as zealous piety, pride showed itself to be man's greatest inherent sin and threatened to overwhelm the true work of the Spirit. After 1741, when Edwards's prayers were answered and another revival did finally come to Northampton, he was forced to admit that the conversions he had long sought could be instruments to destroy the communal holiness that was the most important fruit of genuine piety. Just as the Arminian scare in Hampshire County in 1734 had reminded Edwards of the dangers of preaching too strongly the earthly rewards of conversion, so the extreme, individualistic piety of the Great Awakening in New England illuminated the dangers of the subjectivist definition of conversion he had promulgated in the *Faithful Narrative.* Therefore, the preacher who had once emphasized a somewhat innovative interior religion of sensibility was forced by the mid-1740s to emphasize the need to act out true holiness in traditional Christian behavior.

In the late 1730s, Edwards wrote letters to the Reverend Benjamin Colman of Boston that poignantly revealed the division of his professional life into two parts, a successful career as a propagandist for the revival and a not so rewarding position as a country pastor trying to keep that revival alive among his own people. The letters were primarily concerned with discussing the details of publication of Edwards's *Faithful Narrative* of the Northampton revival, but Edwards also confessed the depths to which his flock had fallen spiritually after their great heights of piety three years earlier. "The work that went on so swiftly and wonderfully while God appear'd in might & irresistible power to carry it on, has seemed to be very much at a stop in these [Valley] towns for a long time, and we are sensibly by little and little, more and more declining." The fall from grace was marked not so much by a return to "lewdness and sensuality," which Edwards felt signified an extreme level of depravity, as by a resurgence of "eagerness after the possessions of this life, and undue heats of spirit among persons of different judgments in publick affairs. Contention and a party spirit has been the old iniquity of this town; and . . . has of late manifestly revived." Such unchristian behavior did not yet dominate the whole town, as it once had done, but Edwards was nevertheless "ready to blush, to speak or think of such an appearance of strife and division of the people into parties as there has been, after such great and wonderfull things as God has wrought for us, which others afar off are rejoicing in, and praising God for, & expecting (as justly they may) to hear better things of us."[1] Such a confession was a pathetic echo of the decade-earlier disparity between Northampton's reputation and its reality, as expressed in the *Faithful Narrative*.

Although Northampton had recently escaped the worst effects of an epidemic (probably diphtheria), a seemingly milder form of which had carried off many children two years previously, God was manifesting his anger with the impious Valley by sending extremely harsh winters and summer droughts to decimate crops and livestock. In sad contrast to the enlivening of worldly and spiritual affairs in the days of revival, the later 1730s were a dying time for Northampton in both agriculture and religion.[2] The town deserved its punishment by Nature: no longer was it a "city on a hill" with all eyes focused on God. In 1736 the office of tithingman, an elected inspector of public behavior (especially illegal drinking), was revived in

Northampton after a lapse of over forty years; eight men were chosen to watch their respective neighborhoods for signs of the blatantly sinful activity that seemed inevitable just one year after the heights of piety in early 1735.[3]

The temper of the times was clearly displayed in the building of a new meetinghouse between 1736 and 1738. The need for a larger edifice had been discussed in town meeting as early as March 1733, but construction was delayed until the summer of 1736 by disagreements over cost and location. The spire was finally raised in July 1737.[4] In March of that year, a "remarkable providence" had underscored the need for a new structure: while Edwards preached in the old building during a Sabbath service, the back gallery collapsed. Hundreds of people were tangled among fallen beams and splintered seats, but miraculously only a few were even slightly injured.[5]

The new meetinghouse promised physical safety but it also brought on a quarrel that had no precedent in the town records. The partisan strife that Edwards described to Colman in the letter quoted above was most distressingly displayed in contention over seating the meetinghouse. Almost all New England Congregationalists before the Revolution assigned meetinghouse seats to all adults on the basis of age and social rank, and in many towns the process of determining the correct order of precedence occasioned significant disturbances of the Christian community.[6] Northampton escaped these troubles until the 1730s. Ever since the building of the second meetinghouse in 1664, a committee of church officers (after 1700 including the pastor) and leading laymen had assigned seats according to a person's age, estate, and "usefulness" (community service, military rank, or other secular distinctions.)[7] Full discretionary powers had always been given to the committee, but in the 1730s the town showed a new distrust of its long-time leaders. In November 1737 three leading citizens were proposed as a seating committee; the town meeting enlarged the group to five by adding two obscure men. The minister was not mentioned: after Solomon Stoddard's death no action had ever been taken to put Jonathan Edwards in his grandfather's place on the standing committee, and he was not included in 1737. The new committee was bound closely by instructions from the townspeople and told at two separate meetings that the plan it drew up would have to be presented to a "legally assembled" town meeting "to be by them approved or disapproved of as they think fit." The most serious departure from custom, however, was the enactment of a new set of criteria for the ranking of persons. The committee was to "have respect principally to men's estate," and only secondarily "to have regard to men's age"; a distinct third in priority was "some regard and respect . . . to men's usefulness."[8] Age had always taken precedence over wealth, but a majority of Northampton's voters implied that property was more respectable than old age, that worldly achievement was more laudable than experience as a humble Christian—and this was only two years after the revival of 1735!

The new emphasis on wealth in the ranking of the congregation was linked to the emergence of family clusterings in the seating arrangements. The old meetinghouse had had benches on either side of a central passage, with adult men on one side and their wives on corresponding seats across the aisle. Younger people, by definition less honorable, sat in the gallery, which was also divided by sex.[9] The 1737 meetinghouse, on the other hand, had pews all around the perimeter of the space and along the side and back aisles, as shown in the diagram on page 127. Seated in these pews were the town's richest men. And they took the further privilege of sitting with their wives and sometimes their daughters in family groups.[10] The town's second-richest man even brought into his pew his twenty-eight-year-old unmarried son, the youngest man (by a decade) on the ground floor of the meetinghouse.

This clustering of families was presumably the desire of the men who led the town to make estate the primary criterion for privilege in seating. At the beginning of the December 1737 town meeting which effected this innovation, a proposal to seat men and their wives together was defeated; but toward the end of that same meeting there was a *negative* vote on forbidding the committee "to seat men and their wives together especially such as incline to sit together."[11] The desire of the rich to assert the importance of the family group while attending divine worship could no longer be denied. Seating would mirror the grouping by families in other, secular aspects of community life: especially for the rich, family was a determinant of wealth and occupation.[12] Brothers sat together more commonly when estate was the criterion than when age was

THE NORTHAMPTON MEETINGHOUSE, 1737

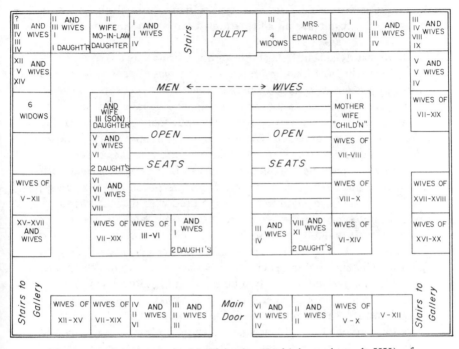

Roman numerals are ranked half-deciles (I=highest, through XX) of total property on 1739 tax-assessment list. Each numeral (or question mark) stands for one man.

"Wives of " = wives of three to six men in tax-range given; their husbands sat upstairs, in the gallery.

In central seats, ranking by estate shows no obvious pattern. Men range from two in top 10% to many in lowest 25%, but only six of forty were in top 25%. Nine of the forty were not listed in 1739.

In central seats, men in first two seats average 74.3 years old. In last two seats, men average 50.8 years old.

considered first. After the quarreling over seating the meetinghouse had ended, after the town as a whole had approved the work of the committee that could not be trusted with traditional discretionary powers, the result was an affirmation of family and a public parade of economic rank.

Significantly absent from these deliberations was the town's pastor. The feelings of Jonathan Edwards, who was not consulted about the new system of arranging persons, were not recorded officially. It is easy to suspect, however, that he would have distrusted the configuration of the pews, for pews put barriers between the preacher and his audience. Within the pews, people sat on benches around the edges on two or more sides of the box shape; and since the Northampton pews contained up to eight people, at least half may have been seated facing away from the pulpit. Families faced each other, and some children were closeted within a wall of protective adults. The pews were cozier in winter, and drowsing was facilitated. It is likely that the Reverend Mr. Edwards would have felt more certain of the full attention of his congregation if they sat on the less-comfortable benches in rows according to the categories by which he divided them when he preached: children, young men, young women, middle-aged, and aged persons. All through the 1730s he advocated family government, but he also warned against too sentimental love of parents for their children, which would interfere with proper discipline and lead to valuation of the child's worldly well-being over its spiritual health.[13] The family unit was the foundation of secular society and was at times an arm of church discipline and evangelism; but within the meetinghouse, where God's minister superseded the role of any other agent, each heart was supposed to be unprotected against the thunder of the Gospel.

Edwards preached at least two sermons about the evils attending the reorganization of the meetinghouse. In May 1737 he took as his text II Samuel 20:19, from which he drew the doctrine: "When a spirit of strife has been prevailing among a visible people of God, and they have been divided into parties, a person may well rejoice, if he can say, he is one, who has been peaceable and faithful among them."[14] Insisting that to be on the winning side is no proof of the righteousness of one's cause, Edwards pointed out that among persons *not* "peaceable and faithful" were those who condemn others for being contentious and "those who seem peaceable after they have obtained their wills, or after they see there is no hope of it." The private slander and abuse of others was the worst sin of all, perfectly visible to God even if hidden from men. "Contention and a party spirit" were Northampton's "old iniquity." "It has been a remarkably contentious town. I suppose for these thirty years people have not known how to manage scarcely any public business without dividing into parties. . . . of late, time after time that old party spirit has appeared again, and particularly this spring [1737]. Some persons may be ready to think that I make too much of things. . . . [but] I do not know but I have trusted too much in men, and put too much confidence in the goodness and piety of the town. . . . It is very likely there are men in this town, who have zealously engaged in every public strife, which has existed for these twenty years, or ever since they have been capable of acting in public affairs. . . ." Edwards closed by asking those (few) who had avoided partisanship to pray for their sinful neighbors.

On "the Sabbath after seating the new meetinghouse," December 25, 1737, Edwards preached from John 14:2: "In my father's house are many mansions."[15] His real purpose was a description of the rewards of heaven, but in passing he made some acerbic comments on the congregation arrayed before him in their economic order. "You that are pleased with your seats in this house because you are seated high in a place that is looked upon hungrily by those that sit round about [,] . . . consider it is but a very little while before it will [be] all one to you whether you have sat high or low here." The same message of eternal equity was also intended as consolation for those who had been seated lower than they felt was appropriate. Nevertheless, Edwards's use of everyday political life to illustrate his doctrines about eternal rewards, with a specificity that he usually eschewed, indicates that heavenly consolations were not so important to the Northampton congregation. If one takes Edwards's *Faithful Narrative* as an accurate picture of the community in 1735—pious and harmonious—one must believe that they would *then* have cared little about where they sat in the meetinghouse. *Then,* Edwards ruefully believed for the rest of his life, they had only been anxious "to drink in the words of the minister as they came from his mouth." Now it was more important to watch each other.

An even stronger blow against the power of the pulpit than the erection of family pews in the new meetinghouse was the decision of March 1738 to build a separate town house for secular meetings. For eighty years the business of the community, religious and worldly, had been organized within the same walls. The pulpit was empty during secular gatherings but it stood as a mute reminder of the position of the minister above the community. After the new town house was finished in 1739, however, the minister's proper sphere was clearly separate from the business of everyday life.[16]

But Jonathan Edwards would never abandon his ambitions to reshape the town into the ideal Christian commonwealth he had once expected it to be. He occasionally thundered from the pulpit against the sins of the marketplace; any economic practice less than charitable he defined as theft. In a sermon of July 1740 he catalogued as many kinds of sly deceits as the human imagination could dream up, including many that were not illegal and may well have been admired as sharp trading. As always, he took care to point out the varieties of the sin under discussion which were the special temptations of children—in this case, stealing fruit from a neighbor's trees.[17]

More importantly, Edwards continued his periodic attacks on the sexual sins of young people and the heinous indulgence of their parents. In a sermon on the temptation of Joseph to adultery with Potiphar's wife, he emphasized that Joseph was "in his youth, a season of life when persons are most liable to be overcome by temptations of this nature." Exhorting his youthful audience to avoid "all degrees of lasciviousness, both in talking and acting," Edwards discussed many varieties of sensual sin but came finally to a custom he considered a great abomination. He did not use the term "bundling," which has since become well known, but he spoke of "young people of different sexes lying in bed together. However light is made of it, and however ready persons may be to laugh at its being condemned, . . . this custom of this country (to which it seems to be peculiar, among people that pretend to uphold their credit) has been one main thing that has led to that growth of uncleanness that has been in the land." Another deplorable custom was one Edwards had worked tirelessly to eradicate in 1734, "young people of both sexes getting together in the night, in those companies for mirth and jollity, that they call frolics; so spending the time together till late in the night, in their jollity." The pernicious effects of frolicking were clearly evident: in those towns where such jollity was rampant, there were also the most "gross sins, fornication in particular." Proof that the practice was sinful could be derived from its eradication from Northampton for several years in the late outpouring of God's Spirit. But frolics had again become popular. Edwards was fighting not only youthful sexuality but also parental permissiveness. To the hypothetical cavil, "if we avoid all such things, it will be the way for our young people to be ignorant how to behave themselves in company," Edwards returned a scornful answer: would his opponents argue that the Spirit that ended frolicking also would "banish all good conduct, good breeding, and decent behavior from among them . . . sink them down into clownishness and barbarity[?]"[18] The pastor was trying to persuade the Northampton parents that he and they shared similar standards for youthful good behavior. His use of the story of Joseph, who eventually became head of Pharaoh's government, might also have been a way to suggest that these problem children would come out all right in the long run—if they remained morally upright. Edwards was trying to enlist the aid of the hitherto ineffective force of family government in another crusade against youthful vice. But the frolicking was to continue, and even to get worse, before the ultimate test of the pastor's standards was made.

In response to the apathy and sin that distinguished Northampton in the late 1730s, Jonathan Edwards, as it appears from the surviving sermons of the period, again altered his rhetorical techniques. In contrast to the "sweet reasonableness" of religion that he preached in the early 1730s, and the beautifully pure doctrines of God's justice and loveliness that filled his sermons in 1734 and 1735, by late 1735 Edwards was preaching unmitigated terror.[19] Really hardened hearts would not be reached by sweet reason or abstract aesthetics, and Edwards's use of the tools recommended by Stoddard to "break the stony hearts of men" revealed the end of his optimism about even the children of Northampton.

A sermon of November 1735 captures the new tone in its doctrine: "indignation, wrath, misery, and anguish of soul, are the portion that God has allotted to wicked men."[20] Unlike most of Edwards's earlier sermons, this work was not an elaboration of a point of doctrine but simply an indictment of the audience, a description of the punishment they would suffer for having rejected the Gospel doctrines of justice and hope that Edwards had previously taken such pains to present. Like the best of his revival sermons, this impreca- tion used the second-person pronoun extensively; the difference was that the primary intent was to describe the future and not the past, and Edwards barely mentioned that there was still time to repent. "This misery is the misery into which you are every day in danger of dropping, you are not safe from it one hour. How soon it may come upon you, you know not: you hang over it by a thread, that is continually growing more and more feeble. . . . How just would it be in God to cut you off, and put an end to your life! . . . You have many and many a time provoked God to do his worst. . . ."

Another sermon, directed particularly at the young people, dwelt at great length on youthful sin. That was, of course, one of the most familiar themes in Northampton by the late 1730s; but whereas the earlier sermons dwelt on the sins that youngsters might commit, the later sermons meditated on the inherent corruption of the human being. From Psalm 71:5—"For thou art my hope, O Lord God, thou art my trust from my youth"—Edwards preached that "it behooves young persons to seek [so] that they may be converted while they are young."[21] So familiar was this doctrine that he could just outline the exposition in his manuscript; but Edwards wrote out the Applica- tion fully, for the message was new, at least in tone. "Consider the miserable state you are in and have been in ever since you was born. You came into the world a child of wrath under guilt," Edwards reminded the children of Northampton. His pessimism was fueled by memories of the piety that a few years before had seemed to portend redemption from that inherently corrupt human condition. He charged his flock to "consider that those unconverted persons that have been at the top of the visible Church in point of privilege in this world will be at the bottom of hell in another world. . . . the inhabitants of this town had the greatest advantage for salvation of perhaps any town in the world." But these children in Edwards's congregation were "not only in danger of hell but . . . in danger of being cast into the bottom of hell."

The sensible dangers of hell, and the precariousness of men's condition in being suspended over it "by a thread" were elements of Edwards's rhetoric that reached a high plane of elaboration in a sermon delivered in the summer of 1741 and published with the title *Sinners in the Hands of an Angry God.*[22] By this time, another wave of revivals had come to the Connecticut Valley, in the wake of the New England tour of the English revivalist George Whitefield. Edwards, famous as the central figure in the regional revival of 1735, was often asked to preach in other towns, and in the late summer of 1741 he traveled down the Valley toward New Haven, preaching in a number of towns, perhaps using *Sinners* in many pulpits. Not only has *Sinners* become Edwards's most famous sermon, or at least the most often anthologized, but it has been used historically as an index to evaluating Edwards—as a mere hellfire preacher, a temporary participant in the excesses that characterized the Great Awakening in New England in 1741–42, or a consistent Calvinist who captured timeless truth when he said that men should be warned of their probable eternal fate with as much vigor as they would be warned that their houses were burning.[23] This often-cited sermon, however, deserves further exploration as a *pastoral* document, for it was first preached at Northampton and it suggests a major change in Edwards's attitude toward his own congregation.

No record was left of the effects of *Sinners* when it was preached in Northampton in June 1741, but in the atmosphere of barely controlled hysteria that pervaded other parts of the Valley in that summer, the bleak rhetoric proved terrifying: the Reverend Stephen Williams of Longmeadow wrote in his diary on the day that Edwards preached at Enfield that "the shrieks and cries were piercing and amazing."[24] The horror derived not from an especially affecting description of hell (Edwards had preached more vividly about the eternal flames on other occasions) but from the emotional tone of the sermon.[25] With an artistry unsurpassed in his other writings, Edwards harmonized the rhetoric with the message. The most striking aspect of the sermon is the description of God's *passivity*. Although it conveys the reek of brimstone, the sermon does not say that God will hurl man into the everlasting fires—on the contrary, doom will come from God's indifference. The focus is not on the eventual pain of the flames but on the moment of exquisite tension before man drops into the fire. God is as wrathful at living sinners as at those already consigned to hell, but His activity is in restraining the punishment that man has incurred. He holds man above the pit as by a spider's thread, and should He become weary of protecting worthless man, that abominable insect will *drop of his own weight.* Man's preservation lay in God's whim of mercy, and the terror of this message derived from the insecurity of being temporarily protected by an all-powerful being who had an infinite anger. (Was the control of such strong feelings something that Edwards's audience found difficult to understand or to trust?) Inevitably, God's anger would be unleashed—in the momentary lapse of His protection, man would plummet to his doom.[26]

No other Edwards sermon conveyed such ultimate terror—to the modern mind, at least, *Sinners* is the strongest of Edwards's statements about the relative powers of man and God, and one is tempted to describe the terror as existential. Although the first sentence of the Application was "The use may be of awakening to unconverted persons," and although the published sermon ends with five paragraphs of exhortation to men to exert themselves for salvation, Edwards's message seemed bleak. How could man climb back up that delicate spiderweb? And if man *did* acknowledge his own powerlessness, thereby doing all that he could to seek salvation, would this indifferent God even notice at the last minute?[27]

The God that Edwards described in *Sinners* showed a rather macabre passivity. Was this a projection of Edwards's own state of mind? During this period he again suffered from the bouts of illness that seemed to afflict him whenever his pastoral labors were unsuccessful. In the autumn of 1735 and again a year later, he had to travel to regain enough strength to resume his preaching.[28] In mid-1738 he described himself as almost too ill to work; and in 1739 another minister described him as unlikely to live more than another two or three years.[29] From about 1740, after he had spent five years trying in vain to whip his flock back to the pitch of piety they had shown in the "little awakening," Edwards revealed a strange kind of professional passivity. Shortly after *Sinners* was revised for publication, Edwards stopped writing out his Northampton sermons, except for very special ones; outlines seemed to suffice, and scrap paper or even tissue paper was now usually substituted for good foolscap for these notes.[30] The steady and well-planned psychological campaign that he had conducted in the mid-1730s was never repeated. Instead, while his private correspondence confessed despair over his inability to keep his congregation on the path of righteousness, his public life was marked by sporadic bursts of activism that were clearly doomed to failure. The early-1740s revivals that have come to be known as the Great Awakening marked a turning point in Edwards's career as important as the upsurge of piety five years earlier. The larger awakening was in many obvious ways a successor to the Valley revivals of 1734–35, but beneath the surface likeness was a critical difference in the pastoral role of Jonathan Edwards.

When the Spirit of God descended on Northampton for the second time in Edwards's ministry, there was no special pride in the revival for either congregation or pastor. Other communities were touched first by the Spirit before it came to Northampton, and even in his own town visiting preachers thundered more effectively than Edwards to arouse the sinful to repentance. In fact, it was depression over his own ineffectiveness that caused Edwards to invite the most famous of all evangelists to Northampton. In February 1740 Edwards wrote to the Reverend George Whitefield, whose evangelical successes in England had earned him many invitations from American ministers, to ask that his "intended journey through New England the next summer" include a visit to Northampton.[31] The famous Anglican itinerant was sorely needed in Northampton, confessed pastor Edwards: "We who have dwelt in a land that has been distinguished with Light, and have long enjoyed the Gospel, and have been glutted with it, and have despised it, are I fear more hardened than most of those places where you have preached hitherto." Even Whitefield's efforts might be in vain.

But neither Whitefield nor his host was disappointed, and the visit of the "grand itinerant" to Northampton catalyzed a revival that lasted (with ups and downs) for almost two years. After a month of triumph in Boston and eastern Massachusetts, Whitefield arrived at the home of Jonathan Edwards on October 17 and stayed for four days. He preached five times in Northampton and once in Hatfield, in meetings that were as "gracious" as any he had experienced in New England. Edwards later recalled that when Whitefield preached, "almost the whole assembly [were] in tears for a great part of sermon time." After Whitefield had left Northampton to bring his message of salvation to sinners in the lower Connecticut Valley, and to continue his tour through all the American colonies, pastor Edwards found that the spark of piety had been rekindled in his own flock.[32]

At first among "professors" who had previously gained hope of their election, and then among the unconverted and especially "those that were very young," religion again became the overwhelming concern of life. The second great revival in Northampton was probably much like the first in its general effects on the community; but this time Edwards chose to describe primarily the "bodily effects" on persons in his congregation. Children left their evening meetings of "social religion" to go home "crying aloud through the streets." By midsummer, "it was a very frequent thing to see an house full of outcries, faintings, convulsions and such like, both with distress, and also with admiration and joy." Often persons "were so affected, and their bodies so overcome, that they could not go home." The influence of the Spirit was strongest among children who had "not come to years of discretion" in 1735 and it "far exceeded" the earlier revival.[33] The full wave of awakening, among both hitherto untouched children and formerly converted adults, did not abate until the fall of 1742. The two-year second revival in Northampton was "great" in its local effects; but its paramount historical significance, of course, lies in its link to the revivals of those years in other New England communities and in the Middle Colonies. The connection was reflected in the Edwards letter quoted above: it was written for *The Christian History,* which appeared weekly in Boston from March 5, 1743, through February, 1744— America's first religious periodical and an intended archive of descriptions of the Awakening.

For pastor Edwards, the second revival—so long prayed for and worked for—was a season of triumph, but one that contained many disquieting undertones. Most important, the work of the Spirit was not so directly controlled by Edwards as the earlier revival had been. Preachers who were strangers were far more effective in arousing the congregation's emotions, in Northampton as elsewhere, than were the local pastors, whose doctrines and rhetorical styles were overly familiar. (Edwards himself found great success as an itinerant, as when he gave his *Sinners* sermon in Enfield.) It was Whitefield's visit in October 1740 that brought the great change in Northampton. In a lull that followed, the next spring, Edwards asked his friend Eleazar Wheelock to come with Benjamin Pomeroy from Connecticut to preach in Northampton. "There has been a reviving of religion among us of late," wrote Edwards, "but your labours have been much more remarkably blessed than mine. . . . and may your coming be a means to humble me, for my barrenness and unprofitableness, and a means of my instruction and enlivening."[34]

It was the preaching of Samuel Buell in the early spring of 1742 that overcame another long abatement of the Spirit's work and brought the congregation to a new pitch of fervor. Buell, a 1741 Yale graduate, had been invited to occupy the pulpit during Edwards's absence for a fortnight on a preaching tour and stayed for two or three weeks after Edwards returned. He preached publicly every day and spent almost all his other waking hours in religious exercises with smaller groups of people, who were "continually thronging him." So successful was Buell that he may have aroused jealousy in pastor Edwards's loyal wife. He certainly inspired her to new heights of piety, and the effects on other people were equally dramatic. "Almost the whole town seemed to be in a great and continual commotion, day and night," Edwards later wrote. Many persons had more extreme "religious affections" than ever before; some even lay in trances for twenty-four hours "with their senses locked up" but enjoying visions of heaven. When Edwards returned to Northampton he found that "a great deal of caution and pains were . . . necessary to keep the people, many of them, from running wild."[35] Indeed, Edwards's role in the later phase of the second awakening was much less one of exhortation to heights of piety, as it had been in 1735, than it was one of restraint on the excesses to which that piety had led.

Edwards deplored the hysteria that touched the revival in Northampton and dominated it in some other towns. By the time the wildness peaked in Northampton, other communities were being torn apart by zealots who would make emotion the sole evidence of holiness, and influential ministerial voices were being raised to indict the entire revival as the work of the Devil because such hysteria could not be produced by God. In 1743 two conservative Hampshire ministers, William Rand of Sunderland and Benjamin Doolittle of Northfield, each published a tract against the recent "upheavals," and from 1743 through 1745 a number of prominent clergymen published condemnations of the revivals.[36] Because Edwards steadfastly believed that the hysterics were just the incidental effects of circumstance upon weak constitutions, and not anything to compromise the holy essence of the work of God's Spirit, he found himself in the awkward position of having to defend the revival from its attackers by saving it from its friends. From 1741 to 1746 Edwards published three treatises of increasingly fine-tuned analysis which have become known as the definitive statement of the judicious pro-revival position. In these works he sought to express the proper role of emotion in religion—as he had experienced it as a pastor and as a convert himself. He also walked the tightrope of trying to preserve ministerial prerogative without denying the New Light position on which his public career and local successes were based.

Edwards's first statement, *The Distinguishing Marks of a Work of the Spirit of God . . .* , was expanded from a sermon he had delivered at the Yale Commencement in September 1741.[37] The timing of this major work of analysis of the revivals is highly significant: only eight days before that Commencement, Edwards had preached the funeral sermon for his uncle, William Williams of Hatfield, the formal leader of the Hampshire clergy since Stoddard's death and the informal leader of the native revival tradition in the Connecticut Valley. He had closed that sermon with a reminder of how a whole generation of Valley clergymen had been taken from their people (at Northampton, Westfield, Deerfield, Springfield, Suffield, and now Hatfield) within little more than a decade.[38] Edwards now seemed to take the leadership of the Hampshire Association, at least the pro-revival contingent within the group, and his invitation to speak at the Yale Commencement was a mark of recognition of his role as leader of the entire revival movement within New England.

In *The Distinguishing Marks,* published late in 1741 under the patronage of a number of clergymen who were moderately pro-revival, Edwards painstakingly analyzed the disturbances of traditional church services, of people's bodies, and of their imaginations; he showed that these things indicated neither that the revival was the product of the Spirit nor that it was the work of Satan. A true work of the Spirit would establish the truth of Jesus as Saviour, turn men away from "worldly lusts," increase regard for Scripture, "lead persons to truth" and "sound doctrine," and foster humility rather than pride. Testing the present revival by these signs, Edwards concluded that it *was* "undoubtedly, in the general, from the Spirit of God." But he did end his treatise by warning his fellow clergymen to exercise charity and to avoid unnecessary "innovations."[39]

By the fall of 1742, extravagant zealots had stolen the spotlight and the clerical community was divided into Old Light and New Light camps. The discord was far more serious in Connecticut than in Massachusetts, for government repressions made enthusiasts more bold; but even in the northern Connecticut Valley, churches were splintering and men were taking sides over the revival. Northampton was blessedly free from this kind of contention, probably because Edwards was moderately New Light and the most flamboyant itinerants (such as James Davenport) did not invade the region.[40] Edwards remained a friend of the revival.

In the second of his three major treatises, *Some Thoughts Concerning the Present Revival of Religion in New England,* written in late 1742, Edwards repeated the essence of the argument put forth in *The Distinguishing Marks.* He denounced extremists of all kinds, pronounced the revival genuine, and even suggested that it might be "the dawning, or at least a prelude" to the millennium, which would begin in America.[41] Edwards began this treatise with a definition of true piety that was the foundation of his attitude toward the revival; it was never understood by his Old Light opponents and formed the real difference between both camps of extremists in the clerical dialogue about the Awakening. "All will allow," Edwards wrote, "that true virtue or holiness has its seat chiefly in the heart, rather than in the head: it therefore follows . . . that it consists chiefly in holy affections."[42] Edwards's use of the head/heart duality here was misleading to his contemporaries and has confused many historians. It should *not* be read as an exact parallel to the traditional faculty-psychology duality of understanding/will: Edwards's use of the word "heart" rather than the narrower concept of "will" is the clue to his attempt to integrate the traditionally divided faculties into one unitary psychological function. In his private theological notebooks, now called the "Miscellanies," Edwards described true conversion as an "indwelling" of the Holy Spirit, which gave the regenerate person a new "sense." The heart was the *locus* of that sense, but it included the operation of newly enhanced natural understanding, as well as will that was itself reborn: regenerate man "is made in the image of God who has understanding and will, which will is the same with the Holy Ghost."[43] In his unpublished writings, Edwards put much more emphasis on the direct action of the Spirit on the will than did his grandfather Stoddard, who had insisted that the will was affected only through the work of grace on the understanding; but Edwards went only so far from the "intellectualist" position on the psychology of conversion as to maintain that both faculties were touched in the same instant. Other revivalists of the Great Awakening may have put so much faith in man's emotions that they became entirely anti-intellectual, but Edwards's great achievement—albeit one never appreciated in his own time (perhaps largely because of the lack of an adequately subtle vocabulary)—was to begin a reintegration of man's psyche.

Edwards was not quite ready in *Some Thoughts* to argue explicitly about the psychology of conversion (he would have much more to say on the subject in 1746), but he followed his brief statement with an impressive illustration of how high emotions could function properly within a mentally healthy person who adhered with the utmost propriety to all the classic doctrines of New England Calvinism. We now know that the instance he cited was his own wife, Sarah. So great were her religious affections that her "soul dwelt on high, and was lost in God, and seemed almost to leave the body." She frequently lost "all ability to stand or speak" and sometimes leapt involuntarily, although there was no trance. This was no "distemper catched from Mr. Whitefield" or childish "giddiness," for this was a woman whose grace had been growing for decades and manifested itself in a "spirit of humility and meekness" as well as the soundest doctrine.[44]

Edwards ended his description of Sarah's remarkable holiness with a compliment that was also a moving confession. "Now if such things are enthusiasm, and the fruits of a distempered brain, let my brain be evermore possessed of that happy distemper! If this be distraction, I pray God that the world of mankind may be all seized with this benign, meek, beneficent, beatifical, glorious distraction!"

Edwards never confessed that he himself enjoyed such transports, although when he wrote the "Personal Narrative" of his own conversion about this time, he attributed to himself a blissful resignation to God's will that was unlike his older autobiographical accounts and much like the state of Sarah's spirit.[45] The real importance of *Some Thoughts,* when it is seen as a companion piece to the "Personal Narrative," is its self-confidence in defining true conversion. We have too few personal documents from these critical years to untangle the strands of experience—Jonathan's, Sarah's, those he observed in his flock—that contributed to this certainty about the nature of conversion. But as we will see, Edwards's success at fitting together experience and doctrine, emotion and idea, would have profound implications for his future as a pastor.

The most complete statement of Edwards's mature thought on conversion came in 1746, when his *Treatise Concerning Religious Affections* was published in Boston.[46] His focus was on the critical line between common and Saving Grace, a distinction every Christian would have to make in self-examination, and a distinction that captured the essence of the task of the pastor as both speculative theologian and community moral officer. Edwards began by insisting, as he did in *Some Thoughts,* that "true religion, in great part, consists in holy affections." He divided the soul's actions into two categories, using the traditional term "understanding" for the actions of "perception and speculation," and using the term "inclination" for the action of making choices: the inclination, he wrote, is called the will where it governs actions (the traditional usage) but is called the heart when expressed through the mind. Here again, but more explicitly than in *Some Thoughts,* is the attempt to describe the reintegration of the faculties of the soul that comes with regeneration. To complete his argument, Edwards asserted that vigorous (sometimes physically sensible) exercises of the inclinations are the "affections," and they are the essential method whereby the converted person connects with the Holy Spirit.[47] Having defined the "affections" that are not merely animal emotion but are the appropriate and necessary *locus* of true religion, Edwards went on to maintain that the "degree of religion" in a person is only to be determined by the "fixedness and strength of the habit" and not "by the degree of the present exercise." True religious affection was not passion, unleashed emotion, for there must also be judgment and control: "Where there is heat without light, there can be nothing divine or heavenly in that heart."[48] This insistence on mental and emotional balance was the hallmark of Edwards's position.

After discussing some signs that could not be a definitive indication of grace, one way or the other, Edwards gave twelve signs that provided a reasonable certainty of the presence of Saving Grace. The first eleven required that the affections proceed from a holy source, turn toward holy things and Gospel truths, and be manifest in a spirit of humility. As *practical* tests of the difference between mere imagination and divine inspiration, they were vague; but Edwards did clearly rule out personal revelations. The twelfth sign was the most critical: it was "Christian practice. . . . universally conformed to, and directed by Christian rules" as the "business of life."[49]

Edwards presented these signs for use in self-examination to root out complacency as well as "enthusiasm." He made no bald statement that a person could *not* be sure of his election; but his implicit position was like Stoddard's, that whatever assurance was possible would come only from a habit of holiness in all its psychological and behavioral dimensions.[50] One would know oneself to be saved by looking back on one's life and seeing a harmony of feeling and action —as Edwards could look back on his own life when he wrote the "Personal Narrative." If we recall Edwards's early struggles to keep his sense of holiness, and how he preached in the mid-1730s that conversion was a new sensibility, we can see how, in the wake of the second revival, he was distancing himself from the potential antinomianism of that sensibility. Sarah Edwards's transports were approved, but only because they were controlled by sound doctrine and conspicuous humility. Edwards's twelve signs of spiritual affections codified what he had felt and observed. Besides working on both the psychological and the doctrinal levels, they also met pastoral exigencies: the criterion of subjective *and* objective Christian life —each part valid only in conjunction with the other—provided an opportunity for a minister to restrain both worldliness and spiritual pride in his congregation.

Equally important as a rein on arrogance was Edwards's series of unequivocal statements about the inability of one man to judge another's heart. This was the most basic and radical of all Stoddard's doctrines, and Edwards quoted his grandfather's *Treatise on Conversion;* but the old warning certainly needed repeating in the new circumstances of such a large and emotional revival as the Great Awakening. There is no evidence that the Northampton congregation was torn by accusations of impiety hurled by those who had experienced violent "affections" against others who had followed a less extravagant road to faith, but Edwards was well aware that many other communities had divided on this very issue. Therefore, he warned that even "true saints have not such a spirit of discerning that they can certainly determine who are godly and who are not. . . . they can neither feel, nor see, in[to] the heart of another." And pastor Edwards pretended to give no absolute criteria for distinguishing spiritual sheep from goats, lest he "be guilty of that arrogance which I have been condemning." For purposes of this world, which included admission to church fellowship, men must judge others with hearts full of charity and not pride.[51]

The man or woman who claimed assurance of salvation, however, would not therefore slip easily into public recognition as a saint. Although Edwards followed Stoddard in acknowledging the inviolable privacy of the experience of grace, he nevertheless insisted in the *Religious Affections* on a voluntary submission by the converted individual to the community of Christians. A profession of Christianity was necessary, and it should include all the essentials—acknowledgment of sinfulness, repentance, and belief in the doctrines of Jesus as Saviour. It could be express or implicit. Not essential was "an account of the particular steps and method, by which the Holy Spirit, sensibly to them," changed their hearts; but some account of the nature of the experience must be given, since "for persons to profess those things wherein the essence of Christianity lies, is the same thing as to profess that they experience those things."[52] Christianity was, in essence, *"heart"* religion.

But wasn't *judgment* of such a profession implicit in this requirement? Professions could, of course, be faked. All these cautions against spiritual pride among the brethren force the overall message of Edwards's treatises on grace into a serious ambiguity. The signs seemed so clear in his mind, but could they not be used to keep hypocrites out of the church? Were church members to abandon discrimination entirely in their exercise of charity toward their neighbors? If so, why was it so important to Edwards to promulgate rules for distinguishing grace in the living person? This was a serious practical problem in the Great Awakening and its aftermath, for piety was now a public stance, as it had not been since the early days of the Puritan commonwealth. In many communities, church membership was a more voluntary and particular association than ever before. Ironically, the emphasis on emotional conversion—essentially a more private matter than the outward morality that had grown fashionable as a mark of holiness—led to the necessity for a converted person to make a choice, to join a church as a convert, not just as the child or grandchild of saints. But then he must be judged worthy by his neighbors. Edwards, so certain of the true signs of holiness, nevertheless warned men that they must *not* judge.

Ultimately, it was impossible to restrain laymen from pretending spiritual powers not legitimized by Scripture without asserting the domination of the minister over his congregation. The combination of abilities that made a good minister—doctrinal expertise and "experimental" understanding of "the inward operations of the Spirit" —gave him an insight into others' souls that was more sophisticated and more sensitive than that possessed by the ordinary lay church member.[53] The only possible solution allowed by Edwards's advice to a "revived" Congregational church infected by hypocrites and yet persuaded by Edwards's logic that there were signs of salvation but not reliable ones for mere mortals would be reliance on the minister in matters of judgment.

Enhanced ministerial power was the real direction in which these treatises on grace and conversion were leading. When *Some Thoughts* listed the most pernicious sins then current, the three Edwards mentioned all concerned the infringement of ministerial prerogatives by laymen. The first was censuring "professing Christians, in good standing in the visible church, as unconverted"; worst of all was daring to censure ministers as graceless. The second abomination was exhorting, or preaching, by laymen; only ministers had the right to assume the authority of speaking in Christ's name or of teaching and exhorting as a calling or full-time occupation. Third among the most dangerous revival practices that Edwards could think of was the attempt of laymen to introduce new practices into the rites of the church without prior consent of "the governing part of the worship-ing society"; the pastor "especially ought to be consulted, and his voice taken, as long as he is owned for their minister."[54] That Jonathan Edwards was the professional heir of his grandfather Stod-dard was never more clear than in these statements about proper church procedures. In spite of his broad and sensitive view of the revival and the good it entailed, Edwards focused on anti-clericalism as the major sign that evil was mixed in with the good.

It was this impure character of even a glorious work of the Holy Spirit that forced the dialectic interaction of theology and pastoral practice in the career of Jonathan Edwards. There is no doubt that as an intellectual he was perpetually fascinated by the search for pure doctrinal truth. But if he had not worked so hard to bring about a revival in his own congregation, and if he had not then seen the resulting heights of piety come close to being unrestrained passion and pride, his concern to find true distinguishing marks of sincere religious affections would have been less pressing and perhaps less fruitful. The second awakening in Northampton had posed a prob-lem which Edwards answered in the mid-1740s with his impressive intellectual and rhetorical skills, in three treatises that became the definitive works on the workings of grace. He managed to harmo-nize the emotions he had felt, and those he had seen in others, with the Calvinist dogma that he acknowledged as truth. But while he was reconciling—theoretically—psychology and behavior, personal piety and community responsibilities, Edwards's real life as a pastor pro-vided a melancholy counterpoint to these elegant doctrinal certain-ties.

CHAPTER SEVEN

Challenges

ALTHOUGH JONATHAN EDWARDS was brilliant at the doctrinal level in defending the revival and identifying its dangers, his accomplishment did not make the solution of the problems he faced in Northampton any easier. In part because he was so confident of the experiential reality and the analytical precision of his doctrine of true faith, Edwards's definition of conversion gradually became in his own mind a norm by which others could be measured and controlled. As he became so certain intellectually, he became insecure professionally. The second awakening in Northampton had threatened Edwards's identity as a pastor; and as the revival waned, Edwards faced again the old challenges to church discipline and ministerial authority. He never gave up trying to re-create the joyous success of the revival of 1735, but by now his once terrifying doctrines were boringly familiar, and his young people were grown up. He was no longer young himself; his charisma faded. As he grew older, and as evangelism failed, Edwards tried to assert the disciplinary powers that he assumed had been enjoyed by Solomon Stoddard. Through the mid-1740s, Edwards's identification with his grandfather became more apparent—and more of a strategic dead end.

By the 1740s, despite the briefly spiritualizing effects of the latest revival, Northampton became more worldly and contentious—a normal eighteenth-century town. Amid the inexorable social changes, we can see the fragmentation of a once integrated body into a mere geographical collection of competitive individuals. Previously public resources were forever committed into private hands, the body politic was divided into active and passive segments, and the once strongly interwoven structures of church and state were separated. In the loss of a unity once imposed by hardship and ideology there came also the separation of morality, and especially piety, into an isolated corner of everyday life.

The most important agricultural change in Northampton was the end of common fields. The last mention of common tillage was in 1743, when the fence around those fields was apportioned for the last time. Later that year a compromise was finally reached over the traditional rights of the town to cut wood on land that had been allocated to individuals but not yet improved. Dispute over these rights had simmered since 1715, when previous land divisions were confirmed without mention of public rights to wood. Jonathan Edwards described this controversy as "above any other particular thing, a source of mutual prejudices, jealousies, and debates, for fifteen or sixteen years past." The problem was not trivial, for these uncleared lands were the only source of firewood within a ten-mile radius (a day's trip with a wagon and oxen). The compromise of 1743 allowed the inhabitants to cut wood on a certain strip of Proprietors' lands for ten years; after another bitter fight in 1754, the agreement was extended for ten more years.[1] After that, private ownership was absolute, and competition was not hindered by remnants of communalism.

Almost equally private was the control of local political offices in the first half of the eighteenth century. The growth of town population was not mirrored by any widening of the pool of officeholders, and the powerful posts of selectman and General Court representative were still held almost exclusively by the same families—Clapp, Clark, Hawley, Hunt, Parsons, Pomeroy, Strong, Wright; Colonel John Stoddard, Dr. Samuel Mather, Colonel Timothy Dwight—who had controlled the town since the late seventeenth century. Most men who held important office were heirs of earlier leaders. Between 1740 and 1749, seven out of nine first-term selectmen were sons of selectmen, and the fathers of these seven had served an average of more than nine terms each. The social leadership that led to election was clearly more easily inherited than earned. A growing elitism was also reflected in the number of selectman's posts held by men with military or courtesy titles (Deacon, Doctor, or Mister): eighty-four percent of the terms in 1740–49 were held by titled gentlemen, almost twice as high a percentage as in 1700–09.[2] There were more titled men in town than there had been earlier, of course, but there were even more citizens without any mark of special status. Although no man in Northampton except Colonel John Stoddard made government service at any level his sole career, by midcentury there were a dozen men who were called on constantly for service, professional politicians in a limited sense. Their sons were also assured of careful consideration for office when other young men were ignored.

The growing restriction of political power to a special class of men was not denounced by Northampton's pastor, for Jonathan Edwards's views on government were those of a Tory. His few sermons on explicitly political themes, given between 1730 and 1748, condemned any democratic scramble for office and inveighed against the contentiousness that he saw pervading Northampton public affairs. He once charged from the pulpit that the community could "manage scarcely any public business without dividing into parties."[3] He felt that a political system that was deferential was a great improvement, but his basis for approval was the old-fashioned ideal of a stable, unified community with "natural" leaders, rather than the faction-oriented politics of the mid-eighteenth century. In an early 1730s sermon on the current unsettled state of public affairs as a sign of sinfulness, Edwards asserted: " 'Tis no part of publick prudence to be often changing the persons in whose hands is the administration of government and 'tis a calamity to have them often changed. . . . The long continuance of the same persons in power if they are fit for their places tends most to the strength and stability of a community."[4] Some men were natural leaders, and their right to govern transcended the petty squabbling of ordinary politics.

Such a man was Edwards's uncle, Colonel John Stoddard, the squire of Northampton, who died in 1748. John was the second son of the Reverend Solomon Stoddard and the only one of the Patriarch's sons to settle in Northampton. A Harvard graduate with no apparent interest in the learned professions (his older brother became a minister), John was primarily a soldier—colonel by 1721 and commander in chief of the western Massachusetts frontier by 1744.

Military prominence brought civil honors: he was also a judge, Northampton's representative to the General Court almost continuously from 1716 to 1748, and a member of the Governor's Council in the 1720s.[5] In the midst of this service to the Province, he found time to dominate Northampton's local politics: he was the most often elected selectman and most often chosen Moderator of the town meeting in the first half of the eighteenth century. Temperamentally aristocratic like his father, he was the undoubted leader of the Court party in the Court-and-Country dichotomy used by Jonathan Edwards to describe Northampton politics, although Colonel John and his allies were so thorough in monopolizing town offices that it is hard to discern another party in the town records.[6]

John Stoddard's influence on his father's and nephew's parishioners cannot be measured only in terms of official position, however. The Colonel was one of the richest men in Massachusetts, and his income derived from the vast amount of speculative land he acquired through government connections.[7] When he died in 1748, Stoddard's real estate alone (much of it frontier land rated at the purchase price, not the sums hundreds of times higher at which his widow would sell acreage after his death) was worth £17,184 Old Tenor—about twenty-five times Jonathan Edwards's yearly salary of £700. Even more important than Stoddard's landholdings as a buttress to his preeminence in Northampton was his lavish display of personal property. In and around the elegant gambrel-roofed mansion that he built next to his father's house on the hill overlooking the town, there was by 1748 more than £18,000 worth of personal property, including many bonds and other forms of money, thirty-five shirts, and Northampton's first gold watch (alone worth £150).[8] He did not marry until 1730, his fiftieth year, and then he chose the daughter of a man much like himself, Major John Chester of Wethersfield, Connecticut. Prudence Chester was known thereafter as Madam Stoddard, a title usually reserved for the wives of ministers as the first ladies of their communities in rural areas. She sat with Madam Edwards in the best pew of the meetinghouse. She entertained guests with the first tea set in Northampton and paraded in the latest feminine fashions from Europe (including the hoopskirts that her father-in-law had denounced). She would perhaps have been happier living in Boston, and her daughters were sent there for "finishing," but she was in all respects a proper consort for the *"de facto* warden of the western marches."⁹ Colonel John Stoddard was, ironically, in his later years an exemplar of all that luxurious living that Solomon Stoddard had railed against in Boston. But his display of wealth actually began with his marriage, which took place (perhaps coincidentally) the year after his father's death. Before that time, he was a powerful but austere man, a military and political leader who eschewed the ostentatious social life he could have afforded.

During his father's lifetime, Colonel John gave every evidence of properly valuing the works of the Spirit, and he later became a valued advisor to his nephew Edwards on religious and political affairs. In April 1742 Edwards communicated to the Hampshire Association of Ministers an essay on the revivals written by his uncle, the manuscript of which has unfortunately been lost; in a letter of advice to a minister in Hartford in 1744, Edwards mentioned that he had discussed the divisions within New England churches very thoroughly with his uncle. When Edwards began to develop new and potentially unpopular doctrines about church admission in the late 1740s, he apparently consulted his uncle before anyone else. And when Stoddard was stricken with his last illness in June 1748, while serving in the government in Boston, Sarah Edwards went to attend his deathbed, leaving her husband and some sick children behind in Northampton.¹⁰

A few days after Stoddard's death, Edwards preached a memorial sermon for his uncle which used the occasion to define the social benefits of natural leaders. In *A Strong Rod Broken and Withered,* Edwards was explicit in trying to remove any stain of mere partisan self-seeking from this man who had led the Court party in Northampton for many decades and who was clearly identified as a Tory in province politics.¹¹ According to Edwards, Stoddard was distinguished by "a genius for government. . . . improved by study, learning, observation and experience. . . . largeness of heart, and a greatness and nobleness of disposition. . . . [and] honorable descent." A "man of estate," he had been "long in authority, so that it is become as it were natural for the people to pay him deference." Rulers like Stoddard restrained ordinary people from their natural inclination to "make a prey of one another" and indulge in "intestine discord, mutual injustice and violence." (Note Edwards's distinction between government—by those commanding natural deference—and intestine discord, or ordinary politics.) In all the virtues fitting a man to rule, John Stoddard left no "superior in these respects, in these parts of the world." (This was a bold statement, for seated among Edwards's audience were at least two contenders for Stoddard's position as leading squire of the upper Connecticut Valley—Israel Williams of Hatfield and Timothy Dwight of Northampton.) Most clearly marking Stoddard off from his competitors for rank was his piety and his connection to men whose vocation was *moral* government. He had been frequently consulted on religious questions by his nephew Edwards, who found him to be "a wise casuist . . . I scarce knew the Divine that I ever found more able to help and enlighten the mind in such cases [applying doctrine to cases of conscience] than he." (This was hardly a compliment to the number of local clergymen present on this occasion.) Stoddard had been unfailingly accurate in doctrine and "intimately and feelingly acquainted" with experimental religion and vital piety. Such a paragon was not to be met with again in Northampton, and Edwards was left sadly alone in defense of religious truth when his uncle went to his eternal reward.

The dual role of exceptional civil leader and patron of religious orthodoxy, reminiscent of the great Puritan, John Winthrop, was claimed by few men in the mid-eighteenth century. Governors and divines still respected each other in New England, but their spheres of power and strategies of dominance had been growing apart for at least half a century. On the local level, at least or perhaps especially in Northampton, the harmony of civil and religious rule was maintained into the eighteenth century by having the same men in both kinds of office. John Stoddard—son of one minister and uncle and patron of the other—was the most visible figure, but there had been others of dual influence in the community. The three elders of the Northampton church—John Strong (*d.* 1699), Preserved Clapp (*d.* 1720), and Ebenezer Strong (*d.* 1729)—the last of whom died on the same day as did Solomon Stoddard, were important men in the secular life of the town: the first and third in order of service, father and son, held a monopoly on the tanning trade in Northampton, and the man who served between them was a commander of the local troops during the Indian wars at the turn of the century. The deacons tended to be wealthy farmers and artisans, although by 1740 they clustered more in the second quartile of taxpayers than at the top of the list. As the community matured, these church officers were much less likely to participate formally in secular town government. Between 1670 and 1699, for example, elders and deacons served over thirty-seven percent of all the selectman terms possible in Northampton; the corresponding figure for 1700–29 was just under twenty-seven percent, and for 1730–54 it was only ten percent.[12] Two of the three deacons chosen in 1739 never served as selectmen, and they were the first church officers not to do so. This unwillingness of the town to give extra powers to the deacons was a significant indication of Northampton's secularization.

Solomon Stoddard had enjoyed a full complement of such formal and informal assistants in his fight to mold the community along the lines of a truly Christian enterprise, but Stoddard's grandson saw the rapid decline of this institution of Christian magistracy. If we did not know that Colonel John Stoddard was the son of the Patriarch, and if Edwards had not told us how actively his uncle had supported the cause of religion, we could see the transition from theocracy to secular leadership as very abrupt—in 1729, when Solomon Stoddard died and his grandson inherited the pulpit without inheriting all the informal power that Stoddard had acquired in threescore years of evangelical success. How lucky was young Mr. Edwards to have the collaboration, rather than the competition for power, of Colonel John.

On the other hand, the balance of allied forces was shifting, and the secular community intruded itself into the church in the 1740s in a way that would have been unthinkable in Solomon Stoddard's day. In June 1740 the church chose a fifteen-member committee to assist the pastor in judging "causes and matters of difficulty," although Edwards never recorded a request for help.[13] The group included the five current deacons, Colonel Stoddard, six men with militia rank of lieutenant or above, a doctor, and one untitled man (who was, however, the son of Northampton's last elder). No record of this committee's work has survived, and there is no mention of a renewal of their appointment until 1748, but the precedent for lay government in the church had been set firmly. Solomon Stoddard, who preached so bitterly against the arrogance of the brethren, would never have allowed this infringement of his own prerogatives. His grandson, who preached just as bitterly but in more guarded language about the pride of laymen and their interference in the church, seems to have had no choice but to accept this committee, at least for a year. The assistants elected by the town did not much ease the burdens on Edwards. As he continued to fight sin, apathy, and pride, he fought alone.

No one in Northampton had any right to expect that the Reverend Mr. Edwards would bow to the inevitable forces of secularization. While he was fighting the emotional excesses of the Awakening on both local and theoretical levels, he gave some attention to a practical step toward moral reform. In March 1742, as the incendiary effects of Buell's preaching were beginning to wear off, Edwards persuaded the congregation to renew ceremonially their covenant with God. Carefully drafted by the pastor, the covenant was so completely oriented toward external morality that the most dedicated Arminian could not have scrupled to sign; Edwards was obviously fighting unethical behavior as well as emotional extremism in that troublesome year. The first nine paragraphs of the new covenant were promises to deal honestly with one's neighbor in financial matters and public affairs and not to seek private gain or revenge. The next two promises were for the young people, who were to vow that their behavior in company would always be consistent with "the devoutest and most engaged spirit in religion." The last specific vow was to perform family duties by "Christian rules." The covenant closed with a supplication to God to assist the brethren "solemnly to devote our whole lives to be laboriously spent in the business of religion."[14] Whatever good this covenant might have done temporarily—and even the sketchy outlines of Edwards's 1740s sermons show that he still had many sins to catalogue—the people of Northampton were never again to be as concerned with the "business of religion" as they had been in 1734–35 and 1741–42. They turned away from their pastor's message, and he knew that winning the small battles was not equal to winning the war.

From about the time of the covenant renewal in 1742 there is some evidence that Jonathan Edwards was rapidly losing the confidence of the community that he served and that he was aware of that loss. Suggesting the psychological atmosphere in the parsonage in that period, Sarah Edwards's narrative of her conversion keeps repeating that she worried about "the esteem and just treatment of the people of this town." She dreamed of "being driven from my home into the cold and snow, of being chased from the town with the utmost contempt and malice." She imagined being "surrounded by enemies, who were venting their malice and cruelty upon me, in tormenting me." She worried that "if our house and all our property in it should be burnt up, and we should that night be turned out naked; whether I could cheerfully resign all to God."[15] Edwards published his wife's narrative to illustrate Christian triumph over temporal hardship, but Sarah's fears were strangely persistent. Jonathan's account of his own conversion, written about the same time as Sarah's, may reveal parallel tension. He confessed that he was "greatly afflicted with a proud and selfrighteous spirit, much more sensibly than I used to be formerly. I see the serpent rising and putting forth its head continually, everywhere, all around me."[16] He was unlikely to be sinfully proud with his small children, or his saintly wife; the objects of his self-assertion must have been his neighbors, his congregation. Now that he was converted, was he less charitable in judging the souls in his care, less patient with the people of Northampton?

About the same time that he published Sarah's dreams of freezing and burning and enduring the contempt of the town, Jonathan Edwards publicly identified himself with Christ the martyr. In an ordination sermon in June 1743, Edwards dwelt on the doctrine that ministers must suffer—even as Christ did, if necessary—to bring the Gospel to the pharisees. This sermon is one of the most revealing documents in Edwards's pastoral career, not only because it was given in the period between the second revival and the first serious outbreak of hostilities between him and his church, but especially because it was given at the installation of Jonathan Judd, the first minister in Southampton, a village recently established on the edge of Northampton by men who were Edwards's own converted young people in 1734–35. Therefore, what he said at Judd's ordination was sure to be communicated to his own flock, and his immediate audience were his former disciples who had turned their backs on him to pursue greater worldly advantages. As a commentary on Edwards's influence that he could not have ignored, the Southampton settlers had passed over the many young New Light clergymen whom Edwards had befriended (Samuel Buell, for example) and hired a minister who was at best neutral about the past revivals.[17] Edwards recorded no dislike of Judd, but he warned that "those people are like to sink the deepest into hell hereafter, that go to hell from under the care of the most faithful ministers."[18] In a fashion uncharacteristic of the ordination sermons he frequently preached, moreover, Edwards spent most of his time not on Scriptural prefigurations of the minister's role but on practical matters of immediate local import.

To get the benefit of a man's ministry, Edwards told the new church at Southampton, they must support it well. "Christ would not have ministers' time and thoughts taken up about providing temporal good things for their own support, but would have them wholly provided for by their people." God would punish even men who gave reluctantly. "And here let me warn you in particular, that you don't only do well by your minister for a while at first, while the relation between you and him is a new thing, and then afterwards, when your minister's necessities are increased, begin to fail, as it too frequently happens."[19] (It was happening, some in the audience knew, even in the first parish of Northampton.) Edwards admitted that some men might say that ministers "love to harp upon this string," because it is to their worldly benefit. "I have not been much in insisting on this duty in my own pulpit, where it would especially concern my temporal interest; and blessed be God that I have had no more occasion." (A month later, if not earlier, Edwards *did* preach in an uncompromising tone about the necessity of tithes.[20]) "But whatever any may judge of the secrets of my heart," he continued, "it is enough for you to whom I have spoke it, that I have demonstrated that what I have delivered is the mind of God." And a lack of money was not the only cross that ministers had to bear: equally "wounding" to pastor and flock were contention about temporal affairs and "quarreling with your minister in matters of church discipline." He also alluded to the presence of "anti-ministerial men" among even the "professors, in some of our towns": "It seems to be as it were natural to 'em to be unfriendly and unkind towards their own ministers, and to make difficulty for them."[21]

The existence of a number of "anti-ministerial men" in a town, therefore, would be good evidence that it was not truly pious and moral, however many revivals it had experienced. And such was the case in Northampton. It was some years before Edwards's persistent challenges forced these reprobates to declare themselves openly, but Edwards knew they were lying in wait, and between 1743 and 1749 he provoked a number of incidents to bring their hypocrisy into open light. Even the full members of Edwards's own church were tried and found wanting in that ultimate requirement of "Christian practice." As he had done at Judd's ordination, Edwards preached "the mind of God" at Northampton; but his flock refused to identify their pastor's voice with the will of their heavenly Father.

The first and clearest manifestation of the Northampton congregation's unwillingness to give its pastor what he regarded as proper homage was in the matter of salary, that traditional battleground between ministers and laymen in eighteenth-century New England.[22] To be sure, Edwards was well paid: in 1749 he even bragged that he was the highest-paid minister in New England outside the city of Boston. His salary started in 1726 at £100 per year, and from 1730 through 1738 he was given that much again as an extra gift each year. Increments to the total sum in 1739 and 1742, however, did not quite keep up with the depreciation of Massachusetts currency from inflation. By 1748 Edwards was being paid £700 per year and was ahead of the inflation rate. That year, too, he was given an extra £170 "to support his family and buy books."[23] But the amounts themselves were not the real problem.

As early as 1734, Edwards had trouble collecting his salary and complained to the town that he had "been put to considerable inconvenience already for want." A scrap of sermon notes, eight years later, preserves a draft of Edwards's response to the "uneasiness" of the town over his family's spending habits, as an introduction to an attempt to justify his various expenses. Tradition has it that the Edwards family displayed tastes for luxuries that could only be purchased in Boston, such as fancy clothes and jewelry. (A bill of £11 for "a gold locket and chane" for "Mrs. Edwards" was used for sermon notes in March 1743.)[24] So parsonage expenses were carefully observed by the town, and even the money that was voted was often paid hesitantly. Sarah Edwards had to write in March 1744 to beg for her husband's past-due salary, for "Mr. Edwards is under such obligations that he can't possibly due without it."[25] The Edwardses would have agreed with Solomon Stoddard, who stated in one of his most famous published sermons that a minister might find "his abilities are clouded, his spirit is sunk and low by refractory persons of his flock, or by his low maintenance for himself and his family."[26]

That the problem was not the amount of the salary, but the embarrassing bickering that accompanied the annual grant, is indicated by a letter Edwards wrote in November 1744 to the first precinct (the civil unit of government for church affairs after the separate parish of Southampton was established). It was but the first of many requests he made for a fixed salary and is worth quoting at length because it shows the tone Edwards took as his difficulties with the town reached a level of permanent bitterness. He used words of condescension, expressed concern for *their* peace and welfare, and clearly indicated that their inquiries into his family budget were impertinent.

Dear Brethren,   What I have to propose to you is not from any uneasiness with my maintenance, or any fault I find with the salary you have given me from year to year; but from a desire that I have, not only of my own, but also of the town's comfort and benefit hereafter. The thing that I would propose is . . . you would settle a certain salary upon me. . . . I look upon it very likely that there will be no great difficulty in our agreeing upon the summ. . . . you will have no further trouble or concern about it. The affair of your minister's support, and the consideration of his families circumstances, won't come over every year, to exercise your minds, & to occasion various opinions & speeches, & to be a constant temptation to persons to look into the way in which the minister spends his money; all occasion for such difficulties will be cut off, which must needs be greatly for the comfort and benefit of the publick society.

I have no aim at leading you into any trap. . . .

In the agreement that is now subsisting between me and the people, the people have obliged themselves, in a general clause, to make my support as shall be suitable . . . ; but there is nothing in that agreement that determines what the support is, nor is it said who shall be the judge.

. . . It can't be expected in so large a society as this is, but that, under these circumstances, there will be some that will be unjustifiably meddling with a minister's affairs: & it may be a temptation even to rational, good sort of men, to look more into a minister's affairs, and his way of spending his money, than is convenient. . . .

I hope that what I propose will not appear to any, a frightfull thing. . . . But however I don't pretend to oblige you to it; but only to request it of you. . . .

If this which I now request of you be done, I hope it may be a means of establishing an Happy Agreement & Peace between me and you, that henceforward we may walk together in Christian Harmony & love engaged with one Heart & Soul to seek & serve the Lord, all traveling the same road towards the Heavenly Canaan, without falling out by the way.

I am, dear Brethren, your affectionate Pastor, being myself, with what I have, devoted to your service, for Jesus sake,

Jonathan Edwards.

Edwards was willing to settle for a fixed wage, which might not be adjusted to keep up with inflation, in return for an end to the embarrassing inquiries into his spending—a method of harassment which did not deceive him.[27]

Edwards's 1744 letter was never recorded in the official deliberations of the first precinct. Only a few months before, Edwards had written to a friend that his congregation were hard-pressed financially: "It is a time of the greatest scarcity of money amongst them, and they have of late been in the most unhappy frame that I have known them to be in." In December 1746, if not earlier, he again pressed for a fixed salary; after "considerable debate" the precinct voted not to give in *even* if they were able to find a way to correct any fixed amount for inflation. A year later Edwards again petitioned for "the reasonableness and expediency" of fixing his salary; but not until March 1748, after many more long and bitter debates, did a majority of the taxpayers agree to settle £700 Old Tenor per year on their pastor, the sum to rise or fall proportionally to the value of certain staples.[28] Edwards would still have to negotiate those values annually, but he had won in principle.

One reason for the town's acquiescence may be surmised from

Edwards's formal letter of acceptance of its terms. In May 1748 he agreed to abide by the rates "so long as I continue in the work of the ministry among them"—this qualification was repeated a number of times in slightly different words. Did the town agree to give him a fixed and high salary because it saw only a short duration to this financial drain?

Edwards may have anticipated leaving Northampton as early as 1744, when he first insisted on a fixed salary.[29] Since he knew the town was hard pressed for money, he may even have been seeking to provoke an open split. But he did not leave until six years later, after more important aspects of his pastoral relationship with the town had soured. The issues that precipitated the ultimate confrontation were Edwards's perennial concerns—discipline of young people and piety in the church—and they exposed the most fundamental problem faced by ministers and congregations in eighteenth-century New England, the unresolved ambiguities of the authority of the minister within the Congregational system.

In the 1740s there arose, as there had in the early 1730s, a problem with the young people of Northampton. Once again it seemed to Edwards that the behavior of this group was so bad as to require a concentrated attack, and once again the youngsters were symbols for the sins of the whole community. This time, however, the results were not reformation and revival but a stalemate in the relationship between pastor and flock.

Edwards continued to preach sermons to the children and young people for moral reform, as well as exhortations to their parents, with apparently little positive result.[30] And then came, in the spring of 1744, the incident of the "bad books," now part of local folklore. According to testimony preserved in Edwards's notes, in early 1744 some girls reported that a group of boys had been reading a midwifery book, and about two dozen young people had been known to laugh and joke over the explicit descriptions and diagrams of female anatomy.[31] The book may have been filched from a local doctor or obtained from a peddler, although one witness heard it described as belonging to a man whose wife had just borne her first child. The reading and laughter were bad enough, but the boys' sin was compounded by their using the information to taunt the girls about what "nasty creatures" they were. The worst miscreant of all, Oliver

Warner, not only offered to show the book to other boys for "10 shillings money" (an apprentice to Deacon Hunt, a hatmaker, Oliver was already learning to strike a good bargain) but ran up to girls in the street and teased them, "when will the moon change, girls, come I'll look on you and see whether there be a blue circle round your eyes."[32]

Oliver Warner, at least, clearly crossed the line between private sin and public lewdness, and when pastor Edwards heard what was going on, he began an inquiry. According to the tradition originated by Samuel Hopkins's biography of Edwards in 1765, Edwards preached against the sin, got the church to appoint an investigative committee, and then angered some of the "considerable families in town" by reading a list of accused persons and witnesses without identifying which was which. Influential parents then determined "that their children should not be called to account in such a way for such things," wrote Hopkins, and "the town was suddenly all in a blaze." By this process, Hopkins concluded, Edwards "greatly lost his influence" with the young people and the town as a whole.[33]

Edwards's notes do not quite support Hopkins's narrative. First of all, the list that Edwards supposedly read from the pulpit contains, from top to bottom, the names of ten boys, then two doctors, then nine girls and one boy.[34] There should not have been any confusion, since all the boys named but none of the girls were accused. In addition to Deacon Pomeroy's son, only one boy was from a "leading family," and his uncle sat with the Deacon on the investigating committee. Whatever the parents' reaction, that committee met at least once; Edwards's notes show that Colonel Stoddard and at least three other leading citizens (the Deacon, a Captain, and a Lieutenant) took formal testimony from the witnesses and examined the suspects. While they deliberated, the young men accused of lewdness waited in an anteroom and compounded their offenses by speaking disrespectfully to and of the committee, playing leapfrog, getting a ladder to peek at the girls waiting upstairs, and finally leaving the parsonage entirely to go to Joseph Lyman's tavern to drink "flip." Ultimately, at least three young men were convicted of serious crimes: cousins Simeon and Timothy Root confessed to "contemptuous behavior toward the authority of this church," and Oliver Warner was charged with "public lewdness."[35]

Edwards's success in pushing the case to such an end not only casts doubt on Hopkins's tale of the obstructiveness of influential citizens, but it may also shed some light on the underlying problem between Edwards and the community. As he had done in 1734–35, Edwards was dealing with a clear failure of family government; and so flagrant was the lack of parental discipline that he overcame scruples about whether the offenses were public or private by asking himself, "Shall the master of a ship not enquire when he hears the ship be running on the rocks?"[36] His analogy was inappropriate, however—he was not the captain of that crew of young men, nor, would it seem, was anyone else. Their parents were absent from the proceedings, never mentioned after the vote to have an inquiry. The only witnesses to the reading of bad books or the lascivious talk on the street were other young people—where were their elders? In spite of their childish behavior, the offenders were not children: Warner was twenty-one, the Root cousins were each twenty-six, and the group of accused males was of an average age of twenty-four![37] These were young adults who seemed to do as they pleased without much adult supervision.

Edwards gathered these young people together away from their families, in his parsonage, as he had done with his converts a decade before; but this time his tactics backfired. Instead of a tractable group of disciples flattered by the attention, eager to maintain their special status, Edwards's inquiry produced a rowdy group of "adolescents" sharing a self-conscious "us-versus-them" camaraderie. Timothy Root was quoted by two witnesses as swearing that he would not "worship a wig" and that he didn't "care a turd" or "care a fart" for the gentlemen of the committee, for they were "nothing but men, molded up of a little dirt." This hostility was directed as much at Colonel Stoddard and Captain Clapp as it was at pastor Edwards. The "boys" were ultimately convicted not of reading bad books but of *lèse majesté*. By implication, the sins they committed at home, and the parental supervision that should have been exercised there, were less important than ever. Edwards's mistake in this case was not in trying to punish the children of "considerable families," but in pointing out to the whole community that their young people were completely out of control.

Edwards's forcing of the issue of discipline had also provided an opportunity for the young men of Northampton to proclaim publicly their lack of respect for traditional authority: he had given them a spotlight in which to perform their ritualized act of rebellion. What were the chances that a young man who had been pushed into announcing that he "didn't care a turd" for the representatives of civil and ecclesiastical authority would ever be polite and deferential again to his own parents? The social authority of "gentlemen" over others, and the deference that was given to ministers because they were wiser than other men, were a fragile web—easily damaged by the first person who would dare point out that the emperor had no clothes.

Even more significantly, Edwards unintentionally revealed in 1744 that he had lost the allegiance of the constituents who had always been most important to him. All but three of the accused young men were church members; they were the product of Edwards's 1735 and 1742 revivals, and their current behavior showed how bankrupt were his hopes for a permanent reformation of the community through grace.[38] With a bitter irony, Edwards's very attention to these young men in an earlier decade had given them the importance they now took for granted. As one acute analyst of adolescence in early America has pointed out, "only young people, it seemed [during the revivals], had the ability to save their communities from corruption." They could, therefore, assert their independence by being bad.[39]

Piety had become ineffective as a force for social control in Northampton by 1744, and the Gospel as taught by Jonathan Edwards no longer had much appeal to these young people. If Edwards's preaching had ever implied any promise of worldly betterment, or escape from social problems, that promise had not been fulfilled. For the young men who scorned the authoritarianism of ministers and squires, life was full of uncertainties that overused rhetoric could not make easier. The culprits of 1744 were acting like boys, and they were in a kind of limbo of protracted adolescence between the security of being a child and the satisfactions of being an adult. They were not married and they owned no property, but most of them were on the verge of making those critical choices of mate, occupation, and residence that would determine the rest of their lives. The lack of parental supervision revealed in their "crimes" may indicate strained relations with their families. It is not possible to confirm Hopkins's account of parental disapproval of Edwards's attempt to discipline these "children," but such protectiveness would be plausible in a community of smaller families and family pews and would not be incompatible with greater dependence and anti-authoritarian feelings among the young people. The very difficulties of transferring traditional customs to the rising generation may have produced both intensity of concern in the parents and resistance in the young people.[40] The youngsters had turned once from their parents to the minister as a friend and guide, but when his message failed them, they in turn failed him. Edwards was able to get three confessions of wrongdoing, but his harsh authoritarianism forfeited the last vestige of trust and reliance between him and the "boys" he had converted. It was no wonder that he wrote treatises about how untrustworthy were the ephemeral manifestations of pious zeal. In 1746 he gave a quarterly lecture to the young people with the text, "I have nourished and brought up children and they have rebelled against me."[41]

If the Hopkins story about an aborted campaign of discipline has any truth in it at all, it is surprising that after the bad-books episode Edwards grew even bolder in his attacks on the kind of sin that laymen wanted to handle privately. Preaching against "lasciviousness" in August 1746, Edwards wanted particularly to observe that the "infection" was spreading among the church, and that "officers" of the church were not doing their duty by pretending to deal privately with such offenses. As in 1744, Edwards seemed to be justifying a minister's right to deal publicly with private activities that were clearly sinful.[42] Was it desperation to assert his own authority that made him create another case of discipline? Like the earlier incident, this second episode is not recorded officially; only private records survive.[43] It started in 1747, when unmarried Martha Root claimed that her illegitimate child (the survivor of a set of twins) had been sired by a dashing young military officer. The alleged father was wealthy Lieutenant Elisha Hawley, a grandson of Solomon Stoddard and the younger son of the Joseph Hawley who had cut his throat in religious despair in 1735. By mid-1748 the Hawley and Root families had settled the matter privately: Martha received a large sum of money and in return gave up all future claim to Elisha's support for herself or the child. But soon thereafter Jonathan Edwards interfered. In December 1748 Elisha Hawley, on duty at Fort Massachusetts in the Berkshires, received a letter from his brother, Joseph Hawley III, who was just beginning to practice law in Northampton. This letter contained the news that the church (*i.e.*, Edwards) was trying to force Elisha to marry Martha but probably would not succeed because Scriptural precedent depended on her proving "absolute virginity" and enticement by Hawley—and because she and her parents did not want the marriage anyway! An undated fragment of notes in Edwards's hand reveals that *his* reading of Scripture taught that a payment of money in lieu of marriage did not end the moral obligation. The main concern, Edwards wrote, was not just repairing the "outward injury" but also preserving "the order, decency and health of human society in general." He was prepared to claim, in essence, that civilization itself depended on Elisha Hawley's being forced to marry Martha Root, even against her will.

In preparation for a church hearing, Edwards made further notes in which he outlined the legal issues: each principal would have to prove the other was lascivious and had used force. Elisha could only defend himself, therefore, by proving that *he* had been seduced. Despite the inexplicable lack of church records about this case, we must assume that the hearing found Hawley guilty, for the next document surviving is the record of a ministerial council called in June 1749 "to hear a matter of grievance between ye Church and Lt. Elisha Hawley." Edwards hoped for support from his professional brethren, but he was disappointed. The ministers of Hampshire voted that it was not Elisha's duty to marry Martha, and they remanded the decision to his own conscience. They also advised that he be received back into the church if he confessed to fornication. No record exists of such a confession, and the only inclusion of Hawley in church records is his original but undated admission. He did not marry the mother of his bastard. His conscience, supported by his brother Joseph's skills as a lawyer, was clearly in conflict with the opinion of the pastor who had tutored and converted both Hawley boys.[44] From Edwards's perspective the two were traitors. They had been disciples of a sort, and they were his own cousins; but they were not ashamed to display just how limited, by the late

1740s, was the pastor's authority. If Edwards could not even count on the morality and the deference of his own converts, there was little hope that he would ever regain spiritual control of the whole community.

The problems of disciplining the young people pushed Edwards by the summer of 1748 into a clear and explicit statement about the failure of the Northampton church as an agency of social control. An unpublished sermon on Deuteronomy 1:13–18, the manuscript labeled June 1748, elaborated on the doctrine: " 'Tis the mind of God that not a mixed multitude but only select persons of distinguished ability and integrity are fit for the business of judging causes." There followed a deliberate attack on the definition of "church" that had been established in Northampton since Stoddard's day. "If Solomon hardly thought himself wise enough," Edwards wrote, "what shall we think of any servant or any youth of 14 or 16 years old in these days that happens to be a member of a church" who sees himself as fit to judge others? Citing both youth and more widespread ignorance among church members, Edwards kept repeating that the church had failed to control sinfulness, that its present method of judging cases (probably both applicants for membership and disciplinary cases) had been the source of "wounds . . . contentions . . . quarreling with their minister, quarreling one with another." In his manuscript, Edwards repeated the charge about "quarreling with your minister" a number of times but crossed many of them out. He closed by asking the church to choose "a number of wise men of understanding" to "assist their pastor," to be "agents for the people"—but not to be judges endowed with any special holy authority. Christ's officers in the church were only the minister and the lay elders, and Edwards was "far from supposing there ought to be such lay elders as used formerly to be in such independent churches." That left the minister with the sole *official* authority, and yet he condescended to outline the proper method of church governance as being by the "concurrence" of both minister and the agents of the people. He closed with a warning that no mistake be made about the role of the people in the church: in answering an objection that it is the "natural right of human nature" for men to be able to admit other men to their assemblies, Edwards answered that churches are not founded on human nature but on the Covenant of Grace.[45]

The Northampton church records show that in the following month the church voted to elect fifteen men to assist the pastor, much in the manner he had outlined in his sermon on Deuteronomy. Fifteen leading citizens were chosen to serve a term of one year. The next record of church action, and the last in the church book during Edwards's tenure, was a vote of August 10, 1749, *not* choosing replacements for the year-old committee or renewing their mandate or mentioning them at all, but insisting that no "contribution" (financial?) should be made by the church without their consent as manifested by the raising of hands. (Was Edwards trying to get his committee of assistants to raise his salary?) It was also voted that any "public fame of scandal in the church" might be brought to the church by the pastor for their deliberation, even if there was no complaint.[46] So far, the church seemed to be giving in to Edwards in his demands for stricter church government. Perhaps the parents of Northampton youth were as disgusted as was their pastor by the perceived increase in immorality.

But Edwards's demands for increased power, or demands for leading citizens in the church to help him exercise the power he felt had been given him by Christ with his pastoral office, were expressions of defensiveness. Whenever he won a small battle, he seemed to be more in danger of losing the war. The confessions of the Root "boys" and Oliver Warner, the harassment of Elisha Hawley, the steady campaign to identify sins of sexuality and contentiousness—none of this was achieving the kind of reformation in Northampton that Edwards demanded. He was growing desperate, and the challenges to his authority kept mounting.

Edwards's response to these challenges came from a complicated interweaving of anxieties about his professional standing. The second round of revivals in Northampton had renewed his professional insecurity by allowing his own earlier successes of 1734–35 to be at least equalled and perhaps surpassed by the evangelism of a young itinerant. Although Northampton itself was not touched by schism in the wake of the revivals, the many contentions and separations in the Connecticut Valley churches had taught Edwards the desirability of keeping a firm hand on his congregation.[47] And as he tried to discipline his own congregation, he probably had almost constantly in mind the turmoil that wracked the other church that he knew well, his father's church in East Windsor.

Once again, Timothy Edwards was battling his congregation for the prerogatives of Christ's minister; and it was just before Jonathan Edwards began his long round of struggle with his own flock that his father's battles had come to a climax and to defeat. In the mid-1720s Timothy Edwards had sided with his wealthy brother-in-law, who tried (in vain) to have his daughter's marriage to an unsuitable man annulled; when the young woman deserted her husband a decade later because he could not support her, her uncle Edwards tried (again in vain) to shield her from church censure.[48] In the late 1730s, Timothy Edwards also took an active role in another parentally disapproved marriage by denying baptism to the child of the couple unless the young father, Joseph Diggens, would confess that he had committed "scandalous sin" by marrying his wife against her father's will.[49] Diggens refused, all but two church members sided with him, and the battle was joined. Timothy Edwards demanded an absolute veto in church discipline and church admissions. He was then formally charged with maladministration by Diggens. In consequence, Edwards suspended the Lord's Supper in his church for almost three years. The real problem was, of course, the imprecision of ministerial authority in the Congregational system. Even after three ministerial councils considered the question, the stalemate continued until Diggens finally gave up. The best primary source on the whole affair ends in 1741 with the confrontation still going on, but Edwards clearly never won the powers he claimed. East Windsor's historian did find some evidence that superficial peace returned with the Great Awakening.

Timothy and Jonathan Edwards were clearly preoccupied with the same issues—young people and their sexual sins, the failure of parents to govern their children, and the need for the pastor to have a decisive vote in matters of church discipline as the ultimate control on community behavior—and their pastoral stance was similar even though Jonathan was never forced to the extreme positions that his father took so eagerly. If Jonathan was ever tempted to accept the worldliness and sin of his own congregation, his father provided an example of a minister who fought valiantly for right principles.

From the experience of the two Edwardses, it appears that revivals were the best opportunity to harmonize the demands of a pastor with the needs of his congregation. It was perhaps the emotional satisfactions offered by publicly praised conversions that made moral obedience easier in times of awakening, and minister and flock engaged in a common endeavor that obscured the underlying problems between them. Unfortunately, revivals were not events that could be created at will. But ministers who had seen the multifaceted betterment of their communities brought by an awakening were bound to strive to re-create that experience.

Jonathan Edwards was such a pastor. The revival of 1735 grew more successful in his mind as he grew older, and the 1742 awakening had had many positive elements mixed in with the newly apparent dangers. The revivals, however, would not come again to Northampton. The now familiar doctrines of justification by faith alone no longer packed an emotional punch. By the late 1740s, Edwards seemed to be left without means to turn his people's attention toward God again. He had tried inspiring them to piety, and he had tried bald discipline; both had failed. But now, just as he seemed to be losing the war against sin and losing the allegiance of his young people, Edwards was able to draw on his newly refined understanding of true holiness to buttress his waning authority in the church. The logic of his theology dictated that if conversion *were* real, sensible, and demonstrable—and he had proved that it was, in *Religious Affections* and other works—then there was no need to maintain Solomon Stoddard's humble refusal to draw lines between sheep and goats because it was too hard to be accurate. His pastoral logic suggested that if church privileges were not open to all men on demand, if full membership and especially the right to have one's children baptized were reserved for those who had been converted and would testify to being so, these privileges would be more eagerly sought. Restricted sacraments had the beautiful advantage of combining an emphasis on genuine piety with an effective tool of moral discipline.

In February 1749 Jonathan Edwards officially announced to the church what had been rumored for some time—that he had decided that his long continuance of Stoddard's open communion was wrong. He could not in good conscience admit any more members to the church who would not make a profession of the essentials of Christian faith, essentials which included evidence of an experiential work of grace as well as sound doctrinal knowledge. Sixteen months later the Northampton congregation would formally and completely reject Jonathan Edwards—his doctrine, his discipline, and his twenty-three years of struggle to make them see the light.

CHAPTER EIGHT

Confrontation

ACCORDING TO THE journal that Jonathan Edwards kept during the communion controversy with his church, he had had difficulties for some years before 1749 in accepting the lax method of admission to full communion in the Northampton church.[1] When he wrote his treatise on the subject, *An Humble Inquiry into the Rules of the Word of God Concerning the Qualifications Requisite to a Complete Standing and Full Communion in the Visible Christian Church,* he confessed that it pained him to go against the principles and practice of his revered grandfather, Solomon Stoddard.

I have formerly been of his opinion, which I imbibed from his books, even from my childhood, and have in my proceedings conformed to his practice . . . deference to the authority of so venerable a man, the seeming strength of some of his arguments, together with the success he had in his ministry, and his great reputation and influence, prevailed for a long time to bear down my scruples. . . . It is far from a pleasing circumstance of this publication, that it is against what my honored grandfather strenuously maintained, both from the pulpit and press. I can truly say, on account of this and some other considerations, it is what I engage in with the greatest reluctance, that ever I undertook any public service in my life.[2]

But Edwards had found that the open communion that had evolved from Stoddard's principles *had* to be an error, for it produced a church that seemed impervious to the truths of Gospel doctrine. Men and women who had been recognized as visible saints in

Northampton still wallowed in clandestine immorality and flagrant pride. The apparent conversions during the revivals of 1734–35 and 1741–42 were proving to be untrustworthy. When Edwards wrote his *Faithful Narrative* in 1735, he had attributed good order and true piety to the inhabitants of Northampton under his grandfather's dominion; he never publicly revised that opinion of the past, but Stoddard's church practices were obviously inappropriate for the people with whom Edwards had to deal in the late 1740s.

Edwards therefore resolved about 1744 not to admit any applicant to full membership in the church unless that person would make a profession of true Godliness by reporting an experience of Saving Grace as well as sound doctrinal knowledge. He told "some" people of his change of heart and strongly hinted at his new principles in the *Religious Affections,* but public controversy was avoided because no new applicants for membership appeared until December 1748.[3] When a man (whose name is unknown) sought admission that winter, he was given a number of sample professions to consider and was informed that Mr. Edwards would not quibble over specific words.[4] Able in conscience to profess a true faith, the man nevertheless declined to do so because it was not necessary by the rules of admission in the Northampton church. Once this gauntlet had been thrown down, Edwards had no choice but to make a formal announcement to the church that he had altered his principles regarding qualifications for the sacraments. In February 1749 he asked permission to explain his ideas from the pulpit—not because the church had a right to refuse, but because he wanted to forestall dissension. His request was denied. He then began to prepare a treatise, the *Humble Inquiry,* which was finished that spring but did not appear in print until August 1749.

Denying any interest in problematic issues such as the degree of membership of baptized infants or the precise definition of conversion, Edwards pretended that such matters were peripheral and attempted only to redefine the visible sainthood that was the criterion for church membership in New England. He assumed, as almost all Christians did, that such a person would have to be an adult and not a flagrant sinner. The real question could be phrased in two ways: Was "visibility" something different from what was *genuine;* or, could a person rightfully profess a faith that he did not hold through the experience of conversion? Edwards answered from Scripture that there were not two kinds of saints, just converted persons and sinners liable to damnation; visibility was only the temporal manifestation of the condition of being saved. Furthermore, a man could not profess a faith that was not living in his heart, for the essence of Christianity was piety and not just obedience to the Law. Rejecting entirely the Stoddardeanism he had publicly espoused for two decades, Edwards wrote that the sacraments were seals of the covenant made between God and man at the moment of conversion.

Edwards took great pains to point out the inconsistencies of Stoddard's claim that the Lord's Supper was a converting ordinance: if unconverted men can be admitted with hopes of being then converted, Edwards argued, why strive at all to distinguish those who have had grace at work in their hearts? This whole argument was really an attack on a straw man: Stoddard would have answered that pious men could not resist searching for grace in themselves, and only those who have some hope of salvation (which is all mortal man, not reading God's mind, can have) should come to the Lord's Supper. Edwards was taking essentially the Stoddardean position when he described reliable signs of grace in the *Religious Affections* but also warned men not to presume to judge each other's hearts. Although he chose to use the vocabulary of theological debate, the ground on which Edwards really fought Stoddard was the practical side of pastoral responsibilities. Stoddard had been willing to let all well-behaved men come to the Table, if they chose to do so, and thereby surrender the disciplinary tool of identifying more particularly the truly "gracious"; he had found more informal means of enforcing his will, and God's moral law, on the town of Northampton. But Jonathan Edwards had tried for twenty years to make Stoddard's methods work for him, and he had failed. He could marshal endless Scriptural evidence for the necessity to distinguish between spiritual sheep and goats in this world. Only those who had been converted in heart, he wrote, could profess a true faith. Only those who so professed should be admitted to full church membership, which included the privileges of the Lord's Supper and baptism for their children.

Edwards was throwing out the Half-Way Covenant, used in almost all the churches of New England; under this system, children of unconverted adults could be baptized. Many churches in western Massachusetts and Connecticut were Stoddardean and even more generous: persons baptized even in their adult years (because their parents had neglected their responsibilities) could then have their offspring baptized and could also attend the Lord's Supper and vote in all church affairs.[5] In the *Humble Inquiry* Edwards spent most of his words on the general question of defining proper church members, and only in passing, in answer to a hypothetical objection that the larger part of the world would then be ignored by the church, did he speak about the consequences of his new definition of visible sainthood. But he was well aware that the clause about baptism was the part of his new system that would be most objectionable. He admitted to a sympathetic colleague: "I am not sure but that my people, in length of time, and with great difficulty, might be brought to yield the point as to the qualifications for the Lord's Supper (tho' that is very uncertain); but with respect to the other sacraments there is scarce any hope of it. And this will be very likely to overthrow me, not only with regard to my usefulness in the work of the ministry here, but everywhere. . . ."[6] Nevertheless, he would not give in on any part of his new scheme.

The *Humble Inquiry* was very explicit about the pragmatic uses of a restriction on church membership.[7] Three main benefits would ensue. Officially recognized saints would serve as models for the unconverted; Edwards had often observed community jealousy at work, and well-publicized conversions were the chief means to convert others. Moreover, a thorough examination of the saint's conversion would inhibit the boasting in private conversation that had grown common under the open admission system; Edwards's late experience had shown this self-selection to be of great mischief in fostering spiritual pride and making the communicant unresponsive to "skilful guides" who could keep him from mistaking mere imagination for true experience of grace. (But had Edwards not been adamant in *Religious Affections* that no man could see into another's heart?) The third and most important benefit would be that adults would have to be converted in order to have their children baptized. The parental responsibility of "instructing, praying for, and governing their children, and setting them good examples" could no longer be ignored; and people could no longer be complacent about their own state without the risk of sending their small children straight to hell if they died.

Edwards was gambling on his understanding of two aspects of community psychology. He was assuming that church membership could safely be made a component of secular status, and that his people would be jealous of those who were certified saints and therefore would strive to join the select group. He turned out to be wrong: in a community where status distinctions were becoming stronger all the time but were resolving themselves into a pattern of wealth and occupations that was at least clear and understandable, the introduction of a new element of status that was independent of all the others would intolerably and unnecessarily complicate the process of mutual ranking. Edwards was also assuming that parents so loved their children that they would have conversion experiences in order to have their offspring included in the covenant under the seals. But what if they loved them so much, and worried about them so much, that the introduction of another responsibility in which parents might fail their young people was too unpleasant to tolerate? What would happen to family government if parents were not able to have their children baptized? How would the family feel about infants who died, or how would children feel about parents who had not provided all possible means of grace for them? What would happen if children did have conversion experiences, if something like the revival of 1735 came again to Northampton; what kind of communion would a regenerate child have with heathen parents? Could the already complicated relationships between parents and children take any more strain?

What Edwards was essentially trying to do, it would seem, was to start another revival. In the early 1730s he had preached doctrines of the narrowness of the gate to heaven that were far harsher than anything his congregation had ever heard. The more he seemed to condemn his people to perdition, while still encouraging them to strive against the odds, the greater grew his list of converts. By now, of course, he knew that most of those conversions had not been genuine. But if he could arouse the community to the same concern for piety again, with his greater experience with both revivals and converts, he could channel the energy of their emotions into true graciousness. Even though he seemed to be losing his former disciples, the young people of 1734–35, to the Devil, perhaps he could draw them back by arousing their concern for the children they had brought into the world. Exclusive sacraments would help to bind their piety to morality, for the communicant would be so conspicuous that he would have to maintain visible sainthood.

All the parts of this new plan of church organization fit together so smoothly in theory—but how would the new system work in practice? Would all church members be reexamined, and those who didn't pass the test be thrown out? More likely, any new applicants for membership would be carefully screened: but would they not thereby become a specially certified class, higher in spiritual/social status than their elders who had joined the church under the lax rules? What would restrain the pride of men who would be given the responsibility to judge each other? And how could a church which was the only church in a large community become an exclusivist, "come-outer" preserve of the elect?

What was missing in Edwards's proposals, most importantly, was an answer to the obvious and most critical question—who would judge? The major obstacle to community acceptance of the new rules was the strong suspicion that Mr. Edwards himself was going to be the judge of their spiritual experiences. He wrote only about *self-*judgment, but then what was the basis for his claims of differing from Stoddard? When a prospective church member made his profession, who would point out brazen hypocrisy?

Unfortunately, the statements made by the town in answer to Edwards's proposals and in the town's charges against him before the two advisory councils have not survived, so it is impossible to produce any explicit testimony of popular aversion to this ambiguity in Edwards's plan.[8] But both of the ministers whom the town asked to prepare a theological answer to Edwards indicated that the strongest objection to Edwards's scheme was the implication that a person could make an absolutely certain judgment about another's spiritual condition and that the chief judge would be the minister. The official answer to Edwards's *Humble Inquiry* was published in 1751 by the Reverend Solomon Williams of Lebanon, Connecticut, son of the late Reverend William Williams of Hatfield and member of the Williams clan that was conspicuous in ministerial politics in the Connecticut Valley. Williams wrote that he assumed from Edwards's argument that the Northampton pastor would insist on judging men's experiences in order to decide on admission, and Williams meant "experiences" in the sense of the emotions and processes of the conversion moment itself, as the word had come to be used with great significance during the Awakening.[9] The Reverend Peter Clark of Salem Village, Massachusetts, the other minister to whom the town sent a messenger pleading for an anti-Edwards treatise, had a similar impression. Actually, Clark had not read Edwards's book when he wrote to Deacon Ebenezer Pomeroy, the manager of the anti-Edwards crusade in Northampton, that Edwards's plan for exclusive sacraments depended on the possibility of his being a final judge of sainthood—and Clark knew that such a clerical prerogative would not be allowed in most Congregational churches.[10] And so it is very clear that the hearsay testimony about Edwards's plan, undoubtedly spread by Northampton residents to their friends and allies, was that Mr. Edwards was going to judge souls—exactly the role that Solomon Stoddard had given up so dramatically, and one which few ministers would dare to assume.

Both Williams and Clark, however, were technically wrong. In the *Humble Inquiry* and in his letters to his opponents, Edwards explicitly denied any special skill in judging hearts. He would rely, he said, on the person's own profession of faith as the criterion for membership.[11] He was, of course, begging the fundamental question of distinguishing sincerity from hypocrisy. In *Misrepresentations Corrected,* his public answer to Williams, Edwards insisted he would not demand certainty in judging a visible saint and that the experience he intended to examine was simply the quality of living faith in an applicant—not just intellectual understanding of classic doctrine.[12] Edwards wrote to Peter Clark and disclaimed any unusual powers of judging souls and any ambition to have a totally pure church. In essence, he was forced to defend himself against charges of being a Separatist.[13]

The fact that Edwards's stance was not as authoritarian as others believed was much less important than the town's readiness to believe the worst. The community which once had followed Edwards in two revivals had come to doubt his motives completely. According to Edwards, few people even read his book when it appeared in August 1749. Williams's rebuttal was not fuel for local hostility to

Edwards, since it did not appear until mid-1751. The anger against Edwards had little to do with fine points of theology. It was based on hearsay and on the *expectation* that, whatever he wrote or preached, he would take an unacceptably authoritarian stance in the church. And it is possible that their suspicions were actually based on firmer ground than their memory of Edwards's assertiveness about salary and discipline in the previous five years.

In his statement before the ministerial council that met in December 1749 to advise the town what to do, Edwards admitted that he wanted a veto over church membership—a claim he did not mention in any other known statement of his plan or principles and that he had actually consistently denied. In this demand Edwards perfectly illustrated the reasons why he was not trusted—having announced his principles in the *Religious Affections,* as he thought, he merely worked out the administrative details in a cavalier fashion as he went along. He discussed restrictions on baptism and ministerial vetoes as though they were easily assumed corollaries of his revival doctrines. But to his church they were revolutionary, unnecessary, and completely unacceptable. To the council of 1749 Edwards announced that it was not he but the church itself that had defected from the Stoddardean principles to which they pretended to cling so zealously. As he recorded his statement in his journal, it read in part:

> *I had as much reason given me by the church in my settlement, to depend upon it, that they would allow me the same power in church government, which I yielded to Mr. Stoddard; as they had to depend on it, that I would allow them the same open door to the Lord's Table.* The church allowed Mr. Stoddard a negative; *and never, so far as I have heard of, disputed it, at least never in the then existing generation. Now they greatly find fault with me for claiming it, and have departed to the length of Brownism.* [14]

If Stoddard had had a veto—and that is entirely believable, although Edwards's is the only direct testimony to the fact—it was surely moral behavior that he would have claimed to judge. Jonathan Edwards, Northampton believed, would be a judge of hearts. And that is why there was no possibility of reconciliation once Edwards had announced his change of mind about the sacraments.

In the six months that followed Edwards's announcement, "several persons" asked to be admitted to the church and even agreed to make a profession, but they were forbidden to do so by the church committee. And until the council of neighboring ministers recommended otherwise in December 1749, Edwards was even denied the right to lecture on the subject of contention. The pastor and his church argued every step of the way—about his preaching, about whether to call a council to advise if he should preach, about who should be members of that council, about the precinct's assuming management of the affair (the precinct was the civil body of all voters, and Edwards insisted that this was a *church* matter, although the church/town distinction had all but lost its meaning with Northampton's hitherto open communion), and about the proper time to invite a council to decide the final outcome of the controversy. A vocal group within the town opposed calling even the preliminary council, for fear it would recommend admitting the voluntary professors or that it would require that Edwards be given a fair hearing. One of the subsidiary issues became whether the church would be subject to a council. The Northampton church had been one of the founders of the advisory Hampshire Association, and the Stoddard it revered had been an outright Presbyterian in ecclesiology, but in these circumstances (and worrying that other clergymen might back Edwards), the church fought to defend Congregational principles.[15]

Edwards sought to maintain a logical position even on these procedural questions, and in many letters to various committees he pointed out in great detail the inconsistencies of his opponents.[16] Logic was, after all, his strong point. But regardless of logic or properly deferential methods, the town was determined to get rid of Edwards, and by late 1749 they were charging him with causing too much trouble and delay. Everyone involved knew he would have to leave. In April of 1749 he had offered to resign if the church so wished, but only after they had read his forthcoming book and if a council mutually chosen by the parties should so advise and should outline proper steps.[17] The next month, Edwards confessed to a friend his despair over achieving a favorable settlement: "I know not but this affair will issue in a separation between me and my people."[18] In December he told the council that he had not intended to cause a great furor in the town, but that he had simply followed his conscience and been candid with his flock—"with the fullest expectation of being driven from my ministerial office, and stripped of a maintenance for my numerous family."[19] Whether or not Sarah was still dreaming of being turned out into the snow to freeze, her husband was determined not to be dismissed by the town like some sort of lackey. He would go, if he must, with due ceremony. And he still had his most potent weapon, oratory.

But when Jonathan Edwards finally preached a series of lectures about his principles in February and March 1750, very few of his own congregation even attended. Among those who did attend were a large number of strangers, including on one occasion the justices of the county court then sitting at Northampton.[20] One of the March sermons expounded the doctrine that a minister who obeys his own conscience but differs from his church is not breaking his bond with them but rather is fulfilling his responsibility to show them the light.[21] This was not a persuasive argument in Northampton. The previous November a majority of the church members had voted their refusal to abide by Edwards's new doctrines, and there is a tradition that only nineteen persons voted for the minister, out of more than six hundred church members.[22]

Edwards was convinced that almost all the Valley ministers would side against him on the substance of the controversy; and he later wrote that because the town was surrounded by Stoddardean churches the narrow-visioned Northamptonites assumed that all the world was against their pastor.[23] During the spring of 1750 the major controversy was whether Edwards would be allowed to get any representatives from outside Hampshire County for the decisive council. The town finally agreed that two out of a total of ten churches represented could be outsiders. A minister and a layman would sit for each church invited. When the final council was convened on June 19, 1750, Edwards's side was one short, because the church at Cold Spring had refused to send representatives, but their pastor, Edward Billings, came to Northampton on his own and took a seat on the council. The sides had been carefully chosen: the votes were ten to nine against Edwards.[24]

The council found that the views of Edwards and his church were diametrically opposed, since Edwards insisted on a "profession of sanctifying grace" for full communion and the church wanted only "competency of knowledge" and a "blameless life." It also decided that a separation between pastor and flock was necessary, and that it should be implemented without delay. But at the same time the council took care to exonerate Edwards personally: stories about his insincerity were judged "false and groundless," he was truly following his conscience, and he was "eminently qualified" to lead a church that shared his sentiments. A minority of the council (four ministers and three laymen) published a protest against the majority decision in which they asserted that Edwards's new principles were the *correct* ones (an issue which had not been debated but of course determined each delegate's vote), that in any case the differences between him and his church were insufficient grounds for a separation, and that the anti-Edwards forces had not allowed themselves to be reasoned with about the fundamental issue.[25]

But Edwards's firing was inevitable. His dismissal from office took place officially on June 22, 1750. This was essentially the end of Jonathan Edwards's pastoral career. He stayed on in Northampton for almost a year and was even hired from week to week as a preacher until November; a church that had fired its pastor over an issue of conscience was not attractive to young candidates for the ministry.[26] Edwards also owned some property in the town which could not be sold quickly. In the midst of his professional tragedy, two of his daughters were married, and their "setting-out" was a large drain on his financial resources. He had to find another job immediately. Of the various offers he received, the best was the position of missionary to the Indian settlement and small white congregation at Stockbridge, in the Berkshires.[27] His adherents had made valiant efforts to keep him in Northampton by organizing another church, but that group was very small and finally gave in to the advice of a council which recommended that Edwards take the position in Stockbridge. The bitterness between Edwards's friends and the majority of the church and town lasted at least two years, during which time the Edwards faction refused to participate in the Lord's Supper with the others. Edwards was kept well informed of the proceedings by his friends, and he may have tried for a time to promote a new church for himself; but he was spared the need to face the disruption he had caused in the community.[28] It took them three years to find a new minister who would settle, and it is significant that the man they chose, John Hooker, was moderate, even colorless, in theology but widely admired as easygoing and affable.[29]

The move to Stockbridge, completed by the autumn of 1751, brought Edwards material hardship, but it also gave him the luxury of time to think and write without serious pastoral distractions.[30] During the next seven years he wrote the great volumes of anti-Arminian theology for which he has become famous. Having lost his twenty-three-year battle against sin and apathy in ordinary human beings, Edwards turned his attention to the fundamental issues underlying the clerical and intellectual opposition he had encountered. From the study at Stockbridge came forth masterful expositions of the Calvinist point of view on the freedom of the will, original sin, the end for which God created the world, and the nature of true virtue. His last project, left unfinished at his death, was the reworking of some late-1730s sermons into a millennialist statement published posthumously as *A History of the Work of Redemption.*[31] In the last years of his life, Edwards was able to see more clearly than ever that the world as he had experienced it in both joy and pain was running along in a perfectly controlled divine design.

How neatly the doctrines could be arrayed in treatises when the practical implications for ordinary laymen did not have to be considered! The Calvinist emphasis on the free quality of God's grace, and the unfree quality of man, could be described so unambiguously when there was no need to preach that men must strive to "take heaven by force" as the best alternative to letting them languish in complacency. In Stockbridge Edwards's pastoral responsibilities, as reflected in the sermon manuscripts, consisted mainly of preaching against the drunkenness and theft to which his Indian congregation seemed prone.[32] He now resumed the intellectual adventures of his youth and became a philosopher. In 1757 he was invited to become president of the College of New Jersey, later renamed Princeton, which had been founded and sustained by the evangelical party within the factionalized Presbyterian Church in the Middle Colonies. Reluctant to give up the freedom from political turmoil for which he had paid such a high price, and even reluctant to give up the work on his treatises that now seemed to be progressing so well, Edwards nevertheless accepted the honor—and then died of a small-

pox inoculation just as he was about to take on these new pastoral
duties in 1758.

Jonathan Edwards's career ended in classic tragedy, and historians
tend to find sufficient justification for his course of action in the logic
of his ideas. By implication, the congregation at Northampton which
dismissed him was too stupid to understand the treasure in their
midst. Or at least, according to Edwards's major biographers, they
were under the influence of forces stronger than their own piety and
common sense. There have been two major interpretations of the
firing, and both discover "villains" in the anti-Edwards crusade. The
older and more popular view, started by Edwards's great-grandson
and major nineteenth-century biographer, Sereno Edwards Dwight,
and elaborated by Perry Miller in his important 1949 biography of
Edwards, attributes Edwards's fall to the personal and ideological
enmity of the Williams clan, descendants of the Reverend William
Williams of Hatfield, who occupied pulpits and government positions of influence throughout the Connecticut Valley. The other
interpretation, arising mainly from Ola Elizabeth Winslow's 1940
Edwards biography, blames Edwards's troubles on his opposition to
a rising tide of democracy in his parish and in the colonies as a whole.
The "evil Williamses" interpretation was a favorite of Edwards himself, it must be noted, although the evidence is at best contradictory.
The Winslow interpretation seems more plausible, but its stress on
the political dimension of the interaction between Edwards and his
enemies is both anachronistic and oversimplified.

Edwards was most inclined during the early Stockbridge years to
tell his correspondents that the Williams clan were the source of all
his problems, and Sereno Dwight elaborated on every reference that
Edwards made to their alleged machinations. Two facts are certain:
Elisha and Solomon Williams wrote the theological answer to Edwards's *Humble Inquiry,* and there was a Williams connection, by
blood and marriage, among the Hampshire ministers.[33] (But so also
was there a Stoddard connection, of which Edwards and the Williamses were both part.) The rest of the case for the Williamses'
villainy is derived from either Edwards's accusations or Dwight's
unsupported assertions. Edwards wrote in 1753 that the Williams
family had been prejudiced against him ever since the revival of

1734–35; Dwight embroidered this statement to a declaration (undocumented in Edwards's manuscripts) that Israel Williams, later called "monarch of Hampshire" but then only twenty-four years old, had ridden into Northampton and "forbidden" his cousin Edwards to preach on justification by faith alone.[34] This story may be true, but fences were soon mended; for it was at the "united request" of William Williams's sons that Edwards preached a laudatory funeral sermon for the pastor of Hatfield in 1741.[35] Edwards also wrote to friends in the 1750s that both Israel Williams and his brother-in-law Jonathan Ashley, pastor at Deerfield, had visited Northampton frequently between 1735 and 1750 and yet never showed the courtesy of calling on the Edwardses. When the communion conflict arose, Edwards later wrote, "this family deeply engaged themselves in this controversy on the side of my opposers, who were primarily upheld, directed, and animated by them." Israel Williams, he insisted, had been the chief family agent and was the behind-the-scenes leader of the anti-Edwards party in Northampton. (But another Williams, the Reverend Stephen of Longmeadow, invited Edwards to preach from his pulpit in October 1750.)[36] Not satisfied to have routed him from Northampton, the Williams clan seemed to Edwards to harass him at Stockbridge, although there he triumphed.

Such was Edwards's version, written mostly while he fought with some Williamses at Stockbridge for control of the Indian school, and as repeated and elaborated by Dwight. Perry Miller used this information in his biography of Edwards; stressing the Williams clan's ideological Arminianism, he asserted that the emotional vehemence behind the battle derived from a feud between Jonathan Edwards's mother and her sister Christian, second wife of William Williams of Hatfield and mother to Israel.[37] There is some evidence of a competition between Jonathan and his cousin Solomon Williams in their earlier years;[38] but beyond this the personal aspects of the feud cannot be documented, and contrary evidence is offered by Jonathan's being asked to preach the sermon at William Williams's funeral in 1741. It is true that many clerical members of the family were opposed to the Great Awakening in its late and peace-breaking stages; but Edwards himself had taken a position that was essentially against those same disturbances and on the same professional grounds. On the other hand, Elisha Williams had been Edwards's own tutor in the precepts of Calvinism, was a leader in the fight against quasi-Arminian Robert Breck in 1735, and was pro-revival in that same year. In his *True State of the Question,* Solomon Williams avowed undying adherence to the doctrines of Solomon Stoddard, who was as staunch a Calvinist as his grandson Edwards.[39] One could be, and most of Edwards's opponents were, Stoddardean in church practice and Calvinist in theology. It was Edwards who defied the family consensus.

A corollary to the assertion that the Williamses were the evil spirits behind the Northampton rebellion against Jonathan Edwards is the attribution to them of a controlling influence over the man who was clearly the intellectual leader of the opposition within Edwards's own church, Joseph Hawley III. Hawley, son of the man of the same name who had committed suicide in June of 1735, probably prepared for college under Edwards's direction, was graduated from Yale in 1742, studied law in Suffield, then returned to Northampton and became a Justice of the Peace in 1749. Although he was a full member of the church, he was not active in the anti-Edwards fight until late in 1749. (He had in 1748 engaged in a fight with Edwards over the duty of his brother Elisha to marry Martha Root.) From late 1749 through the final council in 1751, Hawley was the chief spokesman for the church, precinct, and town against the pastor, although older men who showed venom against Edwards personally took the lead within the precinct meetings.[40] Most biographers of Edwards regard Hawley as the tool of Israel Williams, but there is little evidence for that connection except their association ten years later in the county judiciary and military services.[41] Hawley confessed to Edwards in 1754 that he had assumed his role in the communion controversy out of "vanity and ambition," and he repeated these self-accusations in a public letter to pro-Edwards minister David Hall in 1760.[42] He mentioned no outside influence. Neither did he ever hint that he blamed Edwards for his father's suicide from religious depression. Hawley seems merely to have seized his chance to begin his illustrious career as a popular political leader by adding his educated voice to the general outcry.

Although he did not mention any particular ideological stance in his letters to Edwards and Hall, Hawley may have been an Arminian. Among his manuscripts there is an undated fragmentary confession of Arminianism, which he says began in 1744 while he lived at Cambridge and was sparked by the reading of an eloquent Arminian tract.[43] It is doubtful that his Northampton neighbors shared this ideology—although they were rightfully accused of being lax in practice and apathetic in piety, which is a condition quite independent from belief that man could earn his way into heaven by good works. If Arminianism had crept into Northampton, there would hardly have been revivals as a result of Edwards's doctrines in 1735 and 1741; and Edwards himself would certainly have attacked it head-on, as he did in 1734, instead of just accusing Solomon Williams of being a closet Arminian. In his *Humble Inquiry* Edwards made it very clear that his local enemy was apathy, not Arminianism, though in his Farewell Sermon and in a letter of July 1750 he did mention, among many sins of his congregation, a temptation to Arminianism among the younger people.[44]

The other theory about Edwards's firing, hinted at by Dwight and Miller but most openly espoused by Ola Elizabeth Winslow, presents Edwards as being hounded out of Northampton by the forces of democracy. In Winslow's words, "the church member of 1750 was a democrat, although as yet he did not know it; and a good many of the 'Boys of '76' were already born." Based on Edwards's association with the undoubted Tories Colonel John Stoddard and Timothy Dwight, and Hawley's eventual participation in the Patriot cause fifteen years later, Winslow makes a dramatic case for a "protest against an aristocratic minority. Jonathan Edwards had always had the wrong friends. . . . Besides he lived with too much elegance himself. . . ." And so, concludes Winslow, the town united against Edwards.[45] But that is just the point—the town *was* united against him.

Colonel John Stoddard had never been the subject of public dislike (except perhaps by young Timothy Root); indeed, he was regularly entrusted by the town with the management of their local and provincial public affairs. He won his position by deference, not by force. Timothy Dwight, Edwards's leading ally in 1750, was a similar professional in government, and it is possible that he was not universally beloved. But although Dwight was quite rich, other identifiable pro-Edwards men were much poorer. The anti-Edwards leaders, on the other hand, included three of the four richest men in town. They were not newcomers, potentially arrayed against old families.[46] They were neither significantly younger nor older than the pro-Edwards group. Although Northampton possessed in the 1750s some very rich men whose property was almost all in land, and some equally rich men whose estate was largely commercial, even this dichotomy does not permit us to distinguish between Edwards's supporters and attackers. It is quite easy to believe that wealthy commercial men would find Arminianism congenial and fear the introduction of Edwards's new policies, for any demand for holiness in all aspects of life was potentially a weapon in the hands of the exploited customers and the poorer neighbors of the pluto-crats, at least until the secular ethos of the social benefits of capitalism came to be clearly articulated later in the eighteenth century. But Jonathan Edwards never made any public statements indicating a mistrust of wealthy men—when preaching on the sin of theft, he was more inclined to condemn the stealing of apples from an orchard than the foreclosing of a mortgage on a widow and orphans—and his chief supporter, Timothy Dwight, was as much of a businessman and speculator as Israel Williams—so ideological/occupational cleavages are doubtful.[47] And by the 1770s, Williams proved to be as much of a Tory as the Dwights or Stoddards.[48] This was not even a church/town fight: all the men active in the quarrel on either side were already church members (and "half-way" distinctions had been ignored for generations), and a clear majority of the church voted against Edwards as early as November 1749. Edwards wrote in 1751 that only about twenty heads of families had spoken out against the town's proceedings, which might have been faulted for harshness even by someone opposed to Edwards.[49]

Northampton in 1750 was becoming divided politically on social and economic lines, but one point of unity was opposition to Jonathan Edwards. (A cynical historian might even suggest that if the town were becoming divided, the discovery of a common enemy was a useful coincidence.) Whatever the powers of Israel Williams or Joseph Hawley to influence their neighbors, neither man could have so undermined the position of a minister who still retained his power to reach the hearts of his congregation. When Northampton drew together against Edwards, they showed how much of a threat he was perceived to be to something fundamental to the community, something that transcended the surface differences of wealth and age among the people.

In a letter of 1751 to a Scottish friend, in which he attempted a full analysis of his professional disaster, Jonathan Edwards attested to the unity of the town and the lack of ideological character to his opposition. He identified no particular group within the town as leaders of the movement (although he was convinced that the Williams clan controlled the *ministers* who had opposed him), and he made no charges of Arminianism. The people, he wrote, had always been contentious—they had once even come to blows during a church dispute in Stoddard's time—and were a proud, sinfully proud people. Behind their current outburst of pride was Solomon Stoddard himself, and it was perhaps all his fault: so strong had been his personality that his spirit remained in the town for thirty years after his death. "Mr. Stoddard," wrote his grandson, "though an eminently holy man, was naturally of a dogmatical temper, and the people being brought up under him, were naturally led to imitate him." He had filled their heads with wrong notions, allowed his flock too much reliance on the method and timing of their conversions as grounds for assurance, and had permitted them to boast about their experiences. These were faults that Edwards "could never beat them out of." Stoddard was regarded even three decades after his death with a "vast veneration . . . almost as a sort of deity," and even the younger generation were determined "to esteem his sayings all as oracles."[50]

Ultimately, Jonathan Edwards was fighting the memory of Solomon Stoddard much more than he was fighting Arminianism or democracy in Northampton in 1750. Ultimately, he was fighting the town's reverence for Stoddard with his own—for Stoddard's way was the path he followed. He was much like Stoddard in ideas and temperament—such a staunch Calvinist, and so inclined to authoritarianism when disillusioned with the hypocrisy of his flock. He tried so hard to achieve the evangelistic and disciplinary success of his grandfather. He tried *too* hard—it was his image of Stoddard that kept him trying to use old-fashioned methods to deal with a community that was rapidly changing. Edwards's fundamental problem was that he was much more like Stoddard than the Northampton of 1750 was like the Northampton of 1700.

Northampton was hardly yet modern by the criteria of an economic or social historian, but it was well on its way toward commercial development and popular acceptance of an ideology of individualism. Although no one in 1750 would have welcomed or even believed the idea, the town and the colony of which it was representative were approaching the American Revolution—but that was still a generation away, and only two components of that movement had yet appeared. One was the growing socioeconomic inequalities that were beginning to be perceptible in a town such as Northampton. The other, and the one that Edwards was confronting directly by the late 1740s, was the secularization of morality. Solomon Stoddard had dealt with the sins of his Northampton by separating piety from morality in the institutional church. When the passage of time made that strategic compromise seem unworkable, Jonathan Edwards assumed that he could just take one step backward in ideology and reunite piety and morality.

What Edwards wanted, clearly, was a church with an intensity of voluntary commitment like the Separatists' but also with a community inclusiveness like the Presbyterians'—a "come-outer" spirit in an establishment institution. Edwards's church was still the only one in Northampton, and he wanted a permanent revival of pietism within that church. For whatever the reasons that always make surges of communal piety rather short-lived, Edwards's dream was impossible. There was no way to persuade the community to go back to the "city on a hill," to stake their souls on the approval of their neighbors when the community was so rapidly becoming the arena of honest differences and necessary competition.

It was the Awakening itself that had brought much of the changes in social behavior and attitude into the consciousness of the community. Although there is little evidence of real disagreements over the revivals in Northampton during the period 1734–42, there had been a great deal of discord in many communities not far away. Edwards's pro-revival but moderate stance had kept Northampton unified, but the controversy in 1749 was in some ways a postponed confrontation over the basic revival problem of the relation of a church of regenerate persons to the wider, unregenerate community. As various ministers appealed to wider audiences, through itinerancy or publication of their sermons, the audience began to see that there were many differences in doctrine, some subtle and some great, and that there might be a choice. Open discord among the ministers made it clear to laymen that there was no consensus on the definition of truth. And so they might choose. On the other hand, the evangelists had emphasized the *inner* reality of true piety, and its distinction from mere outward morality: the effect was to make spirituality private. During the revivals, piety also became so emotionally intense that it could not be maintained for long without being translated into some social form. And that form would not be the church, although Edwards could never imagine any alternative.

Jonathan Edwards wanted to renew the effectiveness of the church as a centralizing institution, as he thought it had been when "Pope" Stoddard appeared to rule Northampton. Clearly, he would have liked to see the establishment of a theocracy—that desire grew in part from his millennialism, or contributed to it, and informed his strange description, in the funeral sermon, of Colonel John Stoddard as a minister as well as a magistrate. When Stoddard's death left Edwards without his chief ally in the fight against sin, the man whose authority had derived from socioeconomic status and governmental power as well as quasi-ministerial moral supremacy, the church seemed to be left alone as the potential agency of moral authority. Edwards of course wanted to be the Patriarch, but the institutionalized power at which he grasped would never have been as strong as the largely informal Stoddardean influence that he was denied.

There are two clues, apparently unrecognized by Edwards, to the dimension of social change in eighteenth-century Northampton. One was the power of Colonel John Stoddard—so great that his death made Edwards desperate and the town intractible. The other clue was the character of the leading spokesman for the anti-Edwards party, Edwards's cousin, young Joseph Hawley. Even though it is difficult to make him into a spokesman for democracy against Edwardsean aristocracy, because the party lines were not so clearly drawn, it seems significant that he was a young lawyer. His activity in the case between his brother and Mr. Edwards, over Martha Root's illegitimate child, had shown even more clearly than Elisha Hawley's sexual sins that Edwards's formerly pious young people were going bad. But they were also, after about 1742, refusing to admit that they were bad—they had lost their sense of social shame.

Edwards's special constituency were now not only ignoring his moral advice and his evangelical appeals but, in more polite language and apparently legitimate quarreling over principle, they were telling Mr. Edwards, as Timothy Root had done, that they wouldn't "worship a wig." There is a poignant passage in Edwards's Farewell Sermon to his flock on June 22, 1750, in which—after lengthy and unveiled threats about the controversy being settled at the Day of Judgment, and some special words of encouragement for those in his flock who were seriously pious—the pastor turned his attention to those who had always been most important to him.

Since I have been settled in the work of the ministry, in this place, I have ever had a peculiar concern for the souls of the young people, and a desire that religion might flourish among them; and have especially exerted myself in order to it. . . . This is what I have longed for; and it has been exceedingly grievous to me, when I have heard of vice, vanity and disorder, among our youth. And so far as I know my heart, it was from hence that I formerly led this church to some measures, for the suppressing of vice among our young people, which gave so great offence, and by which I became so obnoxious. I have sought the good and not the hurt of your young people. I have desired their truest honour and happiness. . . . [51]

What is most important to note in this passage is Edwards's defensiveness about a campaign against vice: surely, he could not imagine a true minister who did *not* exert himself to suppress vice, and yet times were changing so much that one who did what a minister had to do could thereby become "obnoxious" to his people and be dismissed. What had changed, perhaps beginning even before the death of the grandfather whose authority Edwards so envied, was the acceptability of the old-fashioned Patriarchal role of the minister. *No one* could be a Stoddard again. In this light, the fact that Joseph Hawley was a lawyer is even more significant. He had planned to be a minister, studied theology after his undergraduate training, recorded about 1743 a vow to preach the truth and save souls, and gone as a chaplain on the military expedition to Louisburg in Canada in 1745.[52] But then, apparently abruptly, Hawley had decided to be a lawyer, instead of a minister. John Adams of Braintree, an even more famous Revolutionary leader, made a similar decision only a few years later. For young men of talent and ambition, the bar was a more promising platform than the pulpit. But personal glory was not the only factor: if a man wanted to influence his neighbors, shape their behavior and ideas, the law was the career to undertake. If there were any young men in Northampton trying to make that vocational decision in the late 1740s, the lessons presented by Mr. Edwards's problems were unmistakable.

Jonathan Edwards's career spanned an era of great but subtle transitions in New England communities in the relationship of authority figures to their potential followers. Edwards never escaped the anachronistic grip of the Patriarchal model, and so all he could do to explain the tragedy that befell him was to describe his opponents as bad and power-hungry individuals. They may have been crypto-Arminians, and logic suggests that they might prefer a theology which stressed man's abilities, but it is more significant that they were men of social influence. The first secular competitors for the ministry's power over the minds and hearts of the populace had been firmly controlled in early New England, but within a generation there began to emerge a class of secular leaders. As long as they worked in concert with the clergy, as did Colonel John Stoddard, the combined forces of church and government and informal social authority could not be challenged successfully. But when piety became a social force that cut across established lines of deference in families and communities, and when ministers tried to make their new constituency into a force to control the whole community, they would find themselves isolated. There would be no more Patriarchs.

The irony of this ministerial dilemma is that the evangelical clergy contributed a major share of the dynamic of change. Jonathan Edwards himself, while extolling family government and preaching Tory politics, had inadvertently drawn young people away from their families and had redefined the value of such politicians as Colonel John on the basis of their usefulness (not just traditional power) to the community. Also inadvertently, because he was experimenting with new evangelical attacks on the sins of Northampton, Edwards redefined the constituency of the minister in terms of the followers of his *ideas:* those groups might well be, and in other towns were much more clearly, particular segments of the community. The "come-outer" spirit inherent in evangelism changed the pastoral model to leader and followers, not shepherd and flock. The sheep had no choice but to follow the shepherd whom God had appointed over them. In Northampton, by 1742, some people might even have chosen one evangelical minister over another—young Samuel Buell over Edwards, perhaps. Edwards saw his role as uniting the community, but even during the revivals it had done that only superficially.

If Edwards had lived into the early nineteenth century, he would have seen how the new role of the ministry developed. Some ministers, particularly those of Arminian views, seemed content to be men of mere Sunday importance, and to legitimize the worldly activities of their congregations without being leaders at all. Other ministers, some Calvinist and some liberal, became leaders of that very moralistic movement for independence from England in the 1770s. Eventually, in the ideological doldrums that followed the Revolutionary era, some ministers would revive the "come-outer" spirit and even lead its transmutation into the moral social crusades of the 1820s and 1830s. Then a minister could be a professional intellectual, for he gathered a constituency around his *ideas*. He would have to give up the old role of father to a community, and eventually the self-conscious intellectual would have to leave the ministry entirely in order to give the fullest scope to his developing ideas. But in the transitional interval, in the eighteenth-century revivals, ministers who could not quite be Patriarchs found followings among young men who could not quite be adult. The rhetoric of absolute submission to an arbitrary God that characterized the Calvinist evangelism of the 1740s turned out to translate rather easily into the parricidal language of the Revolution against an arbitrary King: perhaps 180 degree turns are easier than smaller adjustments in ideas. Whether pious or military, however, revolutionary movements seem to burn themselves out emotionally in a rather short time, and both the Awakening and the Revolution contained the seeds of the conservative reactions that would follow. But somewhere between 1700 (or earlier) and 1800, Patriarchs went out of style: the father figure in clerical garb gave way to the father figure in a military uniform, but he, too, was left behind by sociopolitical progress.

The tragedy of Jonathan Edwards was that he was so clearly a product of the changing patterns of authority and community life in eighteenth-century New England. He was more like a revolutionary than a Patriarch, but he thought of himself as a Patriarch. Self-conscious as he was, introspective as he could be in moments of both triumph and failure, he could nevertheless not reinvent himself. His ideas were potentially far in advance of their time, but he kept all his best insights chained to the service of an antiquated social ideal that few other men shared by 1750. But perhaps, like all good fathers, Edwards gave his children the inner resources to rebel when it came to be time for them to be men.

Manuscript Sources

Jonathan Edwards and Edwards Family MSS. There are two major repositories of Edwards MSS: the Franklin Trask Library of the Andover Newton Theological School in Newton Centre, Massachusetts (listed in the notes as ANTS), which contains some original Edwards writings but mostly family letters and documents; and the Beinecke Rare Book and Manuscript Library at Yale University (listed in notes as Beinecke), which houses the nearly 1,200 MS sermons (filed by Biblical text) and most of the important surviving Edwards MSS, including the theological notebooks known as the "Miscellanies." Many of these writings are currently being prepared for publication in the Yale University Press edition of *The Works of Jonathan Edwards,* of which five volumes have appeared to date. Specific manuscripts will be identified in the notes, as will the various editions of Edwards's published works which have been used. The Edwards MSS have been described by Thomas A. Schafer in "Manuscript Problems in the Yale Edition of Jonathan Edwards," *Early American Literature,* III (1968–69), 159–71. Two readily available bibliographies of Edwards materials and relevant secondary sources can be found in Clarence H. Faust and Thomas H. Johnson's *Jonathan Edwards: Representative Selections,* rev. ed. (N.Y., 1962), cxix–cxlii; and Ola Elizabeth Winslow's *Jonathan Edwards 1703–1758* (N.Y., 1940), 373–93.

Northampton Local Records. "Town Records"—the First Book, 1653–1754, will be cited as Town Records. The MS, a transcription in 1759 from the original (now lost), is in the City Clerk's office, Northampton, and is available on microfilm at Forbes Library. In

February 1742 the town was divided into two precincts, old Northampton and new Southampton, and the Northampton records from that date in "First Precinct Records" (microfilm at Forbes), overlapping somewhat in content with the official Town Record book, will be cited as such. The Northampton Proprietors' Records are on microfilm at Forbes; Vital Statistics are in MS in the City Clerk's office. Hampshire County probate records are in the courthouse annex, Northampton. Land deeds from pre-1786 Hampshire County (including all of what is now the counties of Berkshire, Franklin, and Hampden) are housed in the Registry of Deeds at Springfield.

"Church Records"—original book, unpaginated, is at the First Church of Christ, Northampton; a microfilm copy is at Forbes Library. Unless otherwise noted, all page citations will be to the *second* part of the book, the enactments and other church business; the first section is just lists of members, and its pages will be identified as "first part." In the nineteenth century the Reverend Solomon Clark published a catalogue of the members of the Northampton church since its founding; that list does not precisely correspond to the manuscript record (a few names occur on one list but not the other, and the lists are in rather different order of names), and so it has not been used.

Notes

Introduction

1. There are innumerable works on Edwards as an intellectual, of which the following have been of most use to me: Conrad Cherry, *The Theology of Jonathan Edwards: A Reappraisal* (N.Y., 1966); Edward H. Davidson, *Jonathan Edwards: The Narrative of a Puritan Mind* (Boston, 1966); Roland Andre Delattre, *Beauty and Sensibility in the Thought of Jonathan Edwards: An Essay in Aesthetics and Theological Ethics* (New Haven, 1968); and, most challenging of all, Perry Miller, *Jonathan Edwards* (N.Y., 1949). The standard biographical works are Sereno Edwards Dwight, *The Life of President Edwards* (N.Y., 1829), which is especially valuable for the many documents it includes, some of which are now otherwise lost; and Ola Elizabeth Winslow, *Jonathan Edwards 1703–1758* (N.Y., 1940).

2. The most important works on the Great Awakening as social history are the following: J. M. Bumsted, "Religion, Finance, and Democracy in Massachusetts: The Town of Norton as a Case Study," *Journal of American History,* LVII (1971), 817–31; J. M. Bumsted, "Revivalism and Separatism in New England: The First Society of Norwich, Connecticut, as a Case Study," *William and Mary Quarterly,* 3rd Ser., XXIV (1967), 588–612; Philip J. Greven, Jr., "Youth, Maturity, and Religious Conversion: A Note on the Ages of Converts in Andover, Massachusetts, 1711–1749," *Essex Institute Historical Collections,* CVIII (1972), 119–34; Gerald F. Moran, "Conditions of Religious Conversion in the First Society of Norwich, Connecticut, 1718–1744," *Journal of Social History,* V (1971–1972), 331–43; James Walsh, "The Great Awakening in the First Congregational Church of Woodbury, Connecticut," *William and Mary Quarterly,* 3rd Ser., XXVIII (1971), 543–62; William F. Willingham, "Religious Conversion in the Second Society of Windham, Connecticut, 1723–1743: A Case Study,"

Societas, VI (1976), 109–19. Much criticized but still interesting is John C. Miller, "Religion, Finance, and Democracy in Massachusetts," *New England Quarterly,* VI (1933), 29–58. The major secondary works on the Awakening in New England are: Edwin S. Gaustad, *The Great Awakening in New England* (N.Y., 1957); C. C. Goen, *Revivalism and Separatism in New England, 1740–1800: Strict Congregationalists and Separate Baptists in the Great Awakening* (New Haven, 1962); and Joseph Tracy, *The Great Awakening* (1842; N.Y., 1969). Readers familiar with Richard L. Bushman's provocative book, *From Puritan to Yankee: Character and the Social Order in Connecticut, 1690–1765* (Cambridge, Mass., 1967), will know how indebted I am to its general thesis despite the questions I raise in Chapter 4. The major primary source on the Awakening is the magazine edited by Thomas Prince, Jr., of Boston entitled *The Christian History* (Boston, 1743–45). Documents on the revivals can be found in the following modern collections: Richard L. Bushman, ed., *The Great Awakening: Documents on the Revival of Religion, 1740–1745* (N.Y., 1970); Alan Heimert and Perry Miller, eds., *The Great Awakening: Documents Illustrating the Crisis and Its Consequences* (Indianapolis, 1967); Stephen Nissenbaum, ed., *The Great Awakening at Yale College* (Belmont, Calif., 1972); and Darrett B. Rutman, *The Great Awakening: Event and Exegesis* (N.Y., 1970).

3. Edwards's specification of the meaning of "young people," similar to the definition used by other ministers, can be found in his letter of December 1743 to Thomas Prince, printed in *The Christian History,* and reprinted in C. C. Goen, ed., *The Great Awakening:* Vol. IV of *The Works of Jonathan Edwards* (New Haven, 1972), 544–47, specifically 547. See also Ross W. Beales, Jr., "In Search of the Historical Child: Miniature Adulthood and Youth in Colonial New England," *American Quarterly,* XXVII (1975), 379–98. Testimonies to the involvement of youth in the Awakening can be found throughout *The Christian History;* see especially Vol. I, pp. 133–45, 188, 191, 200, 242, 253, 260, 395, 399–400, 409. The best analytical work on adolescence in colonial America is still N. Ray Hiner, "Adolescence in Eighteenth Century America," *History of Childhood Quarterly* III (1975), 253–80. See also Joseph F. Kett, "Adolescence and Youth in Nineteenth-Century America," *Journal of Interdisciplinary History,* II (1971), 283–99. The problems of rites of passage to adulthood are strongly implied in Bushman, *Puritan to Yankee,* and in Kenneth A. Lockridge, "Land, Population and the Evolution of New England Society 1630–1790," *Past & Present,* No. 39 (April 1968), 62–80.

4. Peter Gregg Slater, *Children in the New England Mind* (Hamden, Conn., 1977), 22–23.

5. Miller, *Jonathan Edwards,* 127–28.

6. For the identification of Edwards's enemies, see *ibid.*, 101–5, 122, 125–26, 218–21; and Winslow, *Jonathan Edwards*, 160, 250–52.

7. An adequate bibliography of important works on the Congregational church in early New England would take another volume, but the following works have been the most useful in this study: E. Brooks Holifield, *The Covenant Sealed: The Development of Puritan Sacramental Theology in Old and New England, 1570–1720* (New Haven, 1974); Paul R. Lucas, *Valley of Discord: Church and Society along the Connecticut River, 1636–1725* (Hanover, N.H., 1976) (although I have many reservations about the use of evidence in this study—see my notes to Chapter 1—it remains the only analytical work on west-central New England besides Bushman's *Puritan to Yankee*); the many works of Perry Miller, especially the two-volume study, *The New England Mind* (Cambridge, Mass., 1939, 1953); Edmund S. Morgan, *Visible Saints: The History of a Puritan Idea* (N.Y., 1963); Norman Pettit, *The Heart Prepared: Grace and Conversion in Puritan Spiritual Life* (New Haven, 1966); Robert G. Pope, *The Half-Way Covenant: Church Membership in Puritan New England* (Princeton, 1969); and Williston Walker, *Creeds and Platforms of Congregationalism* (N.Y., 1893). The best work on the seventeenth-century ministry is David D. Hall, *The Faithful Shepherd* (Chapel Hill, N.C., 1972). The best statement of the widely accepted theory that socioeconomic comfort leads to a loss of emotional piety is Daniel Walker Howe, "The Decline of Calvinism: An Approach to its Study," *Comparative Studies in Society and History*, XIV (1972), 306–27.

8. On infant damnation, see Slater, *Children in the New England Mind;* and David E. Stannard, *The Puritan Way of Death* (N.Y., 1977).

9. On the Synod of 1662 and the Half-Way Covenant, see Walker, *Creeds and Platforms*, 238–339; Miller, *The New England Mind: From Colony to Province*, 93–104; and especially, Pope, *Half-Way Covenant.*

10. Edmund S. Morgan, *The Puritan Family* (Boston, 1956), 90–104.

11. The major biographies of Stoddard are John L. Sibley and Clifford K. Shipton, *Biographical Sketches of Those who Attended Harvard College . . . ,* 17 vols. (Boston, 1873–1975), II, 111–22 [hereafter cited as Sibley, *Harvard Graduates*]; Perry Miller, "Solomon Stoddard, 1643–1729," *Harvard Theological Review*, XXXIV (1941), 277–320; and Ralph J. Coffman, *Solomon Stoddard* (Boston, 1978). The best analytical works on Stoddard are Thomas A. Schafer, "Solomon Stoddard and the Theology of the Revival," in Stuart C. Henry, ed., *A Miscellany of American Christianity* (Durham, N. C., 1963), 328–61; and Holifield, *The Covenant Sealed*, 192–219. Also useful is James A. Goulding, "The Controversy between Solomon Stoddard and the Mathers" (Ph.D. dissertation, Claremont Graduate School, 1971).

Chapter One: Inheritance

1. *Death of a Prophet* (Boston, 1729), quotations 24, 10. On William Williams, see Sibley, *Harvard Graduates*, III, 263–72.

2. JE to Rev. Thomas Gillespie, 1 July 1751, MS at ANTS, included in Sereno E. Dwight, *The Life of President Edwards* (N.Y., 1829), 466.

3. Information on Stoddard's clerical family can be found in the following volumes of Sibley, *Harvard Graduates:* on Anthony Stoddard of Woodbury, IV, 381–83; on Timothy Edwards of East Windsor, IV, 93–99; on Stephen Mix of Wethersfield, IV, 70–72; on Samuel Whitman of Farmington, IV, 315–17; on William Williams of Hatfield, III, 263–72; on William Williams, Jr., of Weston, V, 295–300; on John Williams of Deerfield (widower of Stoddard's stepdaughter Eunice Mather and author of the famous narrative *The Redeemed Captive*), III, 249–62; on Colonel John Stoddard, a member of the Governor's Council that year, V, 96–119; on Israel Williams, VIII, 301–33. Stephen Williams mentioned Stoddard's funeral in his diary, of which a typescript can be found in the Storrs Library, Longmeadow, Mass.; see Vol. 2, 110. On the "River Gods," see Robert J. Taylor, *Western Massachusetts in the Revolution* (Providence, 1954), 11–22; and Robert Zemsky, *Merchants, Farmers and River Gods* (Boston, 1971), passim.

4. Boston, 1729. All quotations are from the Preface, 2. Anglican cleric Timothy Cutler of Boston wrote in 1739 that Stoddard had been "of no great learning and reading, but of a strong brain and thoughtful . . . narrow and odd in his sentiments, self-opinioned, haughty, assuming, and impatient of contradiction, and increased [in] stiffness by living remote from those he could improve by, or [who] dared to oppose him, so that he was [for] many years the oracle of the country, especially in those parts where he lived long. . . ." Douglas C. Stenerson, "An Anglican Critique of the Early Phase of the Great Awakening in New England: A Letter by Timothy Cutler," *William and Mary Quarterly,* 3rd Ser., XXX (1973), 475–88, quotation 480.

5. Some of Stoddard's July lectures were published under the following titles: *The Tryal of Assurance* (1698); *The Necessity of Acknowledgment of Offences in Order to Reconciliation* (1701); *The Danger of Speedy Degeneracy* (1705); *The Falseness of the Hopes of Many Professors* (1708); *Those Taught by God the Father to Know God the Son are Blessed* (1712); *The Way to Know Sincerity and Hypocrisy* (1719). These lectures and others are mentioned in *The Diary of Samuel Sewall, 1674–1729,* ed. M. Halsey Thomas (N.Y., 1973), 525, 597, 639, 693, 720, 762, 897, 924. Apparently Stoddard was a habitué of Sewall's salon of Boston's religious, civic, and business elite. Stoddard also preached the annual Election Sermon in 1703, published as *The Way for a People to Live Long in the Land that God Hath Given Them.*

6. The quotations are from the sermon on Isaiah 3:1–2; the other two written near Stoddard's death are Jeremiah 6:29–30, and II Corinthians 4:7, all MSS at Beinecke. The dates of these are the deductions of Professor Thomas A. Schafer, to whom I am greatly indebted for this information. In subsequent notes, "Schafer date" will indicate the opinion of Professor Schafer; other dates are those in JE's hand on the MS.

7. On JE's illness, see Dwight, *Edwards*, 115; Timothy Edwards to daughter Anne, 12 Sept. and 6 Oct. 1729, ANTS. SS's paradoxical title was bestowed by Increase Mather in his Preface to John Quick, *The Young Man's Claim Unto the Sacrament of the Lord's Supper* (Boston, 1700), 28–29.

8. The settlement of the upper Connecticut Valley and the religious turmoil that accompanied dispersal is described by Paul R. Lucas, *Valley of Discord: Church and Society along the Connecticut River, 1636–1725* (Hanover, N.H., 1976), 3–50. On the economic motives for the Northampton settlement, see James Russell Trumbull, *History of Northampton*, 2 vols. (Northampton, 1898), I, 4–5.

9. On the problems of early Northampton politics, see Trumbull, *Northampton*, I, 200. Lucas, *Valley of Discord*, 83–85, interprets the Northampton records as showing a pattern of townsmen opposing church brethren which also pervaded the lower Valley in this era; but I do not find Lucas's argument for Eleazar Mather's being "engulfed" in controversy at all convincing. Only three men even temporarily objected to Mather. See also note 10, below. There is no evidence that the witchcraft affair became more than a feud between two families.

10. Trumbull, *Northampton*, I, 77–80. On Mather, see Sibley, *Harvard Graduates*, I, 405–09. Lucas, *Valley of Discord*, 84–85, describes Northampton as factionalized but misinterprets the evidence. He says that "few more than the Dorchester people" ever joined the church, there was constant bickering between church and town, and the adoption of the HWC was a victory for the anti-Mather faction. On the contrary, within the very first month of the church's existence, fifty-three of seventy covenant signers were *not* Dorchester people (Church Records, first part, 6ff); town officers were chosen from both groups with no evidence of factional fighting; and the 1668 enactment of the HWC gave all powers of judgment in admission in all categories to the elders, who were the pastor and the Dorchester man chosen Ruling Elder in 1663. Lucas's argument would support my conjectures about the politics of Stoddard's ecclesiology, but I do not find his evidence adequate. Church members have been identified by comparing Mather's lists in the Church Records (first part, 6–20) with Trumbull's Northampton Genealogy (unpublished Volume III of his *History of Northampton*, typescript at Forbes Library). On the HWC, see my note 11

to the Introduction. On Northampton's involvement with Boston's First Church controversy, see Trumbull, *Northampton*, I, 215–17; Hamilton A. Hill, *History of the Old South Church* (Boston, 1890), I, 96, 111n.; and Richard C. Simmons, "The Founding of the Third Church in Boston," *William and Mary Quarterly*, 3rd Ser., XXVI (1969), 241–52.

11. The notebook Stoddard kept while at Harvard contains notes on seventy-two sermons, thirty-three of which are by Mitchell. MS at Union Theological Seminary, N.Y.; microfilm copy in Harvard University Archives. Mitchell's position is best expressed in his *Defense of the Answer* . . . (Boston, 1664). Stoddard's library, as recorded in the same notebook, has been described and annotated by Norman S. Fiering, "Solomon Stoddard's Library at Harvard in 1664," *Harvard Library Bulletin*, XX (1972), 255–69. Among his books were four by the Scottish Presbyterian Samuel Rutherford, who may have been one of the major intellectual sources for Stoddard's later presbyterianism of doctrine; but Rutherford was listed in other Massachusetts clergymen's libraries of the time and was never explicitly cited by Stoddard.

12. On Anthony Stoddard, see Ralph J. Coffman, *Solomon Stoddard* (Boston, 1978), 24–34, 60; and "The Diaries of John Hull," American Antiquarian Society *Transactions and Collections*, III (1857), 198.

13. Town Records, 75–76. Esther was the daughter of the Rev. John Warham of Windsor, on whom see William B. Sprague, *Annals of the American Pulpit*, I (N.Y., 1857), 10–11; Lucas, *Valley of Discord*, 38–40.

14. Church Records, 23. Lucas, *Valley of Discord*, 136, interprets enactment as an automatic and examination-free transition to full membership, but the examination is clearly specified and the two "forms of words" leave no doubt that there were two categories. I have found no supporting evidence for Lucas's plausible assertion (p. 131) that when SS arrived in 1669 he asked the church to give up the conversion-experience test for membership and asked to be the sole judge of admissions but was refused both.

15. Church Records, first part, 6–35. Only sixteen other persons joined the church in full communion in the years 1670–79.

16. Church Records, first part, 1–4. The list begins July 30, 1677, and is begun again Sept. 11, 1706 (with names of survivors from the first list repeated); why these dates were chosen is unknown. Individual entries are not dated.

17. Although Dwight, *Edwards*, 109–10, puts the date at 1704 (without evidence), and each biographer of Stoddard has chosen his favorite date, two letters and a memorandum copied into the notebook of Edward Taylor, pastor at Westfield, give the most probable date for the opening of communion in Northampton and some interesting gossip about the process by

which Stoddard persuaded his congregation. On Feb. 13, 1688, Taylor wrote to Stoddard that he had heard SS was "about to cast off relations and to bring all above 14 years of age that live morally having catechistical knowledge of the principles of religion to the Lord's Supper, and for that end he hath held one day of debate with his church and hath fixed upon another"; Taylor argued against this innovation. Stoddard's reply of June 4 read in part: "I have been abundantly satisfied these many years that we did not offend the Will of God in this matter [open communion] and that our neglect [of the sacrament] is the occasion of the great profaneness and corruption that hath overspread the land[. A]nd therefore [I] thought it both necessary for myself, that I might be found doing the will of God, and necessary for the country, that we might not go on further to forsake God [, to push the revision in church polity]. If I cannot carry it in a way of peace and according to a rule, I am willing to submit to the will of God, but shall look upon it [as] a frown on the land." The next page in the Taylor notebook reads: "Mr. Stoddard having preached up from Gal. 3:1 that the Lord's Supper was a converting ordinance . . . and urged [it], till on an occasion of the Ruling Elder's absence by reason of sickness and many if not all the ancient members of the church were dead, then he and all his church so new covenanting . . . to bring all to the Lord's Supper that had a knowledge of Principles of Religion and not scandalous by open sinful living[. T]his done in the winter 1690." Taylor notebook, Massachusetts Historical Society, Boston, unpaged. Another Taylor memorandum book, at the Boston Public Library, contains notes from a Stoddard sermon on Galatians 3:1, given at Northampton on Oct. 5, 1690, perhaps the sermon to which Taylor referred. The Doctrine is: "The Lord's Supper is appointed by Jesus Christ for ye begetting of Grace as well as for ye strengthening of Grace." This extract from Taylor's notebook has been published by Thomas W. Davis, "Solomon Stoddard's Sermon on the Lord's Supper as a Converting Ordinance," *Resources for American Literary Study*, IV (1974), 205-24. On the Taylor–Stoddard debate, see the many works on Taylor by Norman Grabo, especially "The Poet to the Pope: Edward Taylor to Solomon Stoddard," *American Literature*, XXXII (1960), 197-201. For an intriguing story of SS's adverse reaction to the "extravagant accounts of mystical experiences" recited as part of the organization of the Westfield church in 1679, see John H. Lockwood, *Westfield and Its Historic Influences, 1669-1919* (privately printed, 1922), I, 113, 115.

Stoddard had probably been preaching open communion by 1677, when he changed the format of his church records. That May, Increase Mather's Election Sermon in Boston inveighed against allowing those with only historical and not experiential faith to participate in the Sacrament. *Discourse*

Concerning the Danger of Apostasy (Boston, 1679), 116–17. John Russell, minister at Hadley, wrote to Mather on 28 March 1681 that "our good brother Stoddard hath been strenuously promoting his position concerning that right which persons sound in the doctrine of faith & of (as he calls it) a holy conversation, have to full communion." Massachusetts Historical Society *Collections*, 4th Ser., VIII (1868), 83.

18. Dwight, *Edwards*, 363.

19. On the increasing emphasis on preparation for grace, and the question of how "Arminian" this doctrinal shift was, see Norman Pettit, *The Heart Prepared: Grace and Conversion in Puritan Spiritual Life* (New Haven, 1966); E. Brooks Holifield, *The Covenant Sealed: The Development of Puritan Sacramental Theology in Old and New England, 1570–1720* (New Haven, 1974); and Gerald J. Goodwin, "The Myth of 'Arminian-Calvinism' in Eighteenth Century New England," *New England Quarterly,* XLI (1968), 213–37.

20. *Safety,* 110, 109, 285.

21. SS had written to Mather in late 1685, calling him a "loving brother" (SS's wife was the widow of IM's brother), to ask him to write a preface to *Safety of Appearing;* Mather refused. SS to IM, Prince Papers, Massachusetts Historical Society, 60. On Mather, see Robert Middlekauff, *The Mathers: Three Generations of Puritan Intellectuals, 1596–1728* (N.Y., 1971), Book II. The major Mather tracts in the debate with SS were *The Order of the Gospel* (Boston, 1700), and *A Dissertation, Wherein the Strange Doctrine Lately Published in a Sermon, The Tendency of which, is, to Encourage Unsanctified Persons (while such) to Approach the Holy Table of the Lord, is Examined and Confuted* (Boston, 1708).

Stoddard's 1709 *An Appeal to the Learned,* 93–94, described his debate with Mather during the Synod of 1679. See also Williston Walker, *Creeds and Platforms of Congregationalism* (N.Y., 1893), 409–39.

22. *Tryal,* 13–14; *The Inexcusableness of Neglecting the Worship of God, Under a Pretence of Being in an Unconverted Condition* (Boston, 1708), 14–15; *An Appeal to the Learned, Being a Vindication of the Right of Visible Saints to the Lords Supper, Though They be Destitute of a Saving Work of God's Spirit in their Hearts: Against the Exceptions of Mr. Increase Mather* (Boston, 1709), 74; *A Treatise Concerning the Nature of Saving Conversion, and the Way Wherein it is Wrought* (Boston, 1719), 78–79.

23. *Instituted Churches,* 22.

24. *Inexcusableness,* 28; *Appeal to the Learned,* 25, 70–71; *Safety,* 119; *Instituted Churches,* 22.

25. *Appeal to the Learned,* 53. See also Holifield, *Covenant Sealed,* passim.

26. Walker, *Creeds and Platforms,* 282; Holifield, *Covenant Sealed,* 219. See also SS's *Appeal to the Learned,* 91–92, which cites Thomas Hooker's *Survey*

of the Summe of Church Discipline. Hooker had not opened communion to those without at least a charitable judgment of experiential faith, but he did emphasize the inexact nature of man's knowledge of another's heart. See Frank Shuffelton, *Thomas Hooker 1586–1647* (Princeton, 1977), 168–75, 180–81, 227, 269–71.

27. *Appeal to the Learned,* 17, 21, 22, 23. It would have been easy for SS to take another step in this direction and wax eloquent on the covenanting of New England with God in this external way as a Chosen People, but he did rather less of this than did his opponents. He was simply no optimist about man as a social being. For a fascinating discussion of the "Americanism" that grew out of Puritanism by the late seventeenth century, see Sacvan Bercovitch, *The American Jeremiad* (Madison, Wis., 1978).

28. *An Examination of the Power of the Fraternity* (Boston, 1718), 1, 2; *Appeal to the Learned,* preface; *Inexcusableness,* preface and 20.

29. *Instituted Churches,* 5, 7–8.

30. *Ibid.,* 6–7, 19–20.

31. For the Cambridge Platform, see Walker, *Creeds and Platforms,* 157–237, esp. 212–29. Stoddard, *Instituted Churches,* 9, 12.

32. *Ibid.,* 25, 27, 34.

33. *Examination of the Power of the Fraternity,* 2, 3, 11.

34. Wilson H. Kimnach, "The Brazen Trumpet: Jonathan Edwards's Conception of the Sermon," in Charles Angoff, ed., *Jonathan Edwards: His Life and Influence* (Cranbury, N.J., 1975), 37, 38.

35. *The Efficacy of the Fear of Hell, to Restrain Men from Sin. Shewed in a Sermon . . . on the Occasion of a More than Ordinary Pouring Out of the Spirit of God* (Boston, 1713); and *The Duty of Gospel-Ministers to Preserve a People from Corruption* (Boston, 1718), 24; *The Defects of Preachers Reproved* (New London, 1724), 14; *The Presence of Christ with Ministers of the Gospel* (Boston, 1718), 27–28. Thomas A. Schafer, "Solomon Stoddard and the Theology of the Revival," in Stuart C. Henry, ed., *A Miscellany of American Christianity* (Durham, N.C., 1963), 328–61, esp. 341.

36. Eugene E. White, *Puritan Rhetoric: The Issue of Emotion in Religion* (Carbondale, Ill., 1972), 35.

37. Edwards, *A Faithful Narrative of the Surprising Work of God . . .* (London, 1737; Boston, 1738), reprinted in C. C. Goen, ed., *The Great Awakening,* Vol. IV of *The Works of Jonathan Edwards* (New Haven, 1972), 146.

38. Walker, *Creeds and Platforms,* 282, says that twenty-two or twenty-three of twenty-seven churches in the Hampshire Association (including Hampshire County and a few Connecticut churches) were Stoddardean in 1750.

39. In JE's *The Distinguishing Marks of a Work of the Spirit of God* (Boston, 1741), reprinted in Goen, *Great Awakening,* quotation p. 248.

40. *Safety,* 6; italics in original.

41. Quotation from *Three Sermons,* 8. In seeing this as the quintessential statement on psychology by Stoddard, I agree with Schafer, "Stoddard and the Theology of the Revival," esp. p. 348. See also Norman S. Fiering, "Will and Intellect in the New England Mind," *William and Mary Quarterly,* 3rd Ser., XXIX (1972), 515–58, esp. 556–57.

42. *Guide to Christ* (1735 edition), 10–24, 32–34.

43. *Treatise Concerning Conversion,* 2–3, 30–35, 58–68.

44. *Those Taught by God the Father,* 31–32; *Treatise Concerning Conversion,* 112–13; *Safety,* quotation 180, see also 174–75, 179.

45. *The Falseness of the Hopes of Many Professors,* 16; *Guide to Christ,* 9; *Defects of Preachers,* 9.

46. Quotation, Williams, *Death of a Prophet,* 25. The traditional story can be found in I. N. Tarbox, "Jonathan Edwards as a Man and the Ministers of the Last Century," *The New Englander,* XLIII (1884), 625–26. The major problem with this legend is that Stoddard probably would not have been dispensing the sacrament until after he was ordained, as his stepgrandson Stephen Williams of Longmeadow did not. See Williams Diary, Storrs Library, Longmeadow, I, 37.

47. Stoddard denounced sin most strenuously in his Boston lectures, *The Necessity of Acknowledgment of Offences, The Way for a People to Live Long, The Danger of Speedy Degeneracy;* see also his ordination sermons *The Duty of Gospel-Ministers,* and *The Presence of Christ,* the latter strongly critical of the worldliness of ministers. In his 1722 *An Answer to Some Cases of Conscience* (Boston), 2–15, SS especially denounced people's moving away from their churches, "depreciating the bills of public credit," bringing lawsuits for trivial reasons, and wearing long hair and wigs. When he denounced "HOOPED petticoats," the word "hooped" was printed in letters five times as big as the rest of the text; he described these fashions as having "something of nakedness about them" (apparently they tilted upward and exposed whatever was underneath). "Mixt dancings," he wrote, "are incentives to lust." All these sins were very popular in Boston.

48. See especially *The Efficacy of the Fear of Hell.*

49. *Instituted Churches,* 19–20; Church Records, 25.

50. Middlekauff, *The Mathers,* 133.

51. Edwards, *Faithful Narrative,* in Goen, *Great Awakening,* 190.

52. James Walsh, "Solomon Stoddard's Open Communion," *New England Quarterly,* XLIII (1970), 97–114, argues that facing the traditional New England church dilemma of authority versus purity, SS chose authority. In

terms of the church, this is true. Paul R. Lucas, " 'An Appeal to the Learned':
The Mind of Solomon Stoddard," *William and Mary Quarterly,* 3rd Ser.,
XXX (1973), 257–92, argues that the "real" Stoddard was an evangelical
and that *Instituted Churches* was a temporary aberration. The either/or dilemma—which distorts Stoddard's real meaning—comes only when evangelism is seen as tied to membership; and although it was usually so considered
in New England, Stoddard's ultimate point was to break that tie. He would
discipline the church and win souls for Christ.

53. On Connecticut's presbyterianism, see Lucas, *Valley of Discord,* passim;
on the Saybrook Platform, see Walker, *Creeds and Platforms,* 495–523; and
Richard L. Bushman, *From Puritan to Yankee: Character and the Social Order
in Connecticut, 1690–1765* (Cambridge, Mass., 1967), 150–55.

54. Miller, "Solomon Stoddard, 1643–1729," *Harvard Theological Review,*
XXXIV (1941), 306, 316; Miller, *The New England Mind: From Colony to
Province* (Cambridge, Mass., 1953), 259; Walsh, "Stoddard's Open Commu-
nion," 92–114.

55. Larzer Ziff, *Puritanism in America* (N.Y., 1973), 256. For a bizarre
portrait of Stoddard as an anti-intellectual, see Lucas, *Valley of Discord,*
147–49.

56. Lucas, *Valley of Discord,* Chapters 1–5. Westfield, for example, retained extremely strict standards for admission to the Lord's Supper until
1729. See Norman S. Grabo, *Edward Taylor* (N.Y., 1961), 38–39.

57. Trumbull, *Northampton,* I, 107, 278, 574. Edwards estimated there
were about two hundred families in 1735; *Faithful Narrative,* in Goen, *Great
Awakening,* 114. By 1764 Northampton had 203 families in 186 houses and
a total population of close to 1,300; Southampton, then separate but part of
the original town, had 437 people in 76 families in 66 houses. Evarts B.
Greene and Virginia D. Harrington, *American Population before the Federal
Census of 1790* (N.Y., 1932), 26–27.

58. That third division, called the Long Division, included all the land in
about a seven-mile radius from the village center, which was all the town
except the mountainous southern and western edges of the original nine-
mile-square grant, the hilly and infertile areas not used until the mid-eighteenth century. See Map C, page 17. The Proprietors' Records (microfilm
at Forbes Library) contain the official records of all land grants but do not
always record purchases and deeds of gift. The division lists of 1661 and
1700 (none has survived for the second division in 1684) can be found in
the Proprietors' Records, 1–2, 306–7. All but fifty-two males over twenty-
one known to be in town are listed in 1700; of those missing, the ages of
fifty-one are known and average 26.55 years. Most of them may have been
included in their fathers' grants, and most would have been included in the

next division, if there had been one. Men could have bought land and the commons shares that went with it, and so augmented their own shares in 1700, but there was very little purchasing of land. The similarity of the profiles of 1661 and 1700 therefore reflects what would happen if men did not gain or lose acreage. The lack of a land market makes the 1661 distribution (acres) comparable to the 1700 distribution (values). Land grants are discussed in most of the town studies listed in note 59, below, and broader surveys can be found in Roy H. Akagi, *The Town Proprietors of the New England Colonies* (1924; Gloucester, Mass., 1963); and Melville Egleston, *The Land System of the New England Colonies* (Baltimore, 1886).

59. The most important works on New England colonial communities, each asking different questions but all coordinating into a composite picture of population growth, increasing shortages of good land, and resulting changes of behavior from "Puritan" (community-oriented, self-sacrificing, pious, obedient to authority) to "Yankee" (self-seeking, geographically and economically mobile, independent of authority in family or community), are the following (in approximate chronological order of subject matter): John Demos, *A Little Commonwealth: Family Life in Plymouth Colony* (N.Y., 1970); Sumner Chilton Powell, *Puritan Village: The Formation of a New England Town* (Middletown, Conn., 1963); Kenneth A. Lockridge, *A New England Town: The First Hundred Years* (N.Y., 1970); Philip J. Greven, Jr., *Four Generations: Population, Land, and Family in Colonial Andover, Massachusetts* (Ithaca, N.Y., 1970); Paul Boyer and Stephen Nissenbaum, *Salem Possessed: The Social Origins of Witchcraft* (Cambridge, Mass., 1974); Bushman, *Puritan to Yankee;* Charles S. Grant, *Democracy in the Connecticut Frontier Town of Kent* (N.Y., 1961); James A. Henretta, *The Evolution of American Society, 1700–1815: An Interdisciplinary Analysis* (Lexington, Mass., 1973); Robert A. Gross, *The Minutemen and Their World* (N.Y., 1976). There are many research and review articles on the same topic, of which I would recommend the following: James A. Henretta, "The Morphology of New England Society in the Colonial Period," *Journal of Interdisciplinary History,* II (1971–1972), 379–98; Kenneth A. Lockridge, "Land, Population and the Evolution of New England Society 1630–1790," *Past & Present,* No. 39 (April 1968), 62–80; and Lockridge, "Social Change and the Meaning of the American Revolution," *Journal of Social History,* VI (1972–1973), 403–39. The interrelationship of social change and personality change is addressed by Richard D. Brown in "Modernization and the Modern Personality in Early America, 1600–1865: A Sketch of a Synthesis," *Journal of Interdisciplinary History,* II (Winter 1971–1972), 201–28; and in *Modernization: The Transformation of American Life 1600–1865* (N.Y., 1976).

60. Trumbull, *Northampton,* I, 549.

61. Hampshire County deeds, passim. (Deeds to 1786 are housed in the Hampden County Registry of Deeds, Springfield.)

62. Trumbull, *Northampton,* I, 552; Percy W. Bidwell and John I. Falconer, *History of Agriculture in the Northern United States 1620–1860* (Washington, 1925), 70; Sylvester Judd, *History of Hadley* (Northampton, 1863), 362, 365; Jared Eliot, *Essays upon Field Husbandry in New England and Other Papers, 1748–1762,* ed. H. J. Carman and R. G. Tugwell (N.Y., 1934), 29 and passim; Sylvester Judd MSS, Forbes Library, I, 327. Max G. Schumacher, *The Northern Farmer and his Markets During the Late Colonial Period* (N.Y., 1975), 14, estimates the yield of new land at 20–30 bushels of wheat per acre, and that of long-used land at a mere 6 bushels per acre.

63. Bidwell and Falconer, *History of Agriculture,* 109; Judd, *Hadley,* 368; Joseph Hawley account book quoted in Judd MSS, I, 96, 99.

There is unfortunately no surviving pre-Revolutionary document that gives acreage owned by all Northampton residents at any one time; probate documents seem unreliable because a careful check of a large sample showed no precise correlation of acreage with deeds and other records; tax lists of 1739 and 1759 give valuations for real estate but not acres or types of land. Some idea of what was considered desirable can be obtained by noting that the 1661 division averaged about 40 acres per man of cleared, fertile tilling land, besides a home lot; in the 1730 division of hilly and less fertile Southampton land, home lots were set at 20 acres and the maximum meadow at 70 acres more. Sylvester Judd collected statistics on landholdings for Hadley, South Hadley, Amherst, and Granby in 1771, and although the last three of those towns are much newer than Northampton, the results may yield a Valley pattern in which Northampton shared: Judd found an average of almost 13 acres per house tillage, almost 4 acres mowing, and just over 8 acres meadow and pasture. Judd, *Hadley,* 385–86. Average farm sizes have been reported in Grant, *Kent,* 36–37; Greven, *Four Generations,* 59, 224; Henretta, *Evolution of American Society,* 15; James T. Lemon, *The Best Poor Man's Country: A Geographical Study of Early Southeastern Pennsylvania* (Baltimore, 1972), 150–84; Kenneth A. Lockridge, "Land, Population and the Evolution of New England Society," 66, 68; Darrett B. Rutman, *Husbandmen of Plymouth: Farms and Villages in the Old Colony, 1620–1692* (Boston, 1967), 61.

64. Town Records, 158, 167–68. No official list of the Proprietors survives, and the shares are impossible to follow into the eighteenth century. The Proprietors' Record Book shows that by 1665 between fifty and fifty-eight men were made Proprietors; one man more was admitted, in 1672— Solomon Stoddard.

65. Town Records, 203; Proprietors' Records, 339; Trumbull, *Northampton,* I, 547–52.

66. In the 1750s all the lands within the legal bounds of Northampton were divided officially and forever among private owners. Town Records, 353–54. In 1743 and 1749, small additional grants to the town of Northampton, to straighten boundary lines, were divided up; this very hilly woodland made no significant change in any man's real-estate valuation at the time. Town Records, 278, 281–83, 313–15; Trumbull, *Northampton*, I, 465–66; II, 93–95, 183–90.

67. Town Records, 137 (for 1703), 264. The 1731 grant was four undesirable acres on the steep shoulder of Mt. Tom. Two requests for home lots in March 1739 were refused, although one petitioner was a Proprietor's son.

68. Town Records, 96–97, 199; Proprietors' Records, 21, 60, 113, 130, 139; Trumbull, *Northampton*, I, 312.

69. Town Records, 23, 51, 60, 69, 79, 94; Trumbull, *Northampton*, I, 103.

70. Town Records, 23, 60. Seth Pomeroy's will, written 1755, probated 1777, Hampshire County Probate Records, Box 116, No. 33.

71. Town Records, 148, 173; Trumbull, *Northampton*, I, 454, 473. David J. Rothman, *The Discovery of the Asylum* (Boston, 1971), Chapters I and II, emphasizes the colonial assumption that most of the poor could be cared for within families. Rothman and Demos, *A Little Commonwealth*, follow the theory of Bernard Bailyn's influential *Education in the Forming of American Society* (Chapel Hill, N.C., 1960) that the family was originally the primary educational-charitable institution and gradually lost its functions to the wider community. For a contrary view that I find more plausible, see Henretta, "Morphology of New England Society in the Colonial Period," 397. There were Massachusetts laws enabling a town to "warn out" any potentially indigent person not born there, based on the Elizabethan Poor Laws requiring a town to maintain only its own poor, but the first Northampton warning-out was not recorded until 1742. Hampshire County Court of General Sessions of the Peace and Inferior Court of Common Pleas, IV (1741–45), 70, 84, 101 (microfilm copy at Forbes Library; hereafter cited as Hampshire County Common Pleas). In March 1741 the town had refused to admit a man as an inhabitant. Town Records, 273. The standard secondary work is Josiah H. Benton, *Warning Out in New England* (Boston, 1911).

72. Town Records, 149–50, 200, 156, 225.

73. Town Records, 141.

74. Trumbull, *Northampton*, I, 402–10.

75. Town Records, 133.

76. Trumbull, *Northampton*, I, 290–91.

77. JE to Gillespie, 1 July 1751, in Dwight, *Edwards*, 463–64.

78. Stoddard estate documents, Hampshire County Probate Records, Box 142, No. 53. No inventory of the books, which went to Anthony Stoddard of Woodbury, has survived. Trumbull, *Northampton,* I, 221. Quotation from William Leavitt Stoddard, "Solomon Stoddard: A Liberal Among the Puritans" (unpublished MS, typescript at Forbes Library), 54.

79. Coffman, *Solomon Stoddard,* 105–6, suggests that Northampton was becoming a "closed" society with a problem of prolonged adolescence that Stoddard was tacitly addressing—a plausible theory indeed, but Coffman does not offer source citations and methodological documentation for his fragmentary evidence.

80. Dwight, *Edwards,* 109; Lucas, *Valley of Discord,* 148.

81. Church Records, 21. Hampshire Association Records, Forbes Library. The Association did try in vain to reconcile the pastor and church at Enfield, Conn. See Lucas, *Valley of Discord,* 194.

82. Timothy Dwight, *Travels in New England and New York,* ed. B. M. Solomon (Cambridge, Mass., 1969), I, 240–41.

83. *Faithful Narrative,* in Goen, *Great Awakening,* 146.

Chapter Two: Preparation

1. Town Records, 240, 232, 236–37. James Russell Trumbull, *History of Northampton,* 2 vols. (Northampton, 1898), II, 42–43. JE was given £100 per year salary (with a promise of raises to cover inflation and the increase of his family), 50 acres of land, and £300 for a home lot and house (or more if that would not buy a "suitable habitation"). The following March, JE requested and was granted an extra £80 for his house. (No deed of purchase was ever recorded with the county.) JE's ordination was the last entry in the church book in Stoddard's wavering hand; the Church Records, p. 23, give the date as the 22nd, but the 15th is the date given in JE's autobiographical outline, Beinecke. William Williams preached the ordination sermon, which was not published. Trumbull, *Northampton,* II, 47.

2. Of the many family letters surviving from the era of his youth, there is none addressed to or from JE at Northampton nor any mentioning his being there. In his funeral sermon of 10 Feb. 1736 for his grandmother Stoddard, JE wrote that he would not pretend to describe her character, and otherwise showed no particular knowledge or affection. Revelation 14:13, Beinecke.

3. Sereno E. Dwight, *The Life of President Edwards* (N.Y., 1829), 107, 109.

4. JE was born October 3. On TE, see Sibley, *Harvard Graduates,* IV, 93–99.

5. TE was chaplain to a military expedition to Canada. TE to wife, 3 and 7 August 1711, ANTS. The Aug. 7 letter is in Ola Elizabeth Winslow, *Jonathan Edwards 1703–1758* (N.Y., 1940), 40–42.

6. "The Rainbow" and "Of Insects" (one of two versions of the spider essay) are in Clarence H. Faust and Thomas H. Johnson, eds., *Jonathan Edwards: Representative Selections*, rev. ed. (N.Y., 1962), 13–17 and 3–10. The more polished revision known as "The Flying Spider" can be found in E. C. Smyth, "The Flying Spider: Observations by Jonathan Edwards when a Boy," *Andover Review*, XIII (1890), 1–19. The literary qualities of the revision are cogently discussed in David S. Wilson, "The Flying Spider," *Journal of the History of Ideas*, XXXII (1971), 447–58. Claims have frequently been made that Edwards showed great scientific prowess in these essays (see Dwight, *Edwards*, 22), but the subordination of empirical investigation to the illustration of traditional dogma was persuasively pointed out by Clarence H. Faust, "Jonathan Edwards as a Scientist," *American Literature*, I (1929), 393–404. Perry Miller claimed that in his theology JE spoke "from an insight into science and psychology so much ahead of his time that our own can hardly be said to have caught up with him." Miller, *Jonathan Edwards* (N.Y., 1949), Foreword, 3. The classic rebuttal to Miller, although perhaps misunderstanding Miller's real point about "the artist" and "the meaning of America," is Vincent Tomas, "The Modernity of Jonathan Edwards," *New England Quarterly*, XXV (1952), 60–84. See also Richard Hofstadter's comment on "modernities" in *America at 1750* (N.Y., 1971), 243–44.

Readers interested in Edwards's intellectual development should consult Thomas H. Johnson, "Jonathan Edwards' Background of Reading," Colonial Society of Massachusetts *Publications*, XXVIII (1931), 193–222. Edwards's exposure to Locke's *Essay upon the Human Understanding* was of profound importance: in later life he recalled his pleasure as greater than that of " 'the most greedy miser in gathering up handfuls of silver and gold from some new discovered treasure.' " Quoted in Samuel Hopkins, *The Life and Character of the Late Reverend, Learned and Pious Mr. Jonathan Edwards* (Boston, 1765), 3.

7. The story of Yale's early years is well told in Richard Warch, *School of the Prophets: Yale College 1701–1740* (New Haven, 1973), 1–95; the curriculum before 1740 is described on pp. 186–249. Elisha Williams was the son of the Rev. William Williams of Hatfield and his first wife; his second wife was Christian Stoddard, Esther Stoddard Edwards's sister. Sibley, *Harvard Graduates*, V, 588–98. Edwards described Yale's turmoil in two surviving letters to his family: JE to sister Mary, 26 March 1719, and JE to TE, 24 July 1719, ANTS. Both letters are in Dwight, *Edwards*, 29–32; the July 24 letter

is in Winslow, *Jonathan Edwards,* 60. See also TE to "daughter," 24 Jan. 1717/18, ANTS.

8. Cutler to TE, 30 June 1719, ANTS; in Dwight, *Edwards,* 30–31. By 1739 Cutler, appalled by the Northampton revival, had altered his view of Edwards. He wrote to Bishop Gibson in London that "Mr. Edwards was brought up under my care at Yale College, a person of good abilities, diligence, and proficiency in learning. . . . He was critical, subtle and peculiar, but I think not very solid in disputation." Douglas C. Stenerson, "An Anglican Critique of the Early Phase of the Great Awakening in New England: A Letter by Timothy Cutler," *William and Mary Quarterly,* 3rd Ser., XXX (1973), 475–88, quotation 482. Edwards's M.A. thesis, in the Yale Archives, was titled "A Sinner is not justified before God except through the Righteousness of Christ acquired by Faith."

9. JE's New York and Bolton experiences will be discussed more fully later in this chapter. He was chosen tutor on 21 May 1724. Franklin B. Dexter, *Documentary History of Yale University* (New Haven, 1916), 252. On 29 August 1726 JE was paid by the town of Northampton for "travel and one month's assistance to Mr. Stoddard in the ministry." Trumbull, *Northampton,* II, 42–43.

10. TE account book 1711–1724, Beinecke, 112. JE to Mary Edwards, Dec. 1721, ANTS. On Solomon Williams, see Sibley, *Harvard Graduates,* VI, 352–61. JE's renunciatory diary entry of 10 Jan. 1723 is in Dwight, *Edwards,* 78; the original MS is lost.

11. TE entered Harvard with the class of 1690 but in early 1688 he was marked in the college record for "severe punishments." He went to Springfield to study with the Rev. Pelatiah Glover, who battled his congregation for twenty years over title to his house and land. Sibley, *Harvard Graduates,* I, 558–59; Mason A. Green, *Springfield 1636–1886* (Springfield, 1888), 180–82. In April 1694 TE was paid by Northampton for teaching for an unspecified period. Town Records, 143.

12. The early history of East Windsor and TE's career are depicted in John A. Stoughton, *"Windsor Farmes": A Glimpse of an Old Parish* (Hartford, 1883), passim. TE's settlement and ordination are recorded in the South (then East) Windsor Parish Records, 2, Connecticut State Library (hereafter cited as S. Windsor Records). TE published only one sermon, the Election Sermon of 1732, *All the Living Must Surely Die and Go to Judgment* (New London, 1732). Four unpublished sermons are printed in Stoughton, *"Windsor Farmes,"* 121–45, from MSS not located. The Connecticut Historical Society and ANTS have a few sermon notes. JE mentioned "four or five" revivals in East Windsor before 1735 and a "considerable" one that year in his *Faithful Narrative of the Surprising Work of God . . .* (London, 1737;

214 JONATHAN EDWARDS

Boston, 1738), reprinted in C. C. Goen, ed., *The Great Awakening,* Vol. IV of *The Works of Jonathan Edwards* (New Haven, 1972), 154. Family letters at ANTS describe the revivals of 1716 and 1718; see also the 26 March 1718 entry in the diary of the Rev. Stephen Williams, Storrs Library, Longmeadow. There was another revival during the full tide of the Great Awakening; see "Revivals of Religion," *Contributions to the Ecclesiastical History of Connecticut* (Hartford, 1861), 198. No East Windsor church records before 1830 survive, except a list of members to 1700 and baptisms to 1703 in a TE notebook (MS lost) included in Henry R. Stiles, *The History and Genealogies of Ancient Windsor . . . 1635–1891* (Hartford, 1891), I, Appendix.

13. For TE's salary, see S. Windsor Records, 1–99; for quarrels, 20, 69; and Stoughton, *"Windsor Farmes,"* 59. Comparative figures for Hampshire County are in Mary Catherine Foster, "Hampshire County, Massachusetts, 1729–1754: A Covenant Society in Transition" (Ph.D. dissertation, U. of Michigan, 1967), 299: TE was above the Hampshire average until the 1740s and then slightly below it. JE's salary was explicitly cited in 1735, in the first page of a TE notebook at the Connecticut Historical Society titled "Some things concerning my . . . father. . . ." In 1731 E. Windsor paid 14% less than did Northampton; the difference escalated to 35.7% by 1741 and 100% by 1746. In 1749 JE wrote that he had the highest salary outside Boston. JE to Thomas Foxcroft, 24 May 1749, Beinecke.

14. "Some things concerning my father," C.H.S.; account books for 1695–1718 [sic] at C.H.S. and 1711–1724 at Beinecke, quotation from p. 113 of the latter. Richard Edwards, TE's father, left an estate of £1107 in 1718, and TE's legacy was a mere £60. Richard Edwards estate, Hartford Probate Records, Connecticut Archives. On TE's brothers, rich merchants, see William D. Love, *The Colonial History of Hartford* (Hartford, 1914), 248.

15. See TE's 1711–1724 notebook, Beinecke, 38–47; Stoughton, *"Windsor Farmes,"* 54, 60–65, 71, 86–97, 108–11. From a now lost MS, Stoughton cites a sermon in which TE openly rebuked his congregation for insufficient deference to himself as exemplified by their neglect to " 'remove their hats when they meet their betters upon the street.' "

16. On the Saybrook Platform, see Williston Walker, *Creeds and Platforms of Congregationalism* (N.Y., 1893), 502–14. There is no record of the fight in the extant parish records, and the church records (only full church members would have voted) are lost. See Roger Wolcott, "A Narrative of the Troubles in the Second Church in Windsor from the Year 1735 to the Year 1741 . . . ," MS at Connecticut Historical Society.

17. One student of ministers' professional problems has found that salaries were the single greatest cause of minister-congregation disputes in the eighteenth century. James W. Schmotter, "Ministerial Careers in Eight-

eenth–Century New England: The Social Context, 1700–1760," *Journal of Social History*, IX (1975), 249–67. Some dimensions of the changes in the pastor-flock relation are vividly described in Clifford K. Shipton, "The New England Clergy of the 'Glacial Age,' " Colonial Society of Massachusetts *Publications*, XXXII (1933–37), 24–54.

18. In 1689 Richard Edwards asked a Hartford court for a divorce from his wife of twenty-two years, Elizabeth Tuttle, on grounds of repeated adultery. Shortly after their marriage she had borne another man's child and, he testified, "most of the country" know of the shame. (The baby was taken and raised by the Tuttles in New Haven; in 1718 RE left "Mary, the eldest child of my first wife," two shillings in his will.) RE had perhaps not sought divorce earlier because adultery was a capital crime in Connecticut until 1671. Elizabeth had been forgiven by her husband's "compassionate and pitiful disposition" that overruled his judgment, he later wrote, and they lived together for another eight or nine years until she refused all "conjugal communion" with him and three or four years later boldly confessed her habitual adultery. RE therefore asked the court to relieve him of the "intricate heart breaking miseries" of his marriage, but his petition was denied. For a second petition, Oct. 1690, RE wrote another statement, in which he cited Elizabeth's threats upon his life, answered objections that she was insane (insanity ran in her family but was not grounds for divorce) by saying that her adultery had preceded and probably "forwarded if not occasioned" her "distractions," and pleaded that by lack of a real wife he was "exposed to some of the greatest temptations that our nature is capable of, neither is my strength the strength of stones." A group of ministers favored the divorce, and in Oct. 1691 RE was released from his "conjugal tie" (though not from his financial obligations) to Elizabeth. Shortly thereafter he married Mary Talcott, sister of a future governor. Documents on the divorce can be found in the Conn. Archives, "Crimes & Misdemeanors & Divorces," III, 235–39, and *Public Records of the Colony of Connecticut*, IV, 37, 52–53, 59.

Timothy was a child when the trouble became overt in his family, and he was twenty when the divorce proceedings began. If "most of the country" knew of the scandal, his embarrassment must have been extreme. His mysterious crime at Harvard in 1688 may have been connected to the escalation of tension at home, or anxiety over his own part in the case: in March 1688 he and his sister Abigail made an official deposition against their mother. The unpleasantness of TE's involvement in the case is further suggested by the nature of the biography "Some things concerning my father," original at ANTS, copy of first few pp. in notebook at C.H.S.; excerpts (style "improved") in Dwight, *Edwards*, 654–61. The portrait is of a Puritan never "frightened or scared out of his duty," a hater of "vice and wickedness wherever he saw it" who "abhorred to plead for, justify, or make light of sin, because committed by them that were nearly related to him. . . ." Elizabeth Tuttle was never mentioned in the biography of her honorable husband, although the divorce was the perfect illustration of his principles. There is no record of his mother in any of the extant manuscripts of Timothy Edwards, and no record that he ever saw her after the divorce. The two major fights in TE's church were both precipitated by cases of sexually errant women (one was TE's niece).

19. Law, medicine, commerce, and government service were only slowly being recognized as professions. Warch, *School of the Prophets,* 250–77; and Samuel Eliot Morison, *Harvard College in the Seventeenth Century* (Cambridge, Mass., 1936), 557–63, give percentages of graduates choosing various careers. See also Schmotter, "Ministerial Careers," 249–67.

20. This emphasis, strongest in Perry Miller's *Jonathan Edwards,* remains the most prolific strain in Edwards studies. Continuing interest is reflected in John Opie, ed., *Jonathan Edwards and the Enlightenment* (Lexington, Mass., 1969).

21. Quotation from JE to Thomas Foxcroft, 24 May 1749, Beinecke. A self-consciousness about his intellectual ambitions is revealed in JE's directions to himself in shorthand on the inside of the cover to his "Notes on Natural Science," from his college years, as decoded by William P. Upham, reported in Massachusetts Historical Society *Proceedings,* 2nd Ser., XV (1902), 514–21. Especially interesting is No. 17, "Before I venture to publish in London to make some experiment in my own country [,] to play at small games first." Tutors at Harvard in the seventeenth century were little more than senior students, relatively powerless, low-paid, and transient (a two- or three-year tenure was common). Morison, *Harvard in 17th Century,* 15, 51–53, 122–24, 329, 455–56, 463–65.

22. The "Personal Narrative" was first printed in Hopkins, *Life of Edwards,* 23–39; the MS is lost. It is also in Dwight, *Edwards,* 58–67; and Faust and Johnson, *Edwards Selections,* 57–72.

23. JE's Resolutions and Diary, MSS now lost, are in Dwight, *Edwards,* 67–106. The conscious artistry of the "Personal Narrative" is discussed by Daniel B. Shea, Jr., in "The Art and Instruction of Jonathan Edwards' *Personal Narrative,*" in Sacvan Bercovitch, ed., *The American Puritan Imagination: Essays in Revaluation* (Cambridge, 1974), 159–72. Shea suggests that JE deliberately edited out the melancholy of his experiences because after his uncle Joseph Hawley's 1735 suicide, JE worried about a depressing effect in his writing.

24. Dwight, *Edwards,* 93. JE was living at home at the time, between

preaching jobs, and his anxiety may have grown under implicit pressure from his father, who probably preached a conventional model of conversion and watched his son carefully for signs of regeneration. But there is nothing radical about the "Personal Narrative" except the emphasis on aesthetics.

25. *Ibid.,* 78. Baptismal-covenant renewal as a community ritual grew in popularity in the eighteenth century. See James W. Jones, *The Shattered Synthesis* (New Haven, 1973), 47–49, 86; Paul R. Lucas, *Valley of Discord: Church and Society along the Connecticut River, 1636–1725* (Hanover, N.H., 1976), 93–94; and Stephen Williams Diary, Longmeadow, I, 77–78, 100. Biographer Samuel Hopkins, a close friend, mentions no church-joining in his account of JE; Dwight, *Edwards,* 58, confirms the lack of formal membership before JE went to Northampton. JE would have had to testify to his conversion experience if he joined the East Windsor church as a full member, but not when he joined the Northampton church, which had abandoned "relations" and indeed maintained no public distinctions among categories of membership when JE joined.

26. Dwight, *Edwards,* 80–82, 105–6.

27. Wilson H. Kimnach, "Jonathan Edwards' Early Sermons: New York, 1722–1723," *Journal of Presbyterian History,* LV (1977), 255–66.

28. MSS at Beinecke. I am greatly indebted to Professor Thomas A. Schafer, who is editing the "Miscellanies" for publication by Yale University Press, for allowing me to use his typescripts and sharing with me his deductions about the probable dates of various important entries.

29. Burr letter, incomplete, ANTS. My view of the inconsistencies between the "Personal Narrative" and the diary entries is not shared by Harold P. Simonson, *Jonathan Edwards, Theologian of the Heart* (Grand Rapids, 1974), 19; or by Richard L. Bushman, "Jonathan Edwards as Great Man: Identity, Conversion and Leadership in the Great Awakening," *Soundings,* LII (1969), 15–46, especially 33. The timing of JE's conversion at college graduation is quite similar to other well-known Puritan conversions. See "John Winthrop's Christian Experience," Massachusetts Historical Society, *Winthrop Papers,* I (Boston, 1929), 154–59; Michael McGiffert, *God's Plot: The Paradoxes of Puritan Piety, Being the Autobiography and Journal of Thomas Shepard* (Amherst, Mass., 1972), 40–41; and David Levin, *Cotton Mather: The Young Life of the Lord's Remembrancer, 1663–1703* (Cambridge, Mass., 1978), 58–65. Daniel B. Shea, Jr., has commented that "Puritan autobiographers also suffered chronically from an adolescent disease that masqueraded as true conviction until it disappeared and left good health and a heart more depraved than ever." *Spiritual Autobiography in Early America* (Princeton, 1968), 106.

30. Usually called the "Apostrophe to Sarah Pierrepont," this description

was first printed in Dwight, *Edwards,* 114–15, from a MS now lost; it is also in Faust and Johnson, *Edwards Selections,* 56. Sarah was the daughter of the Rev. James Pierrepont of New Haven, one of the most influential ministers in Connecticut.

31. One analyst, who labels the description of Sarah a "confession," has pointed out that its crux is "its opposition to the formal statements of God's sovereignty. Sarah Pierrepont is a refuge from the harshness, the terror, and the abject feeling of inconsequence which came to Edwards every time he pondered that awesome question of God's infinite majesty." Also, "that he should have put his dream of wonder in the person of a young girl might suggest his unwilling awareness bordering on shame that he was seldom, if ever, in his own life and being, capable of such ecstasy." Edward H. Davidson, *Jonathan Edwards: The Narrative of a Puritan Mind* (Boston, Mass., 1966), 24, 26.

32. "Jonathan Edwards and Puritan Consciousness," *Journal for the Scientific Study of Religion,* V (1966), 383–96, quotations 395, 393.

33. Bushman, "Jonathan Edwards as Great Man," 17–24. A fascinating comparison with John Wesley's experience can be drawn from Robert L. Moore, "Justification without Joy: Psychohistorical Reflections on John Wesley's Childhood and Conversion," *History of Childhood Quarterly,* II (1974), 31–52.

34. Philip Greven, *The Protestant Temperament: Patterns of Child-Rearing, Religious Experience, and the Self in Early America* (N.Y., 1977), 125–29. Sacvan Bercovitch, *The Puritan Origins of the American Self* (New Haven, 1975), 13–23.

35. The most useful works on conversion that I have found are the following: Leon Salzman, "The Psychology of Religious and Ideological Conversion," *Psychiatry,* XVI (1953), 177–87; Salzman, "Types of Religious Conversion," *Pastoral Psychology,* XVII (1966), 8–20; Joel Allison, "Recent Empirical Studies of Religious Conversion Experiences," *ibid.,* 21–34; Allison, "Religious Conversion: Regression and Progression in an Adolescent Experience," *Journal for the Scientific Study of Religion,* VIII (1969), 23–38. The problems of harmonizing adult self-assertion with deference to authority figures are a striking theme in Philip M. Helfaer's study of divinity students, *The Psychology of Religious Doubt* (Boston, 1972). A useful perspective is offered by Howard M. Feinstein, "The Prepared Heart: A Comparative Study of Puritan Theology and Psychoanalysis," *American Quarterly,* XXII (1970), 166–76.

36. Bushman, "Jonathan Edwards as Great Man," 37.

37. "Miscellanies" entry 40; similar sentiments are expressed in No. 45.

38. John Moore, Jr., and Abigail Stoughton (daughter of TE's sister) were

married in Dec. 1724; in Oct. 1723 their child, unnamed and birth date unknown, had died. Abigail's father tried to have the marriage annulled and TE called the local ministerial association to decide the case in Feb. 1725; they upheld paternal authority. But the couple stayed married, although Moore was publicly charged with being idle and was committed to the workhouse, escaped, used force to drag the starving Abigail (and a child) from her refuge in her father's house, then (1738) brought a complaint against her in the church for desertion! The church apparently judged her guilty but TE recorded in his notebook that "she was not convicted, because of my non-concurrence." TE had to call a ministerial council to enforce his view of ministerial power in the East Windsor church, and then he querulously complained to the council that they had not been explicit enough in defending him but had merely exonerated Abigail. This case has been pieced together from *Windsor Vital Records,* II, 176–77; Stiles, *History of Windsor,* II, 501–2; Stoughton, *"Windsor Farmes,"* 71–73; Conn. Archives, "Crimes, etc.," IV, 12, 14–16; and TE notebook, ANTS.

39. In a 1719 note, TE mentioned a loan to a John Smith of 12d. "which he gave into his contribution to the people at New York." 1711–1724 account book, Beinecke. While in New York, JE boarded with a John Smith and his mother. See his diary entries for 1 May and 18 May 1723 in Dwight, *Edwards,* 84–85; "Personal Narrative" in Faust and Johnson, *Edwards Selections,* 64–65.

40. Winslow, *Jonathan Edwards,* 87–88; Thomas Grant to Timothy Woodbridge, Connecticut Historical Society *Collections,* XXI (1924), 404–05.

41. The two letters, JE's of 10 Dec. 1722 and TE's of 16 Jan. 1723, are at the Connecticut Historical Society.

42. Dwight, *Edwards,* 84–85, 71, 86, 72–73, 93.

43. Settlement agreement, Bolton town records, photostat at Beinecke. Other Bolton records are included in Stoughton, *"Windsor Farmes,"* 81–82. There is no record of his leaving. He was probably still there in early December, for his diary entry of the 12th is a resolution to spend more time in the duties of pastoral visiting. Dwight, *Edwards,* 100.

44. Dexter, *Documentary History of Yale,* 252.

45. Diary entry for 6 June 1724, in Dwight, *Edwards,* 103.

46. Describing the aftermath of a speedily quashed student "insurrection" against the college food, Jonathan cited "monstrous impieties, and acts of immorality . . . particularly stealing of hens, geese, turkies, piggs, meat, wood &c,—unseasonable nightwalking, breaking people's windows, playing at cards, cursing, swearing. . . ." He thanked God that he was "perfectly free of all their janglings." JE to TE, 1 March 1721, ANTS; in Winslow,

Jonathan Edwards, 70–72. Typically rowdy student behavior is cited by Warch, *School of the Prophets,* 154, and by Josiah Quincy, *The History of Harvard University* (Boston, 1860), I, 319. Rector Timothy Cutler later remembered JE as "a sober person, but withal pretty recluse, austere and rigid." Stenerson, "Anglican Critique," 482. See also the letters from JE and TE to the Rev. Stephen Mix, n.d. but probably Fall 1720, ANTS.

47. JE's illness is described in his "Personal Narrative," Faust and Johnson, *Edwards Selections,* 66, and in letters from TE to his wife dated 11 Oct., 20 Oct., and 10 Nov. 1725, ANTS. He was so ill that his mother was with him for at least two months. Interesting parallels to JE's physical/emotional collapses at times of great stress can be found in the careers of Elisha Williams and Rector Thomas Clap, Williams's successor. See Warch, *School of the Prophets,* 183; and Louis L. Tucker, *Puritan Protagonist: President Thomas Clap of Yale College* (Chapel Hill, N.C., 1962), 29.

Chapter Three: Strategies

1. *Faithful Narrative* (London, 1737; Boston, 1738) in C. C. Goen, ed., *The Great Awakening,* Vol. IV of *The Works of Jonathan Edwards* (New Haven, 1972), 144–46.

2. *Ibid.,* 146.

3. Elisha Williams was uncompromisingly orthodox in his theology; his 1728 Election Sermon, *Divine Grace Illustrious, in the Salvation of Sinners,* insisted that grace was "wholly free and unearned." As Yale's new Rector in 1725, Williams had to take an oath against "Arminian and Prelatical Principles." Sibley, *Harvard Graduates,* V, 590. JE probably had to take a similar oath to become tutor in 1724.

4. JE to Rev. Thomas Gillespie, 1 July 1751, in Dwight, *Edwards,* 465.

5. Sermon on I Corinthians 11:29, dated Jan. 1732/33, and Psalms 139: 23–24, dated Sept. 1733, MSS at Beinecke; the latter printed in the N.Y. 1844 edition of JE's *Works,* IV, 502–28, see esp. 515. As early as the spring of 1730, perhaps (date deduced by Thomas A. Schafer), JE had written a rather ambiguous description of the requirement of being "Christians really in order to come [to the Lord's Supper] for only the righteous have any right to the privileges of the church"; "Miscellanies" entry 462, MS and Schafer typescript at Beinecke.

6. 3 MSS on Ecclesiastes 9:10, Beinecke; one not dated but probably early 1729 (Schafer), others dated Dec. 1733 and Jan. 1734. The latter two are incomplete. A sermon on Ecc. 4:5, dated Feb. 1733, ANTS, repeats the same charge of men's "negligence." The question of how probable was the reward for striving, according to JE, is discussed by John H. Gerstner, *Steps*

to Salvation: The Evangelistic Message of Jonathan Edwards (Philadelphia, 1960), 96–101.

7. Luke 22:30, ANTS. I Kings 18:21, dated June 1734, included in N.Y. 1844 *Works*, IV, 338–46.

8. JE, "Pressing into the Kingdom of God," Luke 16:16, 1735, printed as No. 2 of *Five Discourses on Important Subjects . . .* (Boston, 1738), reprinted in N.Y. 1844 *Works*, IV, 381–402, see esp. 383–84, 386. Gerstner, *Steps to Salvation*, 74–75.

9. See Norman Pettit, *The Heart Prepared: Grace and Conversion in Puritan Spiritual Life* (New Haven, 1966), passim. Most analysts of New England Puritanism rightly emphasize that there is no fundamental disagreement in theory between Calvinism's doctrine of arbitrary grace and the practice of encouraging men to seek salvation, but it seems more fruitful for analytical purposes to admit the discrepancy in *tone* between the official doctrine and the practical homilies.

10. I Cor. 1:29–31, published in Boston, 1731, reprinted in N.Y. 1844 *Works*, IV, 169–78.

11. "Jonathan Edwards' Sermon Mill," *Early American Literature*, X (1975), 167–78, quotations 171–72.

12. Boston, 1734; reprinted in N.Y. 1844 *Works*, IV, 438–50. MS at Beinecke, dated Aug. 1733. See also Wilson H. Kimnach, "Jonathan Edwards' Early Sermons: New York, 1722–1723," *Journal of Presbyterian History*, LV (1977), 255–66. The "light" metaphor is almost universal in Christian theology, but from the beginning of his career Edwards used it slightly differently than did Stoddard. Stoddard declared that the regenerate person would "know God's glory" through the light of the Spirit (see *Treatise Concerning Conversion*, 30–35, for the essence of Stoddard's "intellectualist" position), whereas Edwards chose to emphasize that the convert would have a "sense" of the loveliness of God's holiness. From his earliest writings on the subject, Edwards tried to emphasize the unification of man's psyche in regeneration (that unity was in fact a definition of regeneration). In his *ca.* 1716–21 "Notes on the Mind," entry No. 14 (in Dwight, *Edwards*, 665), JE stated that "the Scriptures are ignorant of the philosophic distinction of the understanding, and the will; . . . the sense of the heart is there called knowledge, or understanding." In "Miscellanies" entry No. 291, he stated that man since Adam's Fall has had "an inclination contrary to his reason and judgment"; before that, and presumably after regeneration, the will and reason function in perfect unison. The same idea is expressed in entry No. 436, probably written late in 1729 or early in 1730, and in No. 489, perhaps written early in 1731 (Schafer dates). There is no major change in this psychological model of conversion through the rest of Edwards's "Miscella-

nies" and his published writings. What remained to be worked out, and what would only be articulated clearly in the late 1740s, were the implied *behavioral* consequences of this total revitalization of man's faculties by grace.

13. Luke 16:31, MS not extant, included in N.Y. 1844 *Works*, IV, 330–37. Hebrews 11:13–14, preached Sept. 1733 at New Haven, MS at Beinecke, included in *ibid.*, 573–84. Micah 2:11, MS at Beinecke dated Nov. 1733. Ephesians 5:16, MS at Beinecke dated Dec. 1733, included in the two-volume London 1839 edition of JE's *Works*, II, 233–36. Romans 12:17, MS at Beinecke dated July 1733. *Faithful Narrative*, in Goen, *Great Awakening*, 146.

14. Cited in note 5, above, "Miscellanies" entry 462 seems to be testing the idea of using restricted access to the sacraments as a way of punishing bad behavior. "If this way were taken[,] wicked men[,] those that are sensible they are such. . . . would be visibly separate from Christ in that they are separate from the church and don't come and join themselves." But the requirement was defined as a sincere willingness to break off from sin, and the means described for bringing men to that state is not an act of the Holy Spirit but the arguments of the elders and the reading of inspirational books —so whether or not the communicant should be in reality a regenerate person is left unclear.

15. Amos 8:11, dated by Schafer as 20 March 1729; see also the two sermons on Job 1:5, dated by Schafer as early 1730; MSS at Beinecke.

16. Psalms 139:23–24, MS at Beinecke labeled Sept. 1733, included in N.Y. 1844 *Works*, IV, 502–28, quotation 525. Cotton Mather's 1699 tract *A Family Well-Ordered*, 10–11, contained a similar and even deeper appeal to parental guilt: he said that children were under the wrath of God because they had been born in sin, and that was the parents' fault—"Man, thy children are dying of an horrid poison, in their bowels; and it was thou that poisoned 'em."

17. Ecclesiastes 12:1, perhaps very late 1732 (Schafer date). Proverbs 24:13–14, MS dated May 1734. Acts 16:29–30, MS dated Aug. 1734, included in London 1839 *Works*, II, 817–29. Ecclesiastes 7:6, MS dated Nov. 1734, "lecture day night meeting." All MSS at Beinecke.

18. The earlier sermon is Job 21:11, dated March 1733, MS at Beinecke. The later usage was closer to the modern psychologists' distinction between guilt and shame, although Edwards did not use the same words that way.

19. *Faithful Narrative*, in Goen, *Great Awakening*, 147–48. The sudden deaths of two children added to their friends' docility.

20. On Rand, see Introduction to *ibid.*, 17–18. On Breck, see Chapter 5, below. Fears of Arminianism are documented in the Hampshire Association

of Ministers' letter to the Bishop of London, 1734, included in William Stevens Perry, ed., *Historical Collections Relating to the American Colonial Church,* Vol. III: *Massachusetts* (Hartford, 1873), 299–301. See also Hampshire Association Records, MS at Forbes Library, Northampton, 13. A useful comparison is provided by John White, *New England's Lamentations* (Boston, 1734); and J. M. Bumsted, "A Caution to Erring Christians: Ecclesiastical Disorder on Cape Cod, 1717 to 1738," *William and Mary Quarterly,* 3rd Ser., XXVIII (1971), 413–38.

21. *Faithful Narrative,* in Goen, *Great Awakening,* 148.

22. *Ibid.,* 149. The "Justification" sermons were printed, as one, with four others preached thereafter on the same theme, as *Five Discourses on Important Subjects* (Boston, 1738); reprinted in N.Y. 1844 *Works,* IV, 65–132 ("Justification"), 179–201, 226–53, 381–402, 412–21.

23. *Ibid.,* 74, 76–92, 102–28, 128–32.

24. *Faithful Narrative,* in Goen, *Great Awakening,* 149. On 28 April 1735, the Rev. William Williams of Hatfield wrote to the Rev. Benjamin Colman of Boston that "a very general" revival of piety had spread "in most of the towns in our county . . . especially upon the younger sort of people. . . . there is a very sensible reformation among us." Colman Papers, Massachusetts Historical Society.

25. Psalms 46:10, dated June 1735, MS at Beinecke; included in London 1839 *Works,* II, 107–10.

26. The fourth of JE's *Five Discourses,* in N.Y. 1844 *Works,* IV, 232–35.

27. Compare the sermon on Psalms 139:23–24, dated Sept. 1733, MS at Beinecke; included in *ibid.,* 502–28. It is a catalogue of many sins, but its wordiness and elaboration of the circumstances of sin contrast with the rapid-fire trenchancy of the later sermon. The frequent use of "we" and "there are many persons who," rather than the consistent inquisitorial "you" used later, dilutes the emotional effect.

28. Samuel Hopkins, *The Life and Character of the Late Reverend, Learned and Pious Mr. Jonathan Edwards* (Boston, 1765), 52. See also Timothy Dwight, *Travels in New England and New York,* ed. B. M. Solomon (Cambridge, Mass., 1969), IV, 230–31.

29. Cedric B. Cowing, "Sex and Preaching in the Great Awakening," *American Quarterly,* XX (1968), 624–44, points out that anger at the apparent injustice of God's requirements, as measured by common sense, may have served to heighten the susceptibility of emotionally stable men to the ultimate appeal of fear. William Sargant's *Battle for the Mind* (London, 1957) cites the usefulness of anger as a wedge into the mind in classic brainwashing techniques.

30. N.Y. 1844 *Works,* IV, 251.

31. Luke 16:16, MS at Beinecke dated "after the death of Joseph Clark's wife" [Feb. 13, 1735]; printed as No. 2 of the *Five Discourses;* in N.Y. 1844 *Works,* IV, 381–402, see esp. 383–84, 386.

32. I Thessalonians 2:16, MS at Beinecke dated May 1735; included in N.Y. 1844 *Works,* IV, 280–86; the theme was that Puritan favorite, the flight from Sodom. "Pressing into the Kingdom," in *ibid.,* 392, 396, 397.

33. Quoted in David Freeman Hawke, *Franklin* (N.Y., 1976), 160.

34. For an assertion that the New England theological mainstream was consciously and genuinely Calvinist and not crypto-Arminian before the Awakening, see Gerald J. Goodwin, "The Myth of 'Arminian-Calvinism' in Eighteenth Century New England," *New England Quarterly,* XLI (1968), 213–37. In this as in many other studies of theology, putting philosophical labels on what may have been merely circumstantial differences in stress does not help us understand what the preachers were trying to communicate to their congregations.

35. See the works on the social history of the Awakening cited in note 2, Introduction. An essay that has implications for all of New England and particular pertinence to the Valley is Kenneth A. Lockridge, "Land, Population and the Evolution of New England Society 1630–1790," *Past & Present,* No. 39 (April 1968), 62–80. In his influential study of changes in "character and the social order" in eighteenth-century Connecticut, Richard L. Bushman placed great emphasis on the guilt engendered by the ambitions of Puritans who took advantage of a rapidly expanding economy. See Bushman, *From Puritan to Yankee* (N.Y., 1970), 187–95. The eastern part of the state was the most recently developed; there the resulting guilt was perhaps strongest, and there the revivals of 1740–42 were most intense. Although one might question the degree to which Puritan anti-commercial values were still strong in men who had behaved in an entrepreneurial manner for at least half a century, and although Bushman never quite explains why the emotional resolution of conversion was so effective in cleansing the socio-economic conscience, his theory of guilt remains the most satisfactory published attempt to deal with the Awakening as a socio-psychological phenomenon. Philip Greven's *The Protestant Temperament: Patterns of Child-Rearing, Religious Experience, and the Self in Early America* (N.Y., 1977), a marvelously provocative study of the evangelical personality, argues the persistence of that personality type over broad but vague reaches of time and space (see especially pp. 6–7 and 7n.) and so gives us little help in understanding what did seem to be an increase in pietism in the late 1730s and 1740s.

Bushman does not report on the lives of particular converts, and the rather young average age for converts in Northampton and other studied communities (see note 37, below) suggests another psychological drama at work in those "awakened." Young men in their late teens and early twenties, although too young to have had many clashes with legal authorities or to be guilty of economic success, did face problems of incipient rebellion against authority. At that stage in their lives, any remaining Puritan moral economic values would have been focused through the attitudes of their parents, and the tensions a young man might have felt in deciding to be a farmer or an entrepreneur, a stay-at-home or a pioneer, a Puritan or a Yankee, would have translated easily into conflict with parents.

36. For a medical analysis of the throat distemper, see Ernest Caulfield, *A True History of . . . the Throat Distemper . . .* (New Haven, 1939). Philip J. Greven, Jr., "Youth, Maturity, and Religious Conversion: A Note on the Ages of Converts in Andover, Massachusetts, 1711–1749," *Essex Institute Historical Collections,* CVIII (1972), 120–30, points out the rise in church joining in Andover during the years of earthquake and epidemic, although there was no Calvinist revival in those churches.

37. The ages at church joining in Northampton (described in more detail in Chapter 4, note 8) are not far from the average ages reported for other communities. In a study of the Awakening in the northern Connecticut Valley, Kevin Sweeney found that men joining the churches of Longmeadow, Suffield, Northampton, Deerfield, and Springfield First Parish averaged twenty-one to twenty-six years old during the revivals of 1735 and 1741–42; joiners in non-revival years were seven to ten years older. Sweeney, "Unruly Saints: Religion and Society in the River Towns of Massachusetts, 1700–1750" (unpublished honors thesis, Williams College, 1972), 136. Ralph J. Coffman, *Solomon Stoddard* (Boston, 1978), 181, gives figures for Valley churches that are much like Sweeney's, but neither the Sweeney thesis nor any other source is referenced. In Andover, which did not have a revival during the Great Awakening, males joined the two local churches in full communion in their mid-thirties between 1711 and 1729 and about ten years younger in 1730–49; the average age of those "owning the covenant" was about twelve and four years younger, respectively. Greven, "Youth, Maturity, and Religious Conversion," 120–30. In Norton, Mass., before the Awakening the average age at full-communion church joining was 39.7 years for men; it fell to 29.9 years during 1741–42. J. M. Bumsted, "Religion, Finance, and Democracy in Massachusetts: The Town of Norton as a Case Study," *Journal of American History,* LVII (1971), 817–31. In Norwich, Conn., the average age of male church joiners was 30.3 in the years 1718–40, and 25.2 in the Awakening of 1741–44. Gerald F. Moran, "Conditions of Religious Conversion in the First Society of Norwich, Connecticut, 1718–1744," *Journal of Social History,* V (1971–72), 331–43. In the Second Church of Windham, Conn., formed by Andover

men (see Philip J. Greven, Jr., *Four Generations: Population, Land, and Family in Colonial Andover, Massachusetts* [Ithaca, N.Y., 1970]) and other immigrants, men who joined the church during the Awakening averaged 20.9 years old; their fathers had averaged almost eleven years older when they joined the church in the seventeen years preceding the revival. William F. Willingham, "Religious Conversion in the Second Society of Windham, Connecticut, 1723–1743: A Case Study," *Societas,* VI (1976), 109–19. In Woodbury, Conn., the mean age for men admitted to the church during the revival years 1739–42 ranged between 21.2 and 22.9 years, whereas the lowest mean for males admitted in previous periods was 28.3 years old. James Walsh, "The Great Awakening in the First Congregational Church of Woodbury, Connecticut," *William and Mary Quarterly,* 3rd Ser., XXVIII (1971), 543–62.

38. Underlying the assumptions about social psychology which inform this book is, obviously, Erik Erikson's theoretical model, as articulated most clearly in *Identity and the Life Cycle: Selected Papers,* Monograph No. 1 of *Psychological Issues* (N.Y., 1959). Not all historians accept the applicability of this model to historical materials, but a sufficient defense of its usefulness is offered by Cushing Strout in "Ego Psychology and the Historian," *History and Theory,* VII (1968), 281–97. See also Strout, "The Uses and Abuses of Psychology in American History," *American Quarterly,* XXVIII (1976), 324–42; and John Demos, "Demography and Psychology in the Historical Study of Family-life: A Personal Report," in Peter Laslett and Richard Wall, eds., *Household and Family in Past Time* (Cambridge, 1972), 561–69.

The question of the historicity of adolescent experiences is addressed in Kenneth Keniston, "Psychological Development and Historical Change," *Journal of Interdisciplinary History,* II (1971), 329–45. The classic works on adolescent conversion are William James, *The Varieties of Religious Experience* (N.Y., 1903) and Edwin D. Starbuck, *The Psychology of Religion: An Empirical Study of the Growth of Religious Consciousness* (N.Y., 1903). See also the more recent works on the psychology of conversion cited in note 35 to Chapter 2.

One of the best succinct statements of the relationship between evangelical ministers and their followers is that of Cushing Strout, in *New Heavens and New Earth: Political Religion in America* (N.Y., 1974), p. 44: "The precariously seated clergy made an ally out of youth by evoking, interpreting, and legitimating its inner guilt, its public shame, and its ardent hopes for historical meaning and direction."

Chapter Four: Constituency

1. Edwards's Farewell Sermon, II Corinthians 1:14, MS at Beinecke, was first published in Boston in 1751; reprinted in Sereno E. Dwight, *Life of President Edwards* (N.Y., 1829), 630–51, and in Clarence H. Faust and Thomas H. Johnson, eds., *Jonathan Edwards: Representative Selections* rev. ed. (N.Y., 1962), 186–202; quotation from p. 646 or p. 194, respectively.

2. Stoddard, *The Danger of Speedy Degeneracy* (Boston, 1705), 6–7. N. Ray Hiner, "Adolescence in Eighteenth Century America," *History of Childhood Quarterly,* III (1975), 253–80.

3. *A Faithful Narrative of the Surprising Work of God* . . . . (London, 1737; Boston, 1738), reprinted in C. C. Goen, ed., *The Great Awakening,* Vol. IV of *The Works of Jonathan Edwards* (New Haven, 1972), 146.

4. Darrett B. Rutman, *Winthrop's Boston* (Chapel Hill, N.C., 1965), presents early Boston activity quite inconsistent with the communitarian model set forth in Winthrop's sermon on the *Arbella.* A number of other, agrarian, communities exhibited behavior that was much more Puritan in religion and economic life for at least one generation. See Kenneth A. Lockridge, *A New England Town: The First Hundred Years* (N.Y., 1970); Michael Zuckerman, *Peaceable Kingdoms: New England Towns in the Eighteenth Century* (N.Y., 1970).

5. Hampshire County Probate Records, passim; mason Nathaniel Phelps's account book, Historic Deerfield Library; merchant Joseph Hawley's account book, 1712–24ff, Forbes Library; JE to Thomas Foxcroft, 24 May 1749, Beinecke.

6. See Zuckerman, *Peaceable Kingdoms;* E. A. J. Johnson, *American Economic Thought in the Seventeenth Century* (London, 1932); and J. E. Crowley, *This Sheba, Self: The Conceptualization of Economic Life in Eighteenth–Century America* (Baltimore, 1974), for descriptions of the ideal. Zuckerman found the reality in the communities he studied to be much like the ideal, well into the eighteenth century. Northampton men, and probably those in most towns past the frontier stage, behaved much more like the Yankees whom Richard L. Bushman found in Connecticut by the end of the seventeenth century. See Bushman, *From Puritan to Yankee: Character and the Social Order in Connecticut, 1690–1765* (Cambridge, Mass., 1967).

7. It seems logical to modern historians that from the different personalities of the mid-eighteenth-century Yankee frontier entrepreneur and the mid-seventeenth-century Puritan community-oriented saint-in-exile, one might deduce different experiences in early childhood. But substantial information on child-rearing practices in the colonies is lacking. Extremely small samples of data have contributed to the varied interpretations offered by

John Demos and Joseph E. Illick. See Demos, "Developmental Perspectives on the History of Childhood," *Journal of Interdisciplinary History,* II (1971), 315–27; and *A Little Commonwealth: Family Life in Plymouth Colony* (N.Y., 1970), esp. Chap. 9; Illick, "Child-Rearing in Seventeenth-Century England and America," in Lloyd de Mause, ed., *The History of Childhood* (N. Y., 1974), 303–50. Important documents have been published by Philip J. Greven, Jr., in *Child-Rearing Concepts, 1628–1861: Historical Sources* (Itasca, Ill., 1973). Greven's most recent and provocative work, *The Protestant Temperament: Patterns of Child-Rearing, Religious Experience, and the Self in Early America* (N.Y., 1977), presents a broad range of evidence for the existence of an evangelical family and personality type, but also has two important problems. Greven's assertion (pp. 6–7) that there is no change over time (from the mid-sixteenth to mid-nineteenth centuries in England and America) is not really convincing, and his use of pieces of information without any regard to chronological or geographical control makes his evidence hard to use in examining that very question of variation. Moreover, although the evangelical type of family and personality and its opposite, the genteel, do emerge as very distinct, the middle or moderate type seems to be defined only as that which is not either extreme, and so the critical task of distinguishing the eighteenth-century evangelical from the revival-resistant Congregationalist is not made any easier.

The importance of family life as cause or effect of Puritanism or Calvinism has been emphasized by many analyses of that religious movement. See, for example, Michael Walzer, *The Revolution of the Saints* (Cambridge, Mass., 1965), 47–50, 183–91; and Christopher Hill, *Society and Puritanism,* 2nd ed. (N.Y., 1967), 443–81. Even now that we know that the nuclear (husband-wife-unmarried children) family is not new in the modern era (see Peter Laslett's Introduction to Laslett and Richard Wall, eds., *Household and Family in Past Time* [Cambridge, 1972]), it is easy to see the Puritan family fostering notions of individual worth through its emphasis on personal conversion and thereby inadvertently contributing to the rise of liberal thought and democracy. See, for example, James A. Henretta, *The Evolution of American Society, 1700–1815* (Lexington, Mass., 1973), 30–31; and Robert H. Bremner *et al.,* eds., *Children and Youth in America: A Documentary History* (Cambridge, Mass., 1970), I, passim.

The sentimentalization of childhood, the growth of affection toward children as persons (not as economic pawns) has been commented upon in passing in at least two recent studies of the early New England community (which attribute different timing to the process). James Axtell, *The School upon a Hill: Education and Society in Colonial New England* (New Haven, 1974), 92–93, repeats Alexis de Tocqueville's suggestion that partible inheritance (which Axtell and Tocqueville assume was the universal pattern in America) brought the growth of parent-child affection with the absence of competition for scarce resources. Henretta, *Evolution of American Society,* 39, suggests that it was only when (by the late eighteenth century in many areas) the father could no longer provide automatically for all his sons by partitioning his own land, and therefore had to seek actively other means to give his sons a start in life, that there emerged "a new and different type of family life, one characterized by solicitude and sentimentality toward children." The latter view is much more plausible, if only because it was those stern Puritan patriarchs of the first two generations in most towns who had land enough to partition among all their sons. Unless the sources entirely mislead us, the sentimentalization of childhood developed in the eighteenth century, when partition was much more difficult and often very unequal. For a sensitive evaluation of the importance of lineal values in early American agrarian society, see Henretta, "Families and Farms: Mentalité in Pre-Industrial America," *William and Mary Quarterly,* 3rd Ser., XXXV (1978), 3–32. The relationship of certain patterns of family life to different socioeconomic environments, especially types of towns (in terms of geography and age), has yet to be adequately assessed.

8. The church-membership list kept by Stoddard in the front part of the church record book is arranged in four columns, (left to right) male-female-male-female. "Jonathan Edwards" is near the top of the left-most column on page 5, so the date 1727 is assigned to that entry and all subsequent ones on that page and page 43 (no church members on intervening pages) are assumed to be later. The change from Stoddard's hand to Edwards's occurs about one-third of the way down the left-hand two columns. The right-hand two columns on page 5 are each enclosed in a hand-drawn box, and their curvature indicates that they were written later. An attempt was made to identify genealogically every church member (including all of Stoddard's entries); through personal information, such as marriage for women or deaths, individual entries can be identified as necessarily recorded before or after certain dates. By this process the columns in the boxes have been dated January to July 1735. The first two columns are thereafter considered to be 1727–35, and the names on page 43 were entered between mid-1735 and 1746 (JE himself provides the terminal date on the list).

The 1735 males (N-57) averaged twenty-one years old in mid-1735, and the 1727–35 group (N-72) were about five years older in mid-1735; the 1735–46 group (N-129) averaged just over eighteen years old in 1740. (Comparative statistics are given in note 37 to Chapter III.) As far as can be determined from James R. Trumbull's Northampton genealogy (unpublished typescript at Forbes Library) and the Vital Statistics, almost every male in town by 1746 did join the church, although after 1740 there were probably more newcomers and transients who were not recorded in now extant sources.

9. For example, Walter Lee had lived near Boston before going to Windsor, then moved to Northampton for about ten years and left around 1666 to settle at Westfield. Josiah Dewey settled first at Windsor, then lived at Westfield for a while, was living in Northampton from the mid-1660s to 1696, then moved on to Lebanon, Conn. Trumbull, Genealogy.

10. The following statistics on emigration, representing the minimum number of emigrants known, has been drawn from genealogical and other documents from Northampton; the count includes all males known to have been born or lived in Northampton before 1740, most of those born before 1750 to resident families, and all emigration known through the 1760s. I am indebted to Paul V. Rogers of Williams College for his help with this project. Comparative data can be found in Kenneth A. Lockridge, "The Population of Dedham, Massachusetts, 1636–1736," *Economic History Review,* 2nd Ser., XIX (1966), 322–24; Lockridge, *A New England Town,* 64, 139–40, 143n.; Philip J. Greven, Jr., *Four Generations: Population, Land, and*

Table 1: RATE OF EMIGRATION

Decade	Known to move in decade	Date of emigration unknown, but born 30–40 years earlier*	Total
1670s	4	—	4 (?)
1680s	6	14**	20
1690s	3	13	16
1700s	7	12	19
1710s	12	13	25
1720s	9	10	19
1730s***	11	14	25
1740s	14	15	29
1750s	6	7	13
1760s	7	10	17
1770s	—	9	9 (?)

*Two more have birthdates and emigration dates unknown. Five other men, with college degrees, leave town for ministerial posts elsewhere.
**Born before 1660.
***Does not include the approximately twenty men who move to Southampton in the 1730s and early 1740s.

Family in Colonial Andover, Massachusetts (Ithaca, N.Y., 1970), 39, 123, 162–66, 211; and Charles S. Grant, *Democracy in the Connecticut Frontier Town of Kent* (N.Y., 1961), 101–2.

Table 2: PLACES TO WHICH KNOWN EMIGRANTS GO

1670s (N=4): 2 Deerfield, 1 Northfield, 1 Westfield

1680s (N=6): 4 Deerfield, 1 Northfield, 1 Suffield

1690s (N=3): 1 Deerfield, 1 Suffield, 1 Enfield

1700s (N=7): 2 Deerfield, 1 Hatfield, 1 Wethersfield, 2 Durham (Ct), 1 Coventry (Ct)

1710s (N=12): 1 Deerfield, 6 Northfield, 1 Durham, 1 Coventry, 1 Lebanon (Ct), 1 Stamford (Ct), 1 Brookfield (Mass)

1720s (N=9): 4 Suffield, 1 Coventry, 1 Lebanon, 1 Bolton (Ct), 1 Belchertown (Mass), 1 Sunderland (Mass)

1730s (N=11): 2 Suffield, 4 Belchertown, 1 Sunderland, 1 South Hadley (Mass), 1 Farmington (Ct), 1 Goshen (Ct), 1 Lyme (Ct)

1740s (N=14): 3 Hadley or Amherst, 3 Belchertown, 1 Northfield, 1 Berkshires, 3 Farmington, 1 Sharon (Ct), 1 New Hampshire, 1 Maine

1750s (N=6): 1 Hadley or Amherst, 1 Belchertown, 2 Sunderland, 2 Berkshires

Table 3: AGES AT EMIGRATION

	To Deerfield/ Northfield		To Conn.	Other Mass.	Place unk.
	N	(N known) Avg.	N (Nk) Avg.	N (Nk) Avg.	N (Nk) Avg.
1670s	3	(2) 34.5	0	1 (0)	
1680s	5	(5) 29.0	0	1 (1) 36.0	
1690s	1	(1) 31.0	1 (1) 24.0	1 (0)	
1700s	2	(2) 35.5	4 (4) 37.5	1 (1) 26.0	
1710s	7	(5) 29.6	4 (2) 39.0	1 (1) 34.0	
1720s	0		7 (5) 39.2	2 (1) 23.0	
1730s	0		5 (5) 31.8	6 (6) 41.0	
1740s	1	(1) 43.0	4 (4) 44.0	7 (6) 38.3	2 (2) 25.5
1750s	0		0.	4 (4) 38.7	

11. For a statement on the emigrants' desire for neighbors, see Hampshire County Common Pleas, III, 82 (microfilm, Forbes Library); Sylvester Judd MSS, II, 258, Forbes Library.

12. That acreage was given in the 1741 petition for separate precinct status; Massachusetts Archives, XII, 150, 152, 154. See Louis H. Everts, *History of the Connecticut Valley in Massachusetts* (Philadelphia, 1879), I, 30; Trumbull, *Northampton,* II, 38; Southampton General Records, First Book, at Southampton Town Hall.

13. The relative poverty is shown in the 1771 tax-assessment lists that survive for Southampton and part of Northampton. Mass. Archives, Vols. 133 and 134, in alphabetical order of towns. Also testimony to the expectations of poor quality are the large portions granted in 1730. The land did not become really productive until the nineteenth century.

14. Trumbull, *Northampton,* I, 552.

15. For wages, see Nathaniel Phelps's account book, Historic Deerfield Library; Jackson Turner Main, *The Social Structure of Revolutionary America* (Princeton, 1965), 70. Land costs were estimated from prices in a sample of deeds; Map C, page 17, is a topographic map, with prices indicated; compare James T. Lemon, *The Best Poor Man's Country: A Geographical Study of Early Southeastern Pennsylvania* (Baltimore, 1972), 67–68, and Greven, *Four Generations,* 128–29.

16. Margaret E. Martin, *Merchants and Trade of the Connecticut River Valley 1750–1820,* Vol. XXIV of Smith College Studies in History (Northampton, 1939), 7–8, 17. See also the 1760 tax-assessment lists, Town Papers, Forbes Library. For attitudes toward commercial men, see Crowley, *This Sheba, Self,* passim.

An explanation seems in order for the absence in this book of the discussion of community-wide economic stratification that is often offered in community studies. Great emphasis is usually placed on the distribution of property, a statistic easily obtained for those towns whose tax lists have survived, but this kind of information has not been of much use in this study for two reasons. First, the complete assessment lists which survive are from 1676, 1739, and 1759 (the last two separate real and personal estate and enumerate but do not name polls, males over sixteen), but even the last two are too far apart to permit any evaluation of change during the adult years of even a small group of men, so that we cannot really measure movement up and down the economic ladder. Second, a man's place on a tax list at any given moment tells us little about his life. If a man is, let's say, the third richest man in town, or the third poorest, does it not make a difference in our evaluation of his status if he is young or old, a son of a still richer man or the father of six sons who will need to be given property, a man moving up in his personal economic trajectory or on the way down? By the time we take into account all the conditions that give meaning to wealth, we end up with categories of one man each. At an earlier stage of this study, a thorough attempt was made to correlate tax information, Proprietors' records, probate records, and thousands of deeds, in order to construct landholding profiles for at least a few families over a reasonable length of time. But that project foundered on the absence of specific data on acreage and value in many deeds, and the remarkable lack of correlation between a man's holdings as reflected in probate records and in all other sources combined. The few pieces of economic data that seem to have meaning have been included in the text. Graphic representations of the tax lists of 1739 and 1759, and estimated landholdings in 1661, 1700, 1739, and 1759, can be found in the Appendix to my dissertation, "Jonathan Edwards, Pastor," University of Massachusetts, 1977. The only significant change appears when the distribution of personal estate for 1739 and 1759 is charted; the steeper 1759 curve shows the rise of a group of men rich in personal estate (most probably mercantile stock or money at interest)—but this change was probably seen at the time, if at all, as simply the prominence of a few particular men, and not a general realignment of the community social structure. The only deduction which seems reasonable is that amid the subtle but important changes in perceived relations between fathers and sons there was no important change in the measurable overall economic profile of the town.

17. I have found no official records of apprenticeship for Northampton in the period under study (the county court records are silent), although two craftsmen's account books do indicate the presence of a few apprentices. The extent of formal schooling is not known; schools are mentioned at great intervals in the town records, but no count of pupils was ever taken.

18. *Generation to Generation* (Glencoe, Ill., 1956), 30–31. Laslett, "The Comparative History of Household and Family," in Michael Gordon, ed., *The American Family in Social-Historical Perspective* (N.Y., 1973), 28. Conrad M. Arensberg and Solon T. Kimball, *Family and Community in Ireland,* 2nd ed. (Cambridge, Mass., 1968), 55. Darrett B. Rutman, *American Puritanism: Faith and Practice* (Philadelphia, 1970), 54–55. Zuckerman, *Peaceable Kingdoms,* 194, asserts that men without property were excluded from voting even in local matters because they were assumed to be susceptible to improper influence by those on whom they were economically dependent.

No evidence for this practice has been found in Northampton records, but there is also no statement of the criteria for political participation.

19. It should be noted that six men joined the church in the Edwards era along with one or more sons each, so they are listed as both fathers and sons in the statistical analyses. Of the 236 men born to Northampton parents, one was of the second generation (generation of family in the colony, as deduced by Trumbull in his Northampton genealogy, but in most cases the same as "generation in Northampton")—born in 1674, he was the oldest member of the group—and 41 were of the third, 140 of the fourth, and 54 of the fifth generation. This way of measuring generations is similar to that used by Greven in *Four Generations,* except that my survey is backwards in time because the group of church joiners in the 1730s is the real focus of this inquiry. Jonathan Edwards himself is included in the group, as a non-native.

20. Table 4: TOWN LAND GRANTS TO THREE GENERATIONS

	Total N*	Received Grant	
		N	%
Grandfathers	68	64	94.1%
Fathers	121	58**	47.9%
Edwards group	236	3	1.3%

*Native to Northampton out of an unknown total of grandfathers, an estimated 148 total fathers, and 268 total church joiners in the Edwards group.
**Includes three Proprietors.

Table 5: FATHERS WHO RECEIVED TOWN GRANTS

N=55 non-Proprietors, 3 Proprietors
Age at grant (N=51*):
  Range: 14 to 57 years (only 2 under 21)
  Average: 30.4 years
  Median: 27.0 years
Known to be married before grant: 34, or 61.8%

*One grant date and three birthdates unknown, only non-Proprietors counted. Four men, aged 14, 20, 21, and 27, had grants given to their fathers for them.

21. Of the total 268 men, for 47 there is no information, 15 were only

temporary residents in Northampton, 9 others left town before adulthood, 22 died between ages 17 and 46 without forming their own households, and 12 others were eliminated because they are too complicated to categorize. Among the temporary residents were Pelatiah Holbrook, a hatter's apprentice who died in 1738, and Daniel Buckingham, a Yale graduate who was probably studying theology with Jonathan Edwards. Of those who died young, all were still living in their father's house or in a separate house on the father's land; of the 22, no more than 9 were married. Among the 12 remaining uncategorized men were 2 who were perhaps invalids and lived dependent on brothers, 4 who owned land in Northampton but who moved between Northampton and other towns frequently, and others involved in complicated multiple transfers of land and houses among family members.

Table 6: HOW EDWARDS'S CONVERTS ACQUIRED HOMESTEADS

	N	Avg. age at acquisition(N)		Avg. age at marriage(N)	
Town grant in Northampton	3	26.0	(2)	26.5	(2)
Town grant in Southampton	6	22.3	(6)	23.8	(5)
Educated and left town	8	——		27.5	(6)[a]
Own purchase	14	28.6	(14)	25.2	(9)
Inherit from grandfather	1[b]	26.0	(1)		
Gift of land father purchased explicitly for son	3	31.7[c]	(3)	24.5	(2)
Inherit land father purchased for son	2[d]	42.0	(2)	29.0	(1)
Gift or purchase of land (only) from father or grandfather	8[e]	29.1	(8)	28.8	(6)
Gift or purchase from father of father's house	6[f]	38.8	(6)	29.8	(4)[a]
Gift or purchase from father of another house	15[g]	32.4	(15)	25.5	(14)
Inherit part of father's land, house unknown	29[h]	30.5	(29)	30.1	(23)
Inherit with brother(s) father's homestead	19[h]	34.2	(19)	30.9	(13)[i]
Inherit alone father's homestead	23[h,j]	31.1	(23)	28.3	(21)
Inherit a homestead, already lived in, from father (not his own)	24[h,k]	44.6	(24)	27.9	(21)[a]
Total known, of 268	161			28.63	(188)

NOTE: On all inheritances, with no previous deed recorded, father's death date is considered effective date of transfer.

a. One never married, the rest (if any) are unknown.

b. Father dead; house already built on property.

c. Ages: by age 38, 24, by age 33; land at Coventry, Ct., Hadley, Southampton.

d. Two brothers; land out of town; purchase date unknown.

e. Three are purchases.

f. All are purchases: 1 for ld.; 1 for ls; 1 for maintenance; 1 for £40 per year; 1 for £140 lawful; 1 for £200 lawful (the last two approach fair market value; not known if money actually paid or price remitted by father).

g. Four are purchases: £120, £40, £5 and £40/year, £700.

h. On all inheritances, effective ages raised to 21.

i. Two never married, rest unknown.

j. Sisters not counted.

k. Two of these are brothers who share one homestead.

22. One inheritance was from a grandfather; the father was dead.

23. Hampshire County Probate Records, Box 31, No. 10; Trumbull, Genealogy, 106, 114.

24. See *Four Generations,* which contains a superb study of inheritance patterns in Andover. Although I have not yet systematically analyzed patterns of inheritance in Northampton, in the course of examining approximately 500 sets of estate documents I gained the impression that by the mid-eighteenth century fathers tended more to leave their land to only one son and to provide for others through money or apprenticeships. Wealthy fathers bought farms for their sons in other communities; compare Robert A. Gross, *The Minutemen and Their World* (N.Y., 1976), 79–80, 85. Greven, *Four Generations,* 227, found that estates of the third generation were far less divided among sons than those of previous generations.

25. Hampshire Probate Records, Box 31, No. 17.

26. Ed. by Harry J. Carman and Rexford G. Tugwell (N.Y., 1935), 138.

27. 188 known sons, born 1674–1729, married at an average age of 28.63 years; 106 known fathers, born pre-1650 to 1704, married at an average age of 25.65 years. Of the sons, 58 married at an unknown age or perhaps never married, and 22 certainly never married. Of the fathers, 42 married at an unknown age.

Table 7: AVERAGE AGE AT FIRST MARRIAGE IN NORTHAMPTON

a) *Date married*	*Females*	*Males*
Before 1700	20.6	26.1
1700–29	22.7	26.7
1730–49	25.1	28.6
1750–74	26.0	28.9
b) *Date married*		
1691–1710	20.9	25.4
1711–30	23.4	26.6
1731–50	24.5	28.2
c) *Generations*		
First	——	25.4
Second	22.3	26.8
Third	24.1	26.8
Fourth	23.7	27.0

Table 8: NUMBER OF CHILDREN PER COMPLETE FAMILY*

Number of children

	%0–4	%5–9	%10–14	
d) *Date married*				*Sample size*
Before 1700	4.8	57.1	38.2	21
1700–49	24.6	52.3	23.1	65
1750–59	35.1	44.6	20.3	74
e) *Date married*				
1691–1720	18.1	55.5	26.4	72
1721–50	35.0	52.5	12.5	not given

*Husband and wife survive to end of wife's fertility, about age 45.

Sources for Tables 7 and 8:

a) Steven Levy, "A Demographic Analysis of Colonial Northampton, Massachusetts, 1650–1800," Honors thesis, Union College, 1972, p. 27. Sample size not reported.

b) Tiziana Rota, "Marriage and Family Life in Northampton, Massachusetts: A Demographic Study 1690–1750," M.A. thesis, Mt. Holyoke College, 1975, p. 49. Sample size not reported.

c) Russell W. Mank, Jr., "Family Structure in Northampton, Massachusetts, 1654–1729," Ph.D. dissertation, U. of Denver, 1975, pp. 95, 96, 142, 143, 216, 217. Identification of birth or marriage dates for each generation not clearly specified.

d) Levy, p. 18.

e) Rota, pp. 71–72.

For comparative data, see Demos, *A Little Commonwealth*, 193; Lockridge, "Population of Dedham," 330; Daniel Scott Smith, "The Demographic History of Colonial New England," *Journal of Economic History*, XXXII (1972), 177; Robert Higgs and H. Louis Stettler, III, "Colonial New England Demography: A Sampling Approach," *William and Mary Quarterly*, 3rd Ser., XXVII (1970), 282–94; Greven, *Four Generations*, 33–37, 111, 118, 120, 200, 206, 208.

28. The sharing of homes has been deduced from deeds, wills, and tax-assessment lists. Of the nineteen men, eight resided with a brother for ten or more years after inheritance, two for an indefinite time, two for six years or more, one for at least three years, and the other six either sell to or buy out their siblings quickly or leave no evidence. In 1764 Northampton had 203 families in 186 houses, but without the lost enumeration schedules one can't separate households shared by siblings from those with multiple generations (the latter probably more common).

29. There were very few punishments for fornication in Northampton or Hampshire County, and very few "too early" babies in Northampton. The Hampshire Common Pleas records list only twelve cases of fornication before 1755; the most in one year was five, in 1743. The Northampton church disciplined only one person for fornication in the same period, a man, in 1743 (Church Records, 25)—or at least no more were recorded. Rota, "Marriage and Family Life in Northampton," 78–80, reports the following rates of births recorded within eight months of marriage: 1691–1710: 6% of marriages; 1711–30: 10%; 1731–50: 4.7%. These figures are very low compared to those reported by Daniel Scott Smith and Michael S. Hindus, "Premarital Pregnancy in America 1640–1971: An Overview and Interpretation," *Journal of Interdisciplinary History*, V (1975), 537–70; and John Demos, "Families in Colonial Bristol, Rhode Island: An Exercise in Historical Demography," *William and Mary Quarterly*, 3rd Ser., XXV (1968), 40–57. There is no reason to believe that the ministers, magistrates, and parents of the Northampton young people were any less opposed to premarital intercourse than elsewhere. On the other hand, there is no reason to believe that the Northampton young adults behaved differently from their peers to the east. Daniel Scott Smith, "Parental Power and Marriage Patterns: An Analysis of Historical Trends in Hingham, Massachusetts," *Journal of Marriage and the Family*, XXXV (1973), 419–28, offers statistical evidence of parental control of marriage—children marrying in strict birth order—declining after 1740. No comparative data for Northampton have yet been obtained.

30. See Hiner, "Adolescence in Eighteenth Century America," 258–59; Greven, *Four Generations;* Paul Boyer and Stephen Nissenbaum, *Salem Possessed: The Social Origins of Witchcraft* (Cambridge, 1974).

31. Hampshire Probate Records: Alvord, Box 4, No. 9; King, Box 83, No. 48; Wright, Box 165, No. 50; Miller, Box 97, No. 53.

32. In *The Puritan Family: Religion and Domestic Relations in Seventeenth-Century New England,* rev. ed. (N.Y., 1966), Edmund S. Morgan asserted that children lived away from home as a corrective for their parents' affection and the resulting lax discipline; the practice might also have been a way of dealing with various tensions arising from the rearing of adolescents. Only a few references to children living with other families have been found in the Northampton documents, however, and they usually involve a child who is heir to his grandfather's or uncle's property or who is an orphan.

33. Town Records, 248, 259, 275, 276, 283, 296, 314, 341.

34. Town Records, 266–67, 299, 304–5, 308, 309–10, 313.

35. The change was quite similar to that described by Kenneth A. Lockridge and Alan Kreider, "The Evolution of Massachusetts Town Government, 1640 to 1740," *William and Mary Quarterly,* 3rd Ser., XXIII (1966), 549–74. In Northampton the change occurred ten to twenty years later than in eastern Mass., probably because it was ten to twenty years younger than eastern towns.

36. The number of meetings per year besides the annual election meeting in March was greater than three only nine times in the years 1690–1754: years with four or five meetings were 1698, 1702, 1705, 1714, 1735, 1736, 1745, 1746, and 1748; in 1737 there were six meetings. (Adjournments to separate days are counted as separate meetings.)

37. *From Generation to Generation,* 43–46, 116–17; Arensberg and Kimball, *Family and Community in Ireland,* 257–61. Edward Shorter, in *The Making of the Modern Family* (N.Y., 1975), argues that the Western family has become increasingly "domesticated" since the seventeenth century as family members have systematically cut themselves off from various peer groups in the wider community in order to focus their loyalty on the husband-wife-children nuclear unit. If that is an accurate description of the long-range process, the New England experience was an eddy in the flow, for in rural areas at least until the mid-eighteenth century the intention to have a Christian commonwealth tended to blur the lines between family and community until changing economic patterns forced family units to compete rather than cooperate with their neighbors. When Puritan communalism broke down, the economic importance of the nuclear family and the ritualized rebellion that allowed young people to "let off steam" before submitting to family pressures emerged. However much decried by moralists such

as Edwards, the adolescent frolicking was a relatively harmless way for young people to adapt themselves to their inevitable economic subordination.

In the debate as to whether or not adolescence (as a time of tension and disturbing behavior between childhood and adulthood) existed before the industrial era, the affirmative side is taken by Ross W. Beales, Jr., "In Search of the Historical Child: Miniature Adulthood and Youth in Colonial New England," *American Quarterly,* XXVII (1975), 379–98. Beales finds the teens and early twenties in colonial New England to require enough difficult choices that there may have been that sense of a crossroads that brings a consciousness of being neither a child nor an adult. The New England ministers certainly marked an in-between stage as a time of problems; see Hiner, "Adolescence in Eighteenth Century America." The major statements against the existence of adolescence in pre-industrial America are John Demos and Virginia Demos, "Adolescence in Historical Perspective," *Journal of Marriage and the Family,* XXXI (1969), 632–38; Kenneth Keniston, "Youth: A 'New' Stage of Life," *The American Scholar,* XXXIX (1970), 631–54; and Joseph Kett, "Adolescence and Youth in Nineteenth Century America," *Journal of Interdisciplinary History,* II (1971), 283–99. This position generally accepts the argument of Philippe Ariès, *Centuries of Childhood,* trans. Robert Baldick (Paris, 1960; N.Y., 1962). The description of college youth is from Axtell, *School upon a Hill,* 202, 235.

38. Sermon on "Joseph's Temptation," Genesis 39:12, MS at Beinecke dated March 1738, included in N.Y. 1844 *Works,* IV, 585–600.

Chapter Five: Awakening

1. JE wrote his first description of the revival to Benjamin Colman of Boston on 30 May 1735, with a postscript dated 3 June. JE's copy is at ANTS and is included in C. C. Goen, ed., *The Great Awakening,* Vol. IV of *The Works of Jonathan Edwards* (New Haven, 1972), 99–110. For the further history of the *Narrative,* see *ibid.,* 32–46. No other eyewitness account survives except some memories quoted in Timothy Dwight's *Travels,* cited in Chapter 4, and the diary of Deacon Ebenezer Hunt of Northampton, which corroborates Edwards's account and contains a fascinating list of persons regarded as converted that parallels Edwards's church-member list. The original diary MS has not been found, but extracts are in the Sylvester Judd MSS, Forbes Library, I, 23–28.

2. An interesting example of cynicism is quoted in Douglas C. Stenerson, "An Anglican Critique of the Early Phase of the Great Awakening in New England: A Letter by Timothy Cutler," *William and Mary Quarterly,* 3rd

Ser., XXX (1973), 475–88: Cutler repeated a story from Samuel Johnson of Greenwich about the disturbance in his parish in 1735, during which "The Humor . . . took with" a love-crazed old maid and four or five young women, two of whom married shortly thereafter and gave birth to children within six or seven months.

3. Sabbath-night carousing was a perennial worry to religious leaders of Mass. See the 1712 enactment in the Mass. General Court, *Acts and Resolves,* Vol. I, 681; Cotton Mather, *A Good Evening Accommodated with a Good Employment . . .* (Boston, 1716), 10; and the 1717 entry in the diary of the Rev. Stephen Williams. Storrs Library, Longmeadow, I, 91. In Oct. 1733 Edwards and two others were appointed by the Hampshire Assoc. to draw up an address to the county court to ask for the suppression of the "growing vice and immorality, and particularly tavern-haunting, and disorderly night-walking, especially night-walking and company-keeping on the night after the Sabbath." Hampshire Assoc. Records, Forbes Library, 12. The clergy had also discussed a number of fornication cases earlier that day. Their petition never appeared in the county-court records.

4. *Faithful Narrative,* in Goen, *Great Awakening,* 147—hereafter cited as *Faithful Narrative;* sermon on Job 1:5, early 1730 (Schafer), Beinecke, emphasis added.

5. David Levin has pointed out to me that the appearance a generation earlier of this special youthful constituency in Boston, during the pastorate of Cotton Mather, may mark the lag in social development between the city and a country town. See Levin, *Cotton Mather: The Young Life of the Lord's Remembrancer, 1663–1703* (Cambridge, Mass., 1978), 74–75, 273.

6. *Faithful Narrative,* 148.

7. Quoted in Larzer Ziff, *Puritanism in America* (N.Y., 1973), 114. By the time he wrote *Some Thoughts Concerning the Revival* in 1742, JE felt that evening religious meetings of boys and girls should be avoided, since youngsters would "naturally consort together in couples for other than religious purposes" on the way home. JE's *Thoughts* were published in 1743, reprinted in Goen, *Great Awakening,* 289–530, quotation 469.

8. On other towns, see James Axtell, *The School upon a Hill: Education and Society in Colonial New England* (New Haven, 1974), 19–35. Hampshire Assoc. Records, 1.

9. Sereno E. Dwight, *The Life of President Edwards* (N.Y., 1829), 112–13; Samuel Hopkins, *The Life and Character of the Late Reverend, Learned and Pious Mr. Jonathan Edwards* (Boston, 1765), 41–42, 49.

10. Winslow, *Meetinghouse Hill, 1630–1783* (N.Y., 1952), 150–66. JE's sermon on Revelation 14:2, dated 7 Nov. 1734, printed in London 1839 *Works,* I, 913–17; Colossians 3:16, dated 17 June 1736, Beinecke. See also

Faithful Narrative, 151 and note. Suspicion that JE was siding with the young people against their parents is reflected in Timothy Cutler's gossip to the Bishop of London in 1739 that JE took the part of a young man who would not obey his father's commands to cut wood for the family by saying the boy had to "get through" the "extraordinary influence of the Spirit" before he could do his normal chores. Stenerson, "Anglican Critique," 487.

11. *Faithful Narrative,* 148.

12. Although the stories of Abigail Hutchinson and Phebe Bartlett are treated here as literally true, two factors encourage suspicion about possible artistic license taken in the descriptions of the conversions. The first is the convention of dramatic childhood conversion, usually ending in death, created or promoted by James Janeway's *A Token for Children* (London, 1671), edited and enlarged by Cotton Mather and published in Boston in 1700, supposedly a best-seller of the eighteenth century. See William Sloane, *Children's Books in England and America in the Seventeenth Century: A History and Checklist* (N.Y., 1955), 7, 44–45, 50–52, 166–67, 224. For a commentary on the *Token,* see David E. Stannard, "Death and the Puritan Child," *American Quarterly,* XXVI (1974), 461. Second, a striking literary model of the young converts, especially Abigail, is provided by the set of family memorials to Jonathan's sister Jerusha, who died in December 1729 at age nineteen; MSS at ANTS.

13. *Faithful Narrative,* 199–205. Of course, to Puritans the bond between church members, modeled on that between Christ and the saint, was always theoretically stronger than mere natural ties. For examples of practice, see Larzer Ziff, "The Social Bond of the Church Covenant," *American Quarterly,* X (1958), 454–62.

14. *Faithful Narrative,* 149–51, 158, 161. That the congregation was not unanimous is shown by a court case from the following spring, in which Bernard Bartlett, a temporary resident of Northampton frequently charged with vagrancy (and no known relation to Phebe), pleaded guilty to publishing "a libel tending to the defamation of [JE] by saying that the said Edwards was as great an Instrument as the Devil had on this side [of] hell to bring souls to hell." Hampshire Common Pleas, III, 57.

Emory Elliott, *Power and the Pulpit in Puritan New England* (Princeton, 1975), esp. 7, 14, 24–61, sees the widespread concern with young people —with their exclusion from the church until the Half-Way Covenant was accepted, and their inability to achieve the high emotional pitch of conversion—as a reflection of the psycho-social dilemma of the second generation of ministers in New England. Their fathers had been pioneering giants and resisting patriarchs, as had many lay fathers, but they also provided a definition of ministerial success in gathering converts that their sons strove in vain to emulate in the changed religious climate of the late seventeenth century. Grandpaternal images were obviously also a potential challenge, at least for the grandsons of Solomon Stoddard.

15. *Faithful Narrative,* 160–80.

16. *A Divine and Supernatural Light,* in N.Y. 1844 *Works,* IV, 442. Roland Andre Delattre, *Beauty and Sensibility in the Thought of Jonathan Edwards: An Essay in Aesthetics and Theological Ethics* (New Haven, 1968), argues that the objective is more important than the subjective in the thought of Jonathan Edwards, but the criteria for distinguishing one from the other remain vague. Indeed, it seems that Edwards tends to subjectivize the objective, and vice versa, in his struggle to find a vocabulary that would adequately describe the integrated psyche.

17. *Faithful Narrative,* 175.

18. *Ibid.,* 175–76.

19. *Ibid.,* 205–7. Deacon Ebenezer Hunt's journal, quoted in Judd MSS, I, 24, says that Hawley lived for half an hour but did not speak. Northampton tradition is that his wife was turning cheeses (on the Sabbath?) and showed her strong-mindedness by not coming till she finished. She was Lydia Marshall from Windsor; there is no other evidence but JE's remark on mental disorder in her family.

20. Romans 5:6, Beinecke (first 4 pages defective).

21. *Faithful Narrative,* 191, 198, 199, 200, 203, 205–6.

22. *Ibid.,* 208, 211. JE to Thomas Foxcroft, 24 May 1753, Beinecke.

23. *Faithful Narrative,* 209.

24. *Ibid.,* 174, 190. Timothy Cutler commented in 1739 that Stoddard's "sense of the operations of grace, very much resembles what we find in his grandson's book [the *Faithful Narrative*]"; Stenerson, "Anglican Critique," 481.

25. *Faithful Narrative,* 155–56, 205, 210. JE to Rev. Eleazar Wheelock of Lebanon, Conn., 9 Oct. 1740, MS at Forbes Library.

26. The Hampshire JPs were censured by the General Court for interfering with a proper ecclesiastical council. See Mass. Bay House of Representatives, *Journals 1735–1736,* XIII (Boston, 1932), 114–15, 145–46, 151–52, 184, 185, 187.

27. The major sources on the Breck affair are: Hampshire Assoc. Records, 5, 14, 17; Hampshire Common Pleas, III, 80, 133; Sibley, *Harvard Graduates,* VIII, 661–80, on Breck; and the following tracts: (Samuel Hopkins and JE) *A Narrative of the Proceedings of those Ministers of the County of Hampshire, &c. That have disapproved of the late Measures taken in order to the Settlement of Mr. Robert Breck, in the Pastoral Office in the First Church in Springfield. With a Defence of their Conduct in that Affair. Written by Themselves* (Boston, 1736);

(Breck?) *An Examination of and some Answer to a Pamphlet, intitled, A Narrative and Defence. . . . With a Vindication of those Ministers and Churches that approv'd of and acted in the Settlement of said Mr. Breck* (Boston, 1736); (JE) *A Letter to the Author of the Pamphlet Called An Answer to the Hampshire Narrative* (Boston, 1737). The best secondary account is Mary Catherine Foster, "Hampshire County, Massachusetts, 1729–1754: A Covenant Society in Transition" (Ph.D. dissertation, U. of Michigan, 1967), 55–77. See also Dwight, *Edwards,* 125–26.

28. *A Narrative of the Proceedings,* 78–79.

29. Compare Ziff, *Puritanism in America,* 114–15, 198–202, 297.

30. Goen, *Great Awakening,* Introduction, 35, quotes a Colman letter which asserts a belief that JE wrote the November 1736 expanded account of the revival expressly for the international audience.

Chapter Six: Reassessment

1. JE to Benjamin Colman, 19 May 1737, Colman Papers, Mass. Historical Society.

2. JE to Benjamin Colman, 2 May 1738, Stoddard Collection, MHS.

3. Town Records, 250; James Russell Trumbull, *History of Northampton,* 2 vols. (Northampton, 1898), I, 370–74. See also David Flaherty, *Privacy in Colonial New England* (Charlottesville, 1967), 195–201.

4. Town Records, 246, 248, 251–52. Deacon Ebenezer Hunt Diary, quoted in Sylvester Judd MSS, Forbes Library, I, 27.

5. Described by JE to an unidentified recipient, 19 March 1737, in Sereno E. Dwight, *Life of President Edwards* (N.Y., 1829), 139–40.

6. Disturbances resulting from seating the meetinghouse in other towns are described in Ola Elizabeth Winslow, *Meetinghouse Hill, 1630–1783* (N.Y., 1952), 142–49; and in Robert J. Dinkin, "Seating the Meeting House in Early Massachusetts," *New England Quarterly,* XLIII (1970), 450–64. Somewhere in Hampshire County, around 1731, two men fought physically over a seat during a worship service. See Hampshire Assoc. Records, 2.

7. Town Records, 50, 57, 62, 109, 129, 157, 178, 219, 222, 239.

8. Town Records, 257, 258.

9. In other Valley towns, including East Windsor, couples seem not to have sat together until midcentury or later. See Sylvester Judd, *History of Hadley* (Northampton, 1863), 319–20; John Montague Smith, *History of Sunderland* (Greenfield, 1899), 53–54; South Windsor, Conn., Records (MS at State Library, Hartford), 29; John A. Stoughton, *"Windsor Farmes": A Glimpse of an Old Parish* (Hartford, 1883), 100. The Deerfield church,

which had its first box pew about 1710 and pews all around by 1726, voted to seat men and their wives together in 1730. George Sheldon, *A History of Deerfield, Massachusetts* (1896; Somersworth, N.H., 1972), I, 454, 482.

10. The 1737 seating plan is in Trumbull, *Northampton*, II, following p. 75. The 1739 tax list has been used to calculate the estates of all men seated on the ground floor. Pews were more honorific than seats, and even the pews were apparently divided into more and less prestigious locations. Fifty-seven men sat in the pews and 1739 tax assessments are known for fifty-three: all are in the top 75% of taxpayers, 92.5% are in the top half, 71.7% in the top quarter, and 26.4% in the top tenth. To look at the seating from another perspective, the eighteen richest men in town, and thirty-one of the richest thirty-five men, sat in pews. All seven of the men who had daughters sitting with them were in the top quarter of taxpayers. Two women, one a widow and the other married to a man who sat in another pew, also had daughters sitting with them; the married woman's husband was in wealth category III out of XX. The daughters in question were eleven in number and ranged in age from sixteen to forty-three, with an average age of twenty-five.

11. Town Records, 222.

12. There was, of course, a tradition among English gentry to sit in family pews in the village church; but the rest of the seats were not apportioned on the basis of sex, age, or social rank. Philippe Ariès and other writers have pointed out that in the seventeenth and eighteenth centuries the upper-middle class in Europe were the first to be oriented symbolically into a family as we know it today.

13. Job 1:5, early 1730 (Schafer), Beinecke; Luke 17:34, undated but pre-1733, ANTS. When in Oct. 1737 and April 1738 the Hampshire Assoc. discussed the current sickness among children in the Valley as a punishment from God, they decided that their sin was immoderate love of children and indulgence by parents, as well as showing greed by hoarding up material wealth for their children. Hampshire Assoc. Records, 22–27.

14. MS at Beinecke.

15. MS at Beinecke; printed in H. Norman Gardiner, ed., *Selected Sermons of Jonathan Edwards* (N.Y., 1904), 64–77.

16. Town Records, 261–62.

17. Exodus 20:15, Beinecke; in N.Y. 1844 *Works*, IV, 601–14.

18. Genesis 39:12, Beinecke, marked March 1738 and March 1757; in N.Y. 1844 *Works*, IV, 585–600.

19. The essence of JE's mid-1730s style is reflected in the Doctrine from a June 1735 sermon: "The bare consideration, that God is God, may well be sufficient to still all objections and opposition against the divine sovereign

dispensations." Psalms 46:10, Beinecke, in London 1839 *Works*, II, 107–10. JE's "Miscellanies" show the most intense concentration on hell and its torments in the later-500s entries (about 1732) and the early 900s (about 1744?).

20. Romans 2:8–9, dated Nov. 1735, Beinecke; in London 1839 *Works*, II, 878–88.

21. Beinecke, undated but probably late 1738 or early 1739 (Schafer). Other sermons explicit in their attempts to terrify are II Kings 2:23–4, Beinecke, "To the children, at a private meeting, Feb. 1740/41"; and Psalms 34:11, Beinecke, for a "private meeting of children, July 1741."

22. The text was Deuteronomy 32:33. Two other sermons on the same text, undated and probably early, lack the dramatic impact of the later version. The publication of 1741 was expanded from a MS labeled June and July 1741, Northampton and Enfield, respectively. All MSS at Beinecke. The differences between the MS and published versions, showing the attempt to heighten the image of God's wrath and control, are discussed in Franklin B. Dexter, "The Manuscripts of Jonathan Edwards," Mass. Historical Society *Proceedings*, 2nd. Ser., XV (1902), 6; and in Ralph G. Turnbull, *Jonathan Edwards the Preacher* (Grand Rapids, 1958), 100–1.

23. JE defended his use of terror most straightforwardly in *The Distinguishing Marks* (Boston, 1741), reprinted in C. C. Goen, ed., *The Great Awakening*, Vol. IV of *The Works of Jonathan Edwards* (New Haven, 1972), 248. Early twentieth-century historians regarded JE as the last American Puritan, whose hell-fire preaching was the key to his anachronism in an era of enlightenment. Vernon L. Parrington found JE's own conversion to be an un-Puritan transcendental experience of the "inner light," which nevertheless did not keep him from turning his great intellect to the "ignoble ends" of traditional theology. But JE unwittingly doomed the Calvinism that "lay like a heavy weight upon the soul of New England": the "brutal grotesqueries of those dogmas" had only to be exposed to the "common view" to be discredited forever. See Parrington, *Main Currents in American Thought, Vol. I: The Colonial Mind, 1620–1800* (N.Y., 1927), 158–59. In the same vein, Henry Bamford Parkes applied a psychological interpretation to Edwards's Calvinism and found "sadism" lurking there. Parkes, *Jonathan Edwards: The Fiery Puritan* (N.Y., 1930), 102.

24. Stephen Williams diary, Storrs Library, Longmeadow, entry for 8 July, 1741. The rhetorical artistry of *Sinners* has been discussed frequently. See, especially, Edwin H. Cady, "The Artistry of Jonathan Edwards," *New England Quarterly*, XXII (1949), 61–72; and Willis J. Buckingham, "Stylistic Artistry in the Sermons of Jonathan Edwards," *Papers on Language and Literature*, VI (1970), 136–51. A close examination of both the sermon and

its later use by historians can be found in Robert Lee Stuart, "Jonathan Edwards at Enfield: 'And Oh the Cheerfulness and Pleasantness . . .'," *American Literature,* XLVIII (1976), 46–59. Stuart points out (p. 51 n. 25) that JE's defense of terror preaching had a clear class bias: in "Miscellanies" entry 116b, JE says this is the method God usually uses with "the more unthinking people, such as husbandmen and the common sort of people," whereas "in the more knowing and thinking men, the Holy Spirit makes more use of rational deductions" of the value of the reward. "Miscellanies" entry 325 expresses the same sentiment. "Miscellanies," MSS at Beinecke.

25. For vivid terror preaching, see Ezekiel 22:14, "The Future Punishment of the Wicked Unavoidable and Intolerable," MS at Beinecke labeled April 1741, included in N.Y. 1844 *Works,* IV, 234–65, esp. 260. John H. Gerstner, *Steps to Salvation: The Evangelistic Message of Jonathan Edwards* (Philadelphia, 1960), 24, observes that the real terror in the audience may have come from "the realization that they were not hearing a sensationalistic ranter striving for an effect, but a prodigious and cool intellect driven by the purest moral earnestness seeking to approach some adequacy of representation for a transcendently awful fact."

26. An interesting reflection on the psychological impact of *Sinners* can be found in William J. Scheick, *The Writings of Jonathan Edwards: Theme, Motif, and Style* (College Station, Texas, 1975), 76–78: "Edwards wanted the congregation to feel as well as to understand that the unregenerate self lacks any stabilizing context for identity. The wicked walk amid shadows, as if in a dream, where even the apparent solidity of the earth beneath their feet would dissolve upon their walking. They are out of touch with God, Who is reality. . . . nature fails to provide man with any reality by means of which he can attain genuine self-identity. . . . Subjectivity is all man has. . . ."

27. The pessimism of the sermon was unfairly exaggerated in the 1808 Worcester edition of JE's *Works* published by Samuel Austin, which omitted the last five paragraphs. But the 1741 edition was included in full in the S. E. Dwight edition of the *Works* (N.Y., 1829–1830), VII, 163–77.

28. *Faithful Narrative,* in Goen, *Great Awakening,* 155–56, 205, 210.

29. JE to Benjamin Colman, 27 May 1738, Edwards MSS, Princeton University Library. Timothy Cutler to Bishop Gibson, 28 May 1739, in Douglas C. Stenerson, "An Anglican Critique of the Early Phase of the Great Awakening in New England: A Letter by Timothy Cutler," *William and Mary Quarterly,* 3rd Ser., XXX (1973), 482. JE mentioned his "great infirmity of body" in a letter to Deacon Lyman of Goshen, Conn., 31 Aug. 1741, ANTS, included in Goen, *Great Awakening,* 533–34.

30. See Wilson H. Kimnach, "Jonathan Edwards' Early Sermons," *Journal*

of Presbyterian History, LV (1977), 266 n.11. I am grateful to Professor Kimnach for helping me to refine my thoughts about *Sinners* by sharing with me some of the ideas he is including in a forthcoming essay.

31. JE's letter to Whitefield was found in the Methodist Archive and Research Center, London, by Henry Abelove and published in the *William and Mary Quarterly,* 3rd Ser., XXIX (1972), 487–89. In a letter of 9 Oct. 1740 to the Rev. Eleazar Wheelock of Lebanon, Conn., JE spoke of his hopes for Whitefield's success in Northampton; MS in Forbes Library.

32. The only immediate account of the visit is in Whitefield's diary, published as *A Continuation of the Reverend Mr. Whitefield's Journal* (London, 1741); it can be found in *George Whitefield's Journals* (London, 1960), 476–79. JE described the visit briefly in his letter of 12 Dec. 1743 to Thomas Prince, published in *The Christian History, Vol. I* (Boston, 1744), 367–81; reprinted in Dwight, *Edwards,* 160–70; and in Goen, *Great Awakening,* 544–57. The effects of Whitefield on the "common people" can be seen in the Journal of Nathan Cole at the Connecticut Historical Society, excerpts included under the title "Spiritual Travels" in Alan Heimert and Perry Miller, eds., *The Great Awakening: Documents Illustrating the Crisis and Its Consequences* (Indianapolis, 1967), 183–86. JE rode with Whitefield to East Windsor, to the home of Timothy Edwards. GW's diary contains no mention of a supposed conversation with JE that became the ground for a long, bitter debate between JE and Rector Thomas Clap of Yale about whether or not GW had told JE that he intended to bring young men from England to supplant New England parsons who were "unconverted." The story is told in Dwight, *Edwards,* 209–10.

33. JE to Prince, 12 Dec. 1743, in Goen, *Great Awakening,* 545–48. See also JE to Joseph Bellamy, 21 Jan. 1742, MS at Princeton Univ. Library. In a 9 March 1741 letter to Colman (MS in Colman Papers, MHS), JE stated that "all our children that are capable of religious reflections have been under remarkable impressions, and I can't but think that Salvation is come into my house, in several instances: I hope that my four eldest children (the youngest of them between six & seven years of age) have been savingly wrought upon, the eldest some years ago." The youngest persons listed on JE's church-membership list were perhaps about twelve. The list is not dated, except marked "1746" at its end by JE; part of it can be attributed to the period between late 1735 and April 1739, and the youngest person entered by early 1739 was born Oct. 1730.

34. JE to Wheelock, 9 June 1741, in Dwight, *Edwards,* 148.

35. JE to Bellamy, 21 Jan. 1742, describes religion as then "decaying" and himself as praying to God to "improve me as an instrument to revive his work." On Buell's success, see JE to Prince, 12 Dec. 1743, in Goen,

Great Awakening, 549–50. See also Dwight, *Edwards,* 171–86. When Buell was installed at East Hampton, L.I., in 1746, Edwards preached the main sermon, published as *The Church's Marriage to her Sons, and to her God* ... (Boston, 1746). Sarah's jealousy of Buell and the other ministers visiting Northampton in JE's absence is shown clearly in her conversion narrative in Dwight, *Edwards,* 174–75, 178–79. In his letter to Prince, JE also noted that an influx of visitors from other communities, where there was greater "visible commotion," inspired Northamptonites to imitate their "vehement zeal."

36. Doolittle wrote *An Enquiry into Enthusiasm* (Boston, 1743); *The Late Religious Commotions in New-England Considered* (Boston, 1743), long thought to be the work of Charles Chauncy of Boston, is attributed to Rand by Edwin S. Gaustad in "Charles Chauncy and the Great Awakening," Bibliographical Society of America *Papers,* XLV (1951), 125–35. Rand was probably also the author of a hostile address to Whitefield from a group of Hampshire ministers in 1745: see *The Testimony of the North Association in the County of Hartford ... And An Address from Some of the Ministers in the County of Hampshire ...* (Boston, 1745). The ministerial debate over the Awakening was conducted largely in group statements, of which these four are the most important: *The Testimony of the Pastors of the Churches ... May 25, 1743, Against Several Errors in Doctrine, and Disorders in Practice ...* (Boston, 1743); *The Testimony and Advice of an Assembly of Pastors ... at a Meeting in Boston July 7, 1743, Occasioned by the late Happy Revival of Religion in many Parts of the Land* (Boston, 1743; also included in *The Christian History,* 159ff); *The Testimony and Advice of a Number of Laymen Respecting Religion ... September 12, 1743* (Boston, 1743); and *The Testimony and Advice of a Number of New England Ministers met at Boston Sept. 25, 1745, Professing the ancient Faith of these Churches ...* (Boston, 1745). Both Harvard and Yale issued manifestos against Whitefield in 1745.

37. *The Distinguishing Marks,* published in Boston, 1741, is in Goen, *Great Awakening,* 214–88.

38. *The Resort and Remedy of those that are Bereaved by the Death of an Eminent Minister* (Boston, 1741).

39. *Distinguishing Marks,* in Goen, *Great Awakening,* 226–88.

40. According to the count of Separatist churches included by C. C. Goen in *Revivalism and Separatism in New England, 1740–1800: Strict Congregationalists and Separate Baptists in the Great Awakening* (New Haven, 1962), following p. 114, there were schisms in the neighborhood of Northampton only at Sunderland (1749), Westfield (1748)—both Baptist groups who moved to Vermont in the early 1760s—and Suffield, Enfield, Somers, and Stafford (all in Conn.). Three anti-revival Valley ministers had trouble with their

congregations when they differed from the local majority opinion on the revivals: Benjamin Doolittle of Northfield, Grindall Rawson of South Hadley, and William Rand of Sunderland. Most of the ministers in the upper Valley were friendly toward the revival although they shared JE's caution. In May 1742 ministers and lay representatives of seventeen churches in the region gathered to pronounce a favorable verdict on the revival. *A Copy of the Resolves of a Council of Churches, Met at Northampton, May 11, 1742, to Consider what may be done to promote religion, and good order in the Churches* (Boston, 1742). An interesting comment on the radicalism of this document in the minds of more conservative men is in Thomas Clap's letter to Solomon Williams, 8 June 1742, in Stephen Nissenbaum, ed., *The Great Awakening at Yale College* (Belmont, Calif., 1972), 170: the Old Lights assumed the Resolves were Edwards's work, and he was "scarce allowed to be a good man."

Edwards actively sought a rapprochement between the parties. See, for example, his letter to the Rev. Elnathan Whitman of Hartford, 9 Feb. 1744, in Dwight, *Edwards*, 204–9; Thomas Clap's letter to Jonathan Dickinson, in Nissenbaum, *Great Awakening at Yale College*, 117–18; and JE's letter to his wife, 25 March 1743, in which he says he will go with a group of moderate ministers to try to calm down the people of New London, MS at Beinecke, filed by sermon notes on back, Ephesians 4:15–16. JE befriended a number of young men whose New Light sympathies brought them into open conflict with Rector Clap of Yale, the most famous of whom was David Brainerd. Brainerd was expelled from Yale in 1741 for saying that Tutor Chauncey Whittlesey had no more grace than a certain chair; he became an Indian missionary and died of tuberculosis in JE's house in 1748. Edwards preached Brainerd's funeral sermon, *True Saints . . . are Present with the Lord* (Boston, 1747), and edited Brainerd's memoirs, *An Account of the Life of the Late Reverend Mr. David Brainerd . . .* (Boston, 1749).

41. *Some Thoughts . . .* (Boston, 1743), in Goen, *Great Awakening*, 290–530, see esp. 313, 325–30, 353–58. A useful discussion of JE's millennialism is C. C. Goen, "Jonathan Edwards: A New Departure in Eschatology," *Church History*, XXVIII (1959), 25–40. Alan Heimert, *Religion and the American Mind* (Cambridge, Mass., 1966), 59–68, 88–90, 123–39, 152–55, interprets the entire body of Edwards's work from *Some Thoughts* to the end of his life through the theme of an insistent millennialism.

42. *Some Thoughts*, in Goen, *Great Awakening*, 297–98; see also 386–87. Edwards's *Thoughts* were answered by Boston Old Light Charles Chauncy's *Seasonable Thoughts on the State of Religion in New-England . . .* (Boston, 1743). Chauncy charged that the Awakening revived the Antinomianism of the 1630s and wrote at great length against itineracy and emotional extremism;

his major point, on pp. 323–29, was that passion must be governed by the understanding. JE's moderate position between extremes is outlined in Conrad Cherry, *The Theology of Jonathan Edwards: A Reappraisal* (N.Y., 1966), 164–76. JE's contribution to the development of religious psychology in America is discussed in John E. Smith's introduction to the Yale edition of *The Religious Affections,* Vol. II of JE's *Works* (New Haven, 1959).

43. "Miscellanies" entry No. 732, from about 1737–38 (Schafer date). See also No. 436.

44. *Some Thoughts,* in Goen, *Great Awakening,* 332–35. JE regarded his 1749 edition of David Brainerd's memoirs as useful in warning people against "that wild sort of religion" that had prevailed in parts of New England; so he wrote to the Rev. Eleazar Wheelock of Lebanon, Conn., 14 Sept. 1748, MS at Beinecke. See also JE's funeral sermon for Brainerd, *True Saints . . . ,* 26–30. The polemical intent of the Brainerd works is illuminated by Scheick, *Writings of Jonathan Edwards,* 96–111.

45. *Some Thoughts,* in Goen, *Great Awakening,* 341.

46. The definitive modern edition is that edited by John E. Smith for Yale Univ. Press in 1959, hereafter cited as *Religious Affections.* The treatise was expanded from sermons preached in 1742 and 1743.

47. *Religious Affections,* 95–97, 266–91.

48. *Ibid.,* 118, 120. This unity is stressed in both Cherry, *Theology of Jonathan Edwards,* 164–76; and Smith, Introduction to *Religious Affections,* 13–14, 33.

49. *Religious Affections,* Part III, 197–459. JE very clearly insisted that Christian life was a *sign* of spiritual merit, not the *price* of it, so his doctrines were not Arminian.

50. JE's footnote in *ibid.,* 230. See Smith's comments on the relationship between Stoddard's thought and Edwards's, in his introduction to *ibid.,* 57–60. The pragmatism of JE's tests of faith is discussed by Smith in "Jonathan Edwards: Piety and Practice in the American Character," *Journal of Religion,* LIV (1974), 166–80.

51. *Religious Affections,* 181, 182, 193, 420. Page 181 contains the reference to Stoddard's *Treatise on Conversion* (p. 78 of 1735 ed.); see also p. 460. Among the qualities that evidenced true conversion in the case study of a person (Sarah) in *Some Thoughts* was "a peculiar sensible aversion to a judging others that were professing Christians of good standing in the visible church. . . . though before, under smaller discoveries and feebler exercises of divine affection, there had been felt a disposition to censure and condemn others." *Some Thoughts,* in Goen, *Great Awakening,* 335.

52. *Religious Affections,* 412–13, 416–17.

53. Edwards described the ministerial qualifications in his 1744 ordina-

tion sermon for Robert Abercrombie at Pelham, *The True Excellency of a Minister of the Gospel* (Boston, 1744), 12; and in his unpublished 1747 sermon at the ordination of Joseph Ashley in Sunderland, on Zechariah 4:12–14, MS at Beinecke.

54. *Some Thoughts*, in Goen, *Great Awakening*, 474–83, 483–93, 493–95. The professional bias of even so radical an itinerant as Gilbert Tennent is shown in a letter from Tennent to JE in 1741, in Dwight, *Edwards*, 153.

Chapter Seven: Challenges

1. Town Records, 278–83, 286–88. James Russell Trumbull, *History of Northampton,* 2 vols. (Northampton, 1898), II, 93–97. JE to Thomas Prince, 12 Dec. 1743, in C. C. Goen, ed., *The Great Awakening,* Vol. IV of *The Works of Jonathan Edwards* (New Haven, 1972), 544–57.

2. All the men holding major office during Northampton's first hundred years—General Court Representatives, selectmen, town clerks, treasurers, constables, and meetinghouse committeemen—shared fifty-eight surnames, and almost every surname found in any town records was included. But those who served as selectman for more than two one-year terms or in higher office shared only twenty-four surnames; and those who served more than the average number of selectman terms (five) shared only nineteen surnames. A single term was an honor, of course, but because twenty men served ten or more terms during Northampton's first century, the effectiveness of an isolated period of service was minimal. The best index of power was clearly the ability to stay in office long enough to effect policies. Between 1654 and 1754, 102 men served 501 selectman terms. A single term was held by 34 men, and 53 men served two or fewer terms. Six men served more than 15 terms. Most selectmen were in their late forties or fifties; during the period 1675–1754 (when ages are best known), the average age of selectmen serving was 51 years (ranging from about 47 to about 64 for any five-year period); age at first term averaged 43.86 years. From 1745 to 1754, the average age of all selectmen dropped to about 46.8 years, the lowest ever by about two years.

Seven of 11 selectmen in 1700–9, and 7 of 8 in 1720–29, were sons of selectmen; average numbers of terms served by fathers of these 7 were 6.8 terms in 1700–9, 8.1 terms in 1720–29, and 9.2 terms in 1740–49. Titled men held 22 of 50 terms in 1700–9, 25 of 50 in 1720–29, and 42 of 50 in 1740–49.

The best source of comparative data is Edward M. Cook, Jr., *The Fathers of the Towns: Leadership and Community Structure in Eighteenth-Century New England* (Baltimore, 1976), 174–77. Cook took a wide sample of towns (not including Northampton) for statistical analysis. The community studied here would have conformed in the mid-eighteenth century to Cook's category of a major county town, a local market and service center with the top 10% of taxpayers controlling 35–50% of the wealth, some landless poor, officeholding dominated by a dozen or so leading families who also supplied personnel for county and provincial offices.

3. Sermon of May 1737 on II Samuel 20:19, MS at Beinecke.

4. Proverbs 28:2, MS at Beinecke, probably early 1732 (Schafer).

5. Sibley, *Harvard Graduates*, V, 96–119. See also James Russell Trumbull, "John Stoddard" (unpublished essay, 1893, Forbes Library); Sylvester Judd MSS, II, 255–58; Timothy Dwight, *Travels in New-England and New York*, ed. Barbara Miller Solomon (Cambridge, Mass., 1969), I, 241–42; Thomas Hutchinson, *History of the Colony and Province of Massachusetts-Bay*, ed. L. S. Mayo (Cambridge, Mass., 1936), II, 329–30n. No personal nonmilitary papers have come to light. A common soldier in 1704 and a major by 1712, he marked himself as a leader by his success as Commissary to Quebec in 1713 to negotiate the return of the captives taken in the Indian wars. He was first appointed judge in 1725 and declined an appointment to the Superior Court in 1736 because he realized his Tory politics were so unpopular with the mass of citizens that there would be public disturbances. See also note 3 to Chapter 1.

6. Sereno E. Dwight, *The Life of President Edwards* (N.Y., 1829), 464. Trumbull, *Northampton* II, 36, reports an unfruitful search for evidence to corroborate JE's characterization of Northampton politics.

7. For example, in 1716 he bought a share of the "equivalent lands" given to Conn. by Mass. as part of a border settlement; in 1739 he was selling for 2s.7d. per acre what had cost him 1 1/2d. per acre, a profit of over 3000%. Mass. Archives, II, 276–83; Hampshire County Deeds C-139, L-220. His total holdings in the "Equivalent," in common with his nephew Elisha Williams, were 1/16 of the total, or 3306 acres. See Sibley, *Harvard Graduates*, V, 96–119, for other land transactions.

8. Estate inventory in Hampshire Probate Records. According to Sibley, *Harvard Graduates*, V, 118, when JS died his funeral costs "equalled a year's salary for Parson Edwards." See also Trumbull, *Northampton*, II, 177.

9. On JS's wife, see Robert E. Chester-Waters, *Genealogical Notes of the Families of Chester . . .* (privately printed, 1886), 13–20. Quotation about "western marches" from Sibley, *Harvard Graduates*, V, 96.

10. Hampshire Assoc. Records, 1731–47, MS at Forbes Library, 38. JE to wife, 22 June 1748, Beinecke. JE's journal of the communion controversy in Northampton, MS lost, included in Dwight, *Edwards*, 314; see also *ibid.*, 207–8.

11. *A Strong Rod Broken and Withered* (Boston, 1748). On the wider significance of Court and Country viewpoints, see T. H. Breen, *The Character of the Good Ruler: A Study of Puritan Political Ideas in New England, 1630–1730* (New Haven, 1970), 205ff. In "Jonathan Edwards and the Great Awakening," Perry Miller emphasizes the practicality of the skills Stoddard had as a ruler, and therefore his being recognized by JE as a new kind of leader for a new America, where authority would be based on service to the people and judged by them. Miller's essay is in Stanley N. Katz, ed., *Colonial America: Essays in Politics and Social Development* (Boston, 1971), 283–97. Stoddard was nevertheless given a chance to use his modern skills only because of his connections among the magisterial-ministerial elite of Mass., and there is no way to avoid acknowledging that he was truly a Tory. His scorn for service to the people is unabashed in a letter to Governor Dummer in 1724, quoted in Trumbull, *Northampton,* II, 35. Edwards himself was no democrat. In his last sermon notebook for Northampton, MS at Beinecke, there are notes for a quarterly lecture in February 1747 on the doctrine that "a levelling spirit is a very evil and unchristian spirit."

12. The economic rank of then serving elders and deacons on three surviving tax-assessment lists is as follows, with roman numerals indicating half deciles (I is highest, XX is lowest):

1676: I, III, X.

1739: II, III, III, V, and X; one died that year who would have ranked about II or III.

1759: I, VI, VII, IX, XII; one moved to Southampton (was poor). The figures for selectmanship were actually 37.2%, 26.7%, and 10.4%, respectively. If the figures are corrected to show service as selectmen by elders and deacons while holding church office, the figures are 19.2% for 1670–99, 18.7% for 1700–29, and 9.6% for 1730–54.

13. Church Records, 23.

14. The covenant was included in JE's letter of 12 Dec. 1743 to Thomas Prince, published in *The Christian History* and reprinted in Goen, *Great Awakening,* 550–54.

15. Dwight, *Edwards,* 171–86, quotations 172, 174, 183, 184–85.

16. "Personal Narrative," in Clarence H. Faust and Thomas H. Johnson, eds., *Jonathan Edwards: Representative Selections,* rev. ed. (N. Y., 1962), 57–72, quotation 71. In a letter of counsel to Deborah Hatheway of Suffield, JE wrote, "Remember that pride is the worst viper that is in the heart . . . and often creeps insensibly into the midst of religion and sometimes under the disguise of humility." JE to DH, 3 June 1741, MS at Beinecke.

17. *The Great Concern of the Watchman for Souls . . .* (Boston, 1743). Judd was a member of the Yale class of 1741 but not a participant in the evangeli-

cal upheavals that swept through the student body. See Franklin B. Dexter, *Biographical Sketches of the Graduates of Yale College* . . . (N.Y., 1885–1912), I, 677–78. Of the 31 men who signed the Southampton church covenant in 1743, 22 or 71% were listed as JE's own church members and 6 of them were in the group recorded in early 1735, the products of the first great revival in Northampton. The rest of the Southampton covenanters were earlier joiners of the Northampton church, 1706–27. There is no evidence that any of the Southampton church joiners were personally anti-revival.

18. *Watchman for Souls*, 29.

19. *Ibid.*, 34, 37.

20. Malachi 3:10–11, July 1743, MS at Beinecke.

21. *Watchman for Souls*, 38, 39–40.

22. Clifford K. Shipton has reported that of the 400 clergy whose careers between 1680 and 1740 can be documented, 12% had serious financial troubles with their congregations. Shipton, "The New England Clergy of the 'Glacial Age,' " Colonial Society of Mass. *Publications*, XXXII (1937), 50. James W. Schmotter has found that around 1700 and after 1730 salary was the single greatest cause of dispute between pastor and flock. "Ministerial Careers in Eighteenth–Century New England," *Journal of Social History*, IX (1975), 257.

23. JE to Thomas Foxcroft, 24 May 1749, MS at Beinecke. For Edwards's salary amounts and debates, see Town Records and First Precinct Records, passim. The progress of inflation can be seen in the price of an ounce of silver in Massachusetts: 8 shillings in 1710 (that price had long been stable); 12s. by 1720, 18s. in 1730, 30s. in 1740, about 36s. in 1745, and 60s. by 1750. These figures compiled from William B. Weeden, *Economic and Social History of New England, 1620–1789* (1890; N.Y., 1963), II, 473, 677; Andrew McFarland Davis, *Currency and Banking in the Province of the Massachusetts-Bay* (N.Y., 1900–1), I, 90, 367, 378; Sylvester Judd, *History of Hadley* (Northampton, 1863), 331; Judd MSS, Forbes Library, I, 490.

24. Draft letter ending with the words quoted, on the back of notes for a sermon on Ephesians 2:5–7, Dec. 1734, Beinecke; sermon notes on Romans 12:10, March 1742/43, filed at Beinecke as a letter; sermon on Hebrews 2:7–8, Beinecke.

25. MS at Beinecke.

26. *Defects of Preachers Reproved*, ii.

27. Letter in Hawley Papers, New York Public Library.

28. JE to Eleazar Wheelock, 13 July 1744, Historical Society of Pennsylvania; First Precinct Records, 6, 8–11.

29. A letter from JE's daughter Sarah to a friend implied this contempla-

256 JONATHAN EDWARDS

tion of removal; quoted in Ola Elizabeth Winslow, *Jonathan Edwards, 1703–1758* (N. Y., 1940), 213, 361n.

30. Among these sermons were the following: Ephesians 4:29, July 1740; Psalms 144:12, Nov. 1744; Isaiah 30:20–21, Nov. 1746; and Job 36:14, Nov. 1748—all to the "children," all MSS at Beinecke. Among the sermons to the parents were those on Luke 1:17, Aug. 1741, and Joshua 24:15, Feb. 1746—both MSS at Beinecke. These later sermons are mostly outline.

31. There is no record of this case in the church book. The information on the "bad books" episode comes from JE's notes in the ANTS MSS, Box 1, Folder "no date #1." There is a bit of information in the Judd MSS, I, 491. Thomas H. Johnson has included most of these documents in "Jonathan Edwards and the 'Young Folks' Bible,' " *New England Quarterly,* V (1932), 37–54.

32. Testimony of Joanna Clark, in JE notes, ANTS. Oliver was saying that he could tell when they were menstruating. No mention was made in the proceedings as recorded about Oliver's family in Northampton, but Deacon Hunt's journal (Judd MSS, I, 25) identifies him as an apprentice in 1738. Oliver, born in 1723, was the son of a Hadley man and did not settle in Northampton. Oliver's position as an apprentice suggests that he was freer of family social controls than many "boys" his age. In early modern cities, apprentices were the avatars of rebellious youth. See Steven R. Smith, "The London Apprentices as Seventeenth-Century Adolescents," *Past & Present,* No. 61 (November, 1973), 149–61.

33. Samuel Hopkins, *The Life and Character of the Late Reverend, Learned and Pious Mr. Jonathan Edwards* (Boston, 1765), 53–55. The same account, with language somewhat altered, is in Dwight, *Edwards,* 299–300.

34. This list is reproduced in Johnson, "JE and the 'Young Folks' Bible,' " 42–43. There are some unexplained marks next to the names in the MS, which Johnson also includes, that may have been JE's signs for degrees of involvement.

35. The confessions are in JE's hand; Warner's was not signed.

36. Fragment of notes, ANTS, Box 1, Folder "no date #1." In Oct. 1731 the Hampshire Assoc. had decided that private admonition should be used first, and only thereafter should offenses be made matters of church discipline. Hampshire Assoc. Records, 1. We do not know if JE used private counsel in this case; other clergymen might have agreed with his apparent position that a sin so widespread that it reached the minister's attention thereby became by definition a *public* scandal. The pastor of Leicester, Mass., was dismissed in 1729 after being charged with, among other things, " 'bringing cases of private offense before the church.' " David H. Flaherty, *Privacy in Colonial New England* (Charlottesville, 1967), 155.

37. Of the eighteen known ages for the twenty boys accused of some use of the bad books, four were twenty-one, two were twenty-two, two were twenty-three, one each was twenty-four and twenty-five, five were twenty-six, and one each was twenty-seven, twenty-eight, and twenty-nine. Only two were married, and they were only marginally involved in the episode.

38. Of the three nonmembers, one was from out of town and of unknown age, probably an apprentice in Northampton, and the other two were aged twenty-six and twenty-one. Of the church members, one had joined before 1735, one in early 1735, and fifteen since 1736.

39. N. Ray Hiner, "Adolescence in Eighteenth-Century America," *History of Childhood Quarterly,* III (1975), 253–80, quotation 256.

40. See note 27 to Chapter 4, Table 8, for data on smaller families. In the literature on the history of families, it is commonly assumed that limiting the number of children born is an indication of greater love for them as persons—both as cause and effect.

41. Isaiah 1:2, MS at Beinecke.

42. Ephesians 5:5–7, Aug. 1746, Beinecke.

43. There are, in fact, rather few cases of discipline listed in the church records: from 1697 to 1743 only four men and two women were excommunicated, and one man was just admonished; their sins were drunkenness, lying, vilifying their neighbors, and refusing to be examined by the church when accused of fornication. There are no cases listed for 1744–65. Church Records, 25. Three cases of discipline were appealed to the Hampshire Assoc. in Oct. 1741, only one of which is mentioned in the Northampton church records. The clergy sided with the church in all three cases; JE was not present. Hampshire Assoc. Records, 36.

For the Hawley–Root case, see the Joseph Hawley Papers, New York Public Library; and Edwards's notes in Box 1, Folders "no date 1 and 2," ANTS. On this case, see Kathryn Kish Sklar, "Culture versus Economics: A Case of Fornication in Northampton in the 1740s," *Papers in Women's Studies* (U. of Michigan), May 1978, pp. 35–56.

44. Both Elisha and Joseph Hawley are entered in the latter part of the church-membership list that ends with the date 1746 inscribed by JE. In 1751 Elisha married Elizabeth Pomeroy, daughter of Deacon Ebenezer and niece of Seth Pomeroy, both leaders of the anti-Edwards party in 1749–50.

45. MS at Beinecke, quotations 4, 15, 26, 37, 48, 52, 94.

46. Church Records, 23–24.

47. The best account of this disturbance in the churches is C. C. Goen, *Revivalism and Separatism in New England, 1740–1800* (New Haven, 1962).

48. See Chapter 2, note 38.

49. There is a brief account of this case in Sibley, *Harvard Graduates,* IV,

97–98; see also Stoughton, *"Windsor Farmes": A Glimpse of an Old Parish* (Hartford, 1883), 73–75. The major source of information is Roger Wolcott's MS "Narrative of the Troubles in the Second Church in Windsor," Connecticut Historical Society.

Chapter Eight: Confrontation

1. JE's journal, the MS of which is lost, is in Sereno E. Dwight, *Life of President Edwards* (N.Y., 1829), 313–98. The following narrative, except where otherwise noted, is taken from that journal or Dwight's own parallel account, pp. 305–427, which is drawn largely from Samuel Hopkins's *Life and Character of the Late Reverend, Learned and Pious Mr. Jonathan Edwards* (Boston, 1765). Other useful sources are JE's letters to Samuel Hopkins, 3 April 174? [1750]; to Thomas Foxcroft 24 May and 21 Nov. 1749, and 19 Feb. 1750; all MSS at Beinecke. Also, JE to Joseph Bellamy, 6 Dec. 1749, in Stanley T. Williams, "Six Letters of Jonathan Edwards to Joseph Bellamy," *New England Quarterly,* I (1928), 237–50; JE to Rev. Peter Clark of Salem Village, 7 May 1750, in George Peirce Clark, "An Unpublished Letter by Jonathan Edwards," *New England Quarterly,* XXIX (1956), 228–33; and JE to Rev. Thomas Gillespie, 1 July 1751, in Dwight, *Edwards,* 462–68, an abridged version included in C. C. Goen, ed., *The Great Awakening,* Vol. IV of *The Works of Jonathan Edwards* (New Haven, 1972), 561–66. The JE MSS at Beinecke also include a copy of the *Results* of the Dec. 1749 Council and the June 1750 Council with the minority protest to the latter. There is also an account of the firing in James Russell Trumbull, *History of Northampton,* 2 vols. (Northampton, 1898), II, 202ff.

JE's concerns, or his *Religious Affections,* may have influenced the Hampshire Assoc. to discuss "whether an unregenerate person has a right in the sight of God to the Lord's Supper" in April 1746 and Oct. 1747 (question proposed at meetings of Oct. 1745 and Oct. 1746). Unfortunately, no record of their thoughts on the subject survives. Hampshire Assoc. Records, 47, 49.

In Edwards's "Miscellanies," there seems to be an explicit change of principle about the church and the sacraments by early 1736. Schafer suggests that date for entry No. 689, which reads in part as follows: "When persons regularly enter into the visible church we are not to look on their admission as what is done meerly by man . . . nor are they admitted meerly to be treated as some of God's people by man. They are admitted or accepted of God. For the officers of the church when they admit are to act in the name of God in admitting; to them are committed the keys of the kingdom of heaven. . . . and what they do is done in heaven. 2. But God in acting as the Head of the visible church as he transacts by man, so he is wont to conform to man and to transact with us in our own way, as we by reason of our want of omniscience and ability to search the heart are forced to do one with another. . . . So God conforms to man herein and don't act as the Searcher of hearts, but admits and receives persons to be his people, as it were on presumption on their sincerity and faithfulness. . . ." God's people (like Judas) can prove unfaithful, and then will be rejected. The second part of this entry is a strong restraint on the extremism of the first part, but although he still maintains the central Stoddardean principle that men have no infallible knowledge, Edwards is clearly trying to find a way to give the church the power to divide sheep from goats—and here he can do so only by reducing God's omniscience to the level of man.

This was obviously an undesirable compromise, and by "Miscellanies" entry No. 873, written probably in the winter or spring of 1741 (Schafer), Edwards has come to the position he would maintain publicly in the *Humble Inquiry* of 1749, that visible sainthood depends on a true profession of real sainthood: the moral burden is placed on the applicant for membership. The central ideas of No. 873 are as follows: The explicit profession which must be the condition of church membership should include a "conviction that God is just in our damnation. [This conviction of the *justice* of damnation had long been the special product of the work of Saving Grace, as JE so clearly indicated in his own conversion autobiography.] . . . The profession here spoken of is a profession consequent on conversion." Elements of a proper profession "are to varie according to the different times and circumstances of the church," and in Apostolic times professions did not need to be so explicit as now, when the externals of Christianity are traditional and upheld by civil authority. " 'Tis evident that Christians being faithfull to their covenant which they have obliged themselves by entitles them to heaven, and this supposes that in their covenant they profess those things that are the proper qualification and condition of glory."

The central issue for a pastor was still the one of discerning hypocrisy— of having some control over church members short of Judgment Day. As late as entry No. 1138 (late 1740s?), Edwards upheld the inability of mortal men to have perfect knowledge of others' hearts, so there was still no way to mediate between the developing logic of Edwards's theology and the needs of the institutional church.

2. The *Humble Inquiry* is reprinted in the N.Y. 1844 edition of JE's *Works*, I, 83–192, quotation p. 86. All further citations of this work will be to this edition.

3. In June 1750 two men testified that in 1746–47 they heard JE announce his new ideas publicly and that the news was spread throughout the town.

See letter from John Searl to JE, 4 June 1750, incomplete MS at Hartford Seminary Foundation; and statement of Noah Parsons, 13 June 1750, in JE MSS at Beinecke. Both the Searl and Parsons letters refer in passing to a contemporary suspicion that JE had kept his change of mind a secret from his uncle, Colonel John Stoddard, because Stoddard would have disapproved. That question seems to be unanswerable.

4. One of the two sample professions has survived in the JE MSS at Beinecke; two others are quoted by JE in *Misrepresentations Corrected, and Truth Vindicated, in a Reply to the Rev. Mr. Solomon Williams' Book . . .* (Boston, 1752), in N.Y. 1844 ed., *Works,* I, 193–292, esp. 201–2. One is over five hundred words long, and the other two are about sixty words long each, but in essence they are identical—a belief in the standard Christian doctrines (in the longer form), and a commitment of self to obedience to the moral law (in all three). The closest approach to an indication of *experience* in the professions is in the long version, in the phrase "having been made sensible of His divine supreme glory. . . ."

5. James P. Walsh, "The Pure Church in Eighteenth Century Connecticut," (Ph.D. dissertation, Columbia U., 1967), 43–44.

6. JE to Thomas Foxcroft, 24 May 1749, MS at Beinecke.

7. *Humble Inquiry,* 184–91, answer to Objection XIX.

8. This loss is confirmed in Trumbull, *Northampton,* II, 215. At a Hampshire Assoc. meeting (the first recorded after the missing pages for 1748–51), one question posed for consideration was "whether ministers have an exclusive sole right to determine the proper subjects of baptism." Quoted in Ola Elizabeth Winslow, *Jonathan Edwards 1703–1758* (N.Y., 1940), 260.

9. Solomon Williams, *The True State of the Question . . .* (Boston, 1751), 141–42.

10. Peter Clark to Deacon Pomeroy, 4 April 1750, MS at Beinecke.

11. See especially *Humble Inquiry,* 183.

12. *Misrepresentations Corrected,* 204–5.

13. JE to Clark, 7 May 1750, in *New England Quarterly,* XXIX (1956), 228–33. See also Clark to JE, 21 May 1750, MS at Beinecke. JE's 1750 ordination sermon at Portsmouth, N.H., for Northampton native Job Strong, *Christ the Great Example of Ministers* (Boston, 1750), defensively and explicitly warned against Separatism.

14. Dwight, *Edwards,* 363, emphasis added. Brownism was democracy in the church, the minister's vote equal to that of any full member. Joseph Hawley testified to JE's claim of a veto in a statement he prepared for the town to the 1751 Northampton Council. Hawley Papers, New York Public Library.

15. Edwards was a thorough presbyterian; see "Miscellanies" entry Nos.

69, 90, 928; and JE to Rev. John Erskine of Scotland, July 1750, in Dwight, *Edwards,* 412.

16. See especially his letter of 5 Dec. 1749, in Dwight, *Edwards,* 328–32; and letter of 30 March 1750 to Deacon Cook, MS at Beinecke.

17. Autograph draft, Beinecke.

18. JE to Erskine, 20 May 1749, in Dwight, *Edwards,* 273–76.

19. Quoted in JE's journal, *ibid.,* 364.

20. JE to Thomas Foxcroft, 19 Feb. 1750, MS at Beinecke.

21. Isaiah 30:20–21, Beinecke, one of the most fully written out of the late sermons.

22. Dwight, *Edwards,* 325, 467. Solomon Clark, *Antiquities, Historicals and Graduates of Northampton* (Northampton, 1882), 90. Ezra Stiles MSS, Beinecke, Itineraries, I:339, II:94.

23. JE to Thomas Gillespie, 1 July 1751, in Dwight, *Edwards,* 467.

24. See JE to Billings, 11 June 1750, Beinecke; and JE to Erskine, 7 July 1752, in Dwight, *Edwards,* 499. The following were the ministers on the 1750 Council. Pro-Edwards: Robert Abercrombie of Pelham, Billings of Cold Spring, David Hall of Sutton, William Hobby of Reading, Peter Reynolds of Enfield; Anti-Edwards: Joseph Ashley of Sunderland, Robert Breck of Springfield, Jonathan Hubbard of Sheffield, Timothy Woodbridge of Hatfield, Chester Williams of Hadley.

25. The Council Result is in Dwight, *Edwards,* 399–403. A small pamphlet war followed; see *ibid.,* 453.

26. See JE to John Erskine, 15 Nov. 1750, in Dwight, *Edwards,* 415–16; and JE to Thomas Foxcroft, 31 July 1750, MS at Beinecke. Sylvester Judd MSS, Forbes Library, II, 91.

27. He also had offers from Canaan, Conn., Lunenberg, Va., and a tentative offer from Scotland. Perry Miller, *Jonathan Edwards* (N.Y., 1949), 232.

28. Dwight, *Edwards,* 420–21. There are a number of documents in the Edwards MSS at ANTS which pertain to the possibility of a splinter church; see also in the Dwight Papers, Sterling Library, Yale, 3 letters from Timothy Dwight to Thomas Foxcroft of Oct. 1750 to Dec. 1751; also Hawley's statement to the 1751 Council, Hawley Papers, NYPL.

29. On John Hooker, see Franklin B. Dexter, *Biographical Sketches of the graduates of Yale . . .* (N.Y., 1885–1912), II, 254–56.

30. JE did fight for about three years with some of the Williamses over the running of the Indian school, and he won. On JE's later years, see Dwight, *Edwards,* 449–583, and Winslow, *Jonathan Edwards,* 268–324.

31. *A Careful and Strict Enquiry into . . . Freedom of the Will . . .* was begun in 1753 and published in 1754. *The Great Christian Doctrine of Original Sin Defended* appeared in 1758. Posthumously published were *Two Dissertations:*

I, Concerning the End for which God Created the World; II, The Nature of True Virtue (Boston, 1765); *A History of the Work of Redemption* (Edinburgh, 1774); and a treatise on grace was included in Alexander B. Grosart, ed., *Selections from the Unpublished Writings of Jonathan Edwards of America* (Edinburgh, 1865). Jonathan Edwards, Jr., subsequently published many selections and sermons from the MSS.

Useful commentaries on these writings as theology can be found in Conrad Cherry, *The Theology of Jonathan Edwards: A Reappraisal* (N.Y., 1966); Conrad Wright, "Edwards and the Arminians on the Freedom of the Will," *Harvard Theological Review,* XXXV (1942), 241–61; and Norman S. Fiering's review of books about Edwards in *William and Mary Quarterly,* 3rd Ser., XXVIII (1971), 655–61. The most important volume discussed by Fiering is Clyde A. Holbrook's edition of *Original Sin,* Vol. III of *The Works of Jonathan Edwards* (New Haven, 1970). The authoritative modern edition of *Freedom of the Will* was edited by Paul Ramsey for the Yale series in 1957.

32. JE apparently wrote almost no new sermons for use at Stockbridge. Wilson H. Kimnach, "Jonathan Edwards' Sermon Mill," *Early American Literature,* X (1975), 168.

33. Part of the network can be seen through the marriages of William Williams's children; see Sibley, *Harvard Graduates,* III, 263–69.

34. JE to Sir William Pepperell, 30 Jan. 1753, ANTS; JE to William Hogg, 25 Nov. 1752, Beinecke; JE to Thomas Foxcroft, 19 Feb. 1750, Beinecke. Dwight, *Edwards,* 122n., 433–34.

35. JE, *The Resort and Remedy of Those that are Bereaved by the Death of an Eminent Minister* (Boston, 1741), 1.

36. JE to Pepperell, 30 Jan. 1753, ANTS. Dwight, *Edwards,* 434. MS sermon on Malachi 1:8, Beinecke, dated Oct. 1750 and labeled as preached at Longmeadow.

37. See Miller, *Jonathan Edwards,* 101–5, 125–26, 218 (on Williamses); 15, 104 (on feud between Christian and Esther).

38. See, especially, JE to "Dear Sister" [Mary], 12 Dec. 1721, ANTS, and discussion in Chapter II. George Henry Merriam, "Israel Williams, Monarch of Hampshire, 1709–1788" (Ph.D. dissertation, Clark Univ., 1961), 74–75, 152–58, attempts to exonerate IW from culpability in the JE dismissal, but the direct evidence is inconclusive either way.

39. Sibley, *Harvard Graduates,* VI, 352–61, describes Solomon Williams as a "true moderate" in the Awakening. On Elisha Williams, see *ibid.,* V, 592, and Richard Warch, *School of the Prophets: Yale College, 1701–1740* (New Haven, 1973), 180–82.

40. The only biography of Hawley is E. Francis Brown, *Joseph Hawley: Colonial Radical* (N.Y., 1931), which contains most of this information; see

esp. pp. 26–38. Edwards described Hawley and his role in the controversy in a letter to John Erskine of 5 July 1750: "The people, in managing this affair on their side, have made chief use of a young gentleman of liberal education and notable abilities, and a fluent speaker, of about seven or eight and twenty years of age, my grandfather Stoddard's grandson, being my mother's sister's son, a man of lax principles in religion, falling in, in some essential things, with Arminians, and is very open and bold in it. He was improved as one of the agents for the church, and was their chief spokesman before the Council. He very strenuously urged . . . the necessity of an immediate separation. . . ." Quoted in Dwight, *Edwards,* 410.

41. See Merriam, "Israel Williams," 78; IW to Joseph Hawley, 10 Aug. 1759, Hawley Papers, NYPL; Brown, *Joseph Hawley,* 76–78.

42. The first Hawley letter to JE, dated 11 Aug. 1754, is lost, but its general content can be inferred from JE's answer, 18 Nov. 1754, in the Hawley Papers, NYPL, which also contain Hawley's second and last letter to JE, 21 Jan. 1755. The MS of Hawley's letter to David Hall of Sutton, 9 May 1760, is also lost; but that letter was printed in the *Boston Evening Post,* 19 May 1760; in Hopkins's *Life of Edwards,* 66–72; and (with grammar "corrected") in Dwight, *Edwards,* 421–27.

43. In undated items, Hawley Papers, NYPL. JE, on the other hand, wrote in his Nov. 18 letter to Hawley (p. 6) that a major aggravation of Hawley's fault was that he *agreed* with JE on the basic issue! Hawley never confirmed this. The confession says that Hawley gave up his Arminian views in 1754.

44. JE to John Erskine, 5 July 1750, in Dwight, *Edwards,* 411.

45. Winslow, *Jonathan Edwards,* 244, 252.

46. The list of pro people is easier to determine, because they were fewer in number. Drawing on the Judd MSS and some other documents now lost, Trumbull, *Northampton,* II, 205–6, 234, gives a list of pro and anti men, on which the description in the text was based. These men appeared as follows on the 1749 tax list (in half deciles, I the highest, arabic numerals indicate the rank out of 259 persons listed): Pro: II-#17, II-#19, II-#22, III, V, VIII, VIII, IX, XII. (Two of these men married JE's daughters in 1750.) Anti: I-#1, I-#3, I-#4, II-#14, II-#15, II-#18, II-#23, III, IV, VII, VII, IX (Joseph Hawley; if his estate were joined with that of his widowed mother, it would be a IV), XI. (One of these men was accused of reading the midwifery book in 1744 but was not a major culprit.) Miller, *Jonathan Edwards,* 218, says that Dwight and Dr. Mather were a "remnant of the old gentry." They were really the opposite: Dwight had come to town as a child in 1711 and was the son of a merchant; Mather was the son of the minister at Windsor and had come to Northampton about 1730. If there were gentry in Northamp-

ton, they were more prominent among Edwards's opposers—including Joseph Hawley, not rich but a grandson of Solomon Stoddard.

47. The businessman-Arminian link is suggested by Miller, *Jonathan Edwards*, 122–23, 210, 218.

48. In early 1750 he had supposedly called Edwards a tyrant for preaching his doctrines; JE to Thomas Foxcroft, 19 Dec. 1751, Beinecke. But in the Revolution he was a Tory. Merriam, "Israel Williams," 96–140; Robert J. Taylor, *Western Massachusetts in the Revolution* (Providence, 1954), 66–67. Elderly Seth Pomeroy was a Patriot in the Revolution, but most of the other identifiable activists of 1750 were too old to be participants in the war except as officers, and most officers were chosen from the richer men, so the firing-revolutionary-democracy link is obscure at best. Joseph Hawley was an intellectual leader of the Whigs until 1766, when he succumbed to the melancholia that afflicted most of the males in his family.

49. JE to Thomas Gillespie, 1 July 1751, in Dwight, *Edwards*, 462–68, and in Goen, *Great Awakening*, 561–66.

50. *Ibid.* There is no supporting evidence for this.

51. First printed in Boston, 1751; in Dwight, *Edwards*, 630–51, quotation 646. Both Dwight (p. 404) and Winslow (*Jonathan Edwards*, 364) read this sermon as charitable and forgiving. The tone strikes me as harsh and threatening, much like JE's letter of forgiveness to Joseph Hawley in 1754, which reads in part: "And as you, sir, distinguished yourself as a head and leader to that people in those affairs, at least the main of them, so I think the guilt that lies on you in the sight of God is distinguishing, and that you may expect to be distinguished by God's frown, unless there be true repentance, and properly expressed and manifested, with endeavors to be a leader of the people in the affair of repentance, as in their transgression." Hawley Papers, NYPL. It is possible that Edwards wanted to be recalled in moral triumph to Northampton.

52. Brown, *Joseph Hawley*, 17–23.

Index